D0774501

THE
BRITISH ARMY
GUIDE
2008–2009

Editor – Charles Heyman

Copyright © R & F Defence Publications 2007

ISBN 978-1-84415-280-3

Price £6.99

Pen & Sword Books Ltd
47 Church Street
Barnsley S70 2AS

Telephone: 01226-734222   Fax: 01226-734438
www.pen-and-sword.co.uk

The information in this publication has been gathered from
unclassified sources

Front Cover: A soldier from The Rifles takes aim. The largest of the new Infantry
Regiments, The Rifles has five Regular and two Territorial Army Battalions
(Copyright Fovea)

Rear Cover: Watchkeeper UAV will probably enter service in 2010 and be
operated by 32 Regiment Royal Artillery (Copyright Thales UK Ltd)

Printed and bound in Great Britain by Biddles Ltd, King's Lynn, Norfolk

Contents List

CHAPTER 1 – THE MANAGEMENT OF DEFENCE

GENERAL INFORMATION

Populations – European Union – Top Five Nations (2007 estimates)

Germany	82 million
France	60 million
Italy	58 million
United Kingdom	60 million
Spain	40 million

Finance – European Union – Top Five Nations (2006 Figures)

	GDP	Per Capita Income
Germany	US$2,970 bn	US$36,100
United Kingdom	US$2,430 bn	US$40,233
France	US$2,270 bn	US$37,300
Italy	US$1,880 bn	US$32,400
Spain	US$1,250 bn	US$30,900

UK Population – 58.7 million (2001 census)

England	–	49.6 million	Wales	–	2.9 million
Scotland	–	5.06 million	Northern Ireland	–	1.68 million
Total	–	59.3 million			

The population split in Northern Ireland is approximately 56% Protestant and 41% Roman Catholic with the remaining 3% not falling into either classification (2001 Census).

UK Area (in square kilometres)

England	–	130,423
Wales	–	20,766
Scotland	–	77,167
Northern Ireland	–	14,121
Total	–	242,477

UK Population Breakdown – Military Service Groups
(2007 estimates)

Age Group	Total	Males	Females
15–19	3.6 million	1.8 million	1.8 million
20–24	3.6 million	1.8 million	1.8 million
25–29	3.6 million	1.8 million	1.8 million
30–64	28.4 million	14.5 million	13.9 million

There are about 10.9 million in the 0–14 age group and about 9 million in the age group 65+.

Government

The executive government of the United Kingdom is vested nominally in the Crown, but for practical purposes in a committee of Ministers that is known as the Cabinet. The head of the Ministry and leader of the Cabinet is the Prime Minister and for the implementation of policy, the Cabinet is dependent upon the support of a majority of the Members of Parliament in the House of Commons. Within the Cabinet, defence matters are the responsibility of the Secretary of State for Defence. The Secretary of State for Defence has three principal deputies; the Minister for the Armed Forces; Minister for Defence Equipment and Support Parliamentary Under-Secretary of State for Defence and Minister for Veterans Affairs.

TOTAL BRITISH ARMED FORCES

Regular: 190,420 (1 Apr 2007) Regular Reserves 201,650 (1 Apr 2006); Volunteer Reserves 39,600 (1 Apr 2006); Cadet Forces 132,700 (1 Apr 2006); MoD Civilians 98,050 (1 Apr 2007).

Regular Army 106,200 (1 Apr 2007 – trained and untrained but excluding Gurkhas); Royal Navy 38,860 (1 Apr 2007 – including 7,400 Royal Marines); Royal Air Force 45,360 (1 Apr 2007).

Strategic Forces:

Strategic Forces are provided by the Royal Navy:

4 x Vanguard Class submarines each with up to 16 x Trident (D5) Submarine Launched Ballistic Missiles (SLBM) deploying with up to 48 x warheads per submarine. If necessary a D5 missile could deploy with 12 MIRV (multiple independently targetable re-entry vehicles). Future plans appear to be for a stockpile of 200 operationally available warheads and 58 missile bodies.

Royal Navy: 38,860 (including 7,400 Royal Marines) 10 x Tactical Submarines; 3 x Aircraft Carriers; 1 x Helicopter Carrier; 2 x Assault Ships; 3 x Landing Ships; 26 x Destroyers and Frigates; 16 x Mine Warfare Vessels; 5 x Survey Ships; 24 x Patrol Craft; 1 x Antarctic Patrol Ship. **Royal Fleet Auxiliary:** 2 x Fast fleet tankers; 3 x Small fleet tankers; 4 x Support tankers; 4 x Replenishment ships; 1 x Aviation training ship; 1 x Forward repair ship; 6 x Ro-Ro Ships (4 under civil management). **Naval Aircraft:** 2 x Fixed wing (Harrier GR7/GR9) squadrons; 8 x Helicopter squadrons with 38 x Merlin Helicopters; 12 x Sea King MK6. 23 x Lynx Helicopters; 11 x AEW Sea King Helicopters; 41 x Sea King Commando Helicopters; 6 x Lynx Helicopters. Anti-Tank role; 8 x Gazelle Helicopters.

Royal Marines: 1 x Commando Brigade Headquarters; 3 x Royal Marine Commando (Battalion Size); 3 x Commando Assault Helicopter Squadrons; 1 x Commando Light Helicopter Squadron; 1 x Commando Logistic Regiment; 1 Commando Assault Group (Landing-Craft); 1 x Fleet Protection Group; 4 x Special Boat Service Squadrons: Supported by the following army major units – 1 x Commando Regiment Royal Artillery; 1 x Commando Regiment Royal Engineers; 1 x Infantry Battalion (1 Rifles).

Royal Air Force: 45,360; 5 x Strike/Attack Squadrons (includes 1 x reserve squadron); 1 x Offensive Support Squadron; 4 x Air Defence Squadrons; 3 x Maritime Patrol Squadrons (includes 1 x Reserve Squadron); 5 x Reconnaissance Squadrons; 2 x Airborne Early Warning

Squadrons; 9 x Transport and Tankers Squadrons; 10 x Helicopter Squadrons; 6 Ground (Field) Defence Squadrons.

Regular Army: 106,200 trained and untrained but excluding 3,360 Gurkhas; 1 x Corps Headquarters in Germany (ARRC); 1 x Armoured Divisional HQ in Germany; 1 x Mechanised Divisional HQ in UK; 3 x Non-deployable divisional type HQ in UK; Germany: 3 x Armoured Brigade Headquarters (to be two by mid 2008) and 1 x Logistics Brigade HQ; UK: 4 x Deployable Combat Brigade HQ and 1 x Logistics Brigade HQ; 10 x Regional Brigade HQ; Major Units: 11 x Armoured Regiments; 36 x Infantry Battalions; 15 x Artillery Regiments; 14 x Engineer Regiments; 12 x Signal Regiments; 4 x Army Air Corps Regiments; 7 x Equipment Support Battalions; 18 x Logistic Regiments; 5 x Medical Regiments and 3 x Field Hospitals.

Territorial Army: 32,150 (1 Apr 2006); 14 x Infantry Battalions; 4 x Yeomanry Regiments; 7 x Artillery Regiments; 5 x Engineer Regiments; 2 x Special Air Service Regiments; 11 x Signals Regiments; 4 x Equipment Support Battalions; 15 x Logistic Regiments; 2 x Intelligence Battalions; 2 x Army Aviation Regiments; 12 x Field Hospitals and 3 x Medical Regiments; 2 x Military Police Battalions.

BRITISH ARMY EQUIPMENT SUMMARY

Armour: 345 x Challenger 2; 136 x Sabre; 48 x Striker (with Swingfire ATGW); 320 x Scimitar; 1,492 x Fv 432/430 family; 793 x MCV 80 Warrior; 478 x Spartan; 622 x Saxon; 108 x Mastiff; 11 x Fuchs (NBC).

Artillery and Mortars: 450 x 81 mm mortar (including 110 x self-propelled); 2093 x 51 mm Light Mortar; 146 x AS 90; 63 x 227 mm MLRS; 136 x 105 mm Light Gun.

Air Defence: 57 x Rapier C Fire Units (including 24 x SP); 145 x Starstreak (LML); 84 x HVM (SP).

Army Aviation: 112 x Lynx; 107 x Gazelle; 6 x BN-2; 67 x WAH-64D Apache; 4 x A109.

JOINT FORCES

Joint Force Harrier: 2 x Royal Navy Squadrons; 2 x Royal Air Force Squadrons.

Joint Helicopter Command: 4 x Royal Naval Helicopter Squadrons; 6 x Army Aviation Regiments (including 1 x Volunteer Reserve); 7 x Royal Air Force Helicopter Squadrons (including 1 x RAuxAF Helicopter Support Squadron).

Joint Special Forces Group: 1 x Regular Special Air Service (SAS) Regiment; 2 x Volunteer Reserve Special Air Service Regiments; 4 x Special Boat Service (SBS) Squadrons; 1 x Special Reconnaissance Regiment; 1 x Special Forces Support Group.

Joint Nuclear, Biological and Chemical Regiment.

National Police Forces: England and Wales 125,000, Scotland 14,000, Northern Ireland 11,000.

The Missions of the Armed Forces

The MoD mission statement for the armed forces reads as follows "Defence policy requires the provision of forces with a high degree of military effectiveness, at sufficient readiness and with a clear sense of purpose, for conflict prevention, crisis management and combat operations. Their demonstrable capability, conventional and nuclear, is intended to act as an effective deterrent to a potential aggressor, both in peacetime and during a crisis. They must be able to undertake a range of Military Tasks to fulfil the missions set out below, matched to changing strategic circumstances." These missions are not listed in any order of priority:

Peacetime Security: To provide forces needed in peacetime to ensure the protection and security of the United Kingdom, to assist as required with the evacuation of British nationals overseas, to afford Military Aid to the Civil Authorities in the United Kingdom, including Military Aid to the Civil Power, Military Aid to Other Government Departments and Military Aid to the Civil Community.

Security of the Overseas Territories: To provide forces to meet any challenges to the external security of a British Overseas Territory (including overseas possession and the Sovereign Base Areas) or to assist the civil authorities in meeting a challenge to internal security.

Defence Diplomacy: To provide forces to meet the varied activities undertaken by the Ministry of Defence to dispel hostility, build and maintain trust, and assist in the development of democratically accountable armed forces (thereby making a significant contribution to conflict prevention and resolution).

Support to Wider British Interests: To provide forces to conduct activities to promote British interests, influence and standing abroad.

Peace Support and Humanitarian Operations: To contribute forces to operations other than war in support of British interests and international order and humanitarian principles, the latter most likely under UN auspices.

Regional Conflict outside the NATO Area: To contribute forces for a regional conflict (but on an attack on NATO or one of its members) which, if unchecked, could adversely affect European security, or which could pose a serious threat to British interests elsewhere, or to international security. Operations are usually under UN or Organisation for Security Co-operation in Europe auspices.

Regional Conflict inside the NATO Area: To provide forces needed to respond to a regional crisis or conflict involving a NATO ally who calls for assistance under Article 5 of the Washington Treaty.

Strategic Attack on NATO: To provide, within the expected warning and readiness preparation times, the forces required to counter a strategic attack against NATO.

This mission statement is further sub-divided into a number of Military Tasks (MT) which accurately define the way in which these missions are actually accomplished.

MINISTRY OF DEFENCE (MoD)

In 1963, the three independent service ministries (Admiralty, War Office and Air Ministry) were merged to form the present MoD.

The UK MoD is the government department that is responsible for all defence related aspects of national policy. This large organisation, which directly affects the lives of about half a million servicemen, reservists and MoD employed civilians, is controlled by The Secretary of State for Defence and his deputies.

The Secretary of State for Defence has three principal deputies;

Minister of State for the Armed Forces

Minister of State for Defence Equipment and Support

Parliamentary Under-Secretary of State for Defence and Minister for Veterans Affairs

The Secretary of State is assisted by two principal advisers:

Permanent Under-Secretary of State (PUS): The PUS is responsible for policy, finance and administration in the MoD. As the MoD's Principal Accounting Officer he is personally responsible to Parliament for the expenditure of all public money voted to the MoD for Defence purposes.

Chief of the Defence Staff (CDS): The CDS acts as the professional head of the Armed Forces and he is the principal military adviser to the Secretary of State and to the Government.

Both the PUS and the CDS have deputies; the Second Permanent Under-Secretary of State (2nd PUS), and the Vice-Chief of the Defence Staff (VCDS).

In general terms defence is managed through a number of major committees that provide corporate leadership and strategic direction:

Defence Council
Defence Management Board
Chiefs of Staff Committee
Single Service Boards

DEFENCE COUNCIL

The Defence Council is the senior committee which provides the legal basis for the conduct and administration of defence and this council is chaired by the Secretary of State for Defence. The composition of the Defence Council is as follows:

The Secretary of State for Defence
Minister of State for the Armed Forces
Minister of State for Defence Equipment and Support
Parliamentary Under-Secretary of State for Defence and Minister for Veterans Affairs
Permanent Under-Secretary of State for Defence
Chief of the Defence Staff
Vice-Chief of the Defence Staff

Chief of the Naval Staff and First Sea Lord
Chief of the Air Staff
Chief of the General Staff
Chief of Defence Procurement
Chief Scientific Adviser
Second Permanent Under-Secretary of State

DEFENCE MANAGEMENT BOARD

This board is chaired by the PUS and is the MoD's senior non-ministerial committee. In essence the Defence Management Board is the MoD's main corporate board providing senior leadership and direction to the implementation of defence policy.

Chiefs of Staff Committee

This committee is chaired by the CDS and is the MoD's senior committee that provides advice on operational military matters and the preparation and conduct of military operations.

Single Service Boards

There are three single service boards: Admiralty Board, Army Board and the Air Force Board all of which are chaired by the Secretary of State for Defence. In general the purpose of the boards is the administration and monitoring of single service performance. Each of these three boards has an executive committee chaired by the single service chief of staff; Navy Board, Executive Committee of the Army Board and the Air Force Board Standing Committee.

CHIEF OF THE DEFENCE STAFF

The Chief of the Defence Staff (CDS) is the officer responsible to the Secretary of State for Defence for the coordinated effort of all three fighting services. He has his own Central Staff Organisation and a Vice Chief of the Defence Staff who ranks as number four in the services hierarchy, following the three single service commanders. The current CDS is:

Air Chief Marshal Sir Jock Stirrup KCB AFC ADC FRAeS FCMI RAF

Air Chief Marshal Stirrup was educated at Merchant Taylors' School, Northwood and the Royal Air Force College Cranwell, and was commissioned in 1970.

After a tour as a Qualified Flying Instructor he served on loan with the Sultan of Oman's Air Force, operating Strikemasters in the Dhofar War. Returning to the United Kingdom in 1975 he was posted to No 41(F) Squadron, flying Jaguars in the Fighter Reconnaissance role, before taking up an exchange appointment on RF-4C Phantoms in the United States. He then spent two years at RAF Lossiemouth as a flight commander on the Jaguar Operational Conversion Unit, and subsequently attended the Joint Service Defence College in 1984. He commanded No II(AC) Squadron, flying Fighter Reconnaissance Jaguars from Royal Air Force Laarbruch, until 1987 when he took up the post of Personal Staff Officer to the Chief of the Air Staff. He assumed command of Royal Air Force Marham in 1990, just in time for Operation GRANBY, and then attended the 1993 Course at the Royal College of Defence Studies. He completed No 7 Higher Command and Staff Course at Camberley prior to becoming the Director of Air Force Plans and Programmes in 1994. He became Air Officer Commanding No 1 Group in

April 1997 and was appointed Assistant Chief of the Air Staff in August 1998. He took up the appointment of Deputy Commander-in-Chief Strike Command in 2000. At the same time he assumed the additional roles of Commander of NATO's Combined Air Operations Centre 9 and Director of the European Air Group. He spent the last few months of his tour, from September 2001 to January 2002, as UK National Contingent Commander and Senior British Military Advisor to CINCUSCENTCOM for Operation VERITAS, the UK's contribution to the United States led Operation ENDURING FREEDOM in Afghanistan.

Air Chief Marshal Stirrup was appointed KCB in the New Year Honours List 2002 and became Deputy Chief of the Defence Staff (Equipment Capability) in March 2002. He was appointed Chief of the Air Staff, on promotion, in March 2005 and was appointed as the Chief of the Defence Staff during May 2007 following the retirement of General Sir Michael Walker.

Air Chief Marshal Sir Jock Stirrup

CHAIN OF COMMAND

The Chief of the Defence Staff (CDS) is the principal service advisor to HM Government and he commands and coordinates the activities of the three services through the three single service commanders. These single service commanders exercise command of their single services through their respective headquarters.

However, the complex inter-service nature of the majority of modern military operations, where military, air and naval support must be coordinated has led to the establishment of a permanent tri-service Joint Headquarters. The chain of command resembles the following:

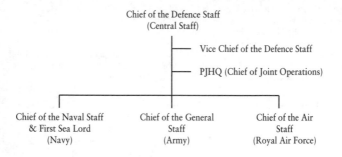

Chief of the Defence Staff
(Central Staff)

Vice Chief of the Defence Staff

PJHQ (Chief of Joint Operations)

Chief of the Naval Staff & First Sea Lord (Navy)

Chief of the General Staff (Army)

Chief of the Air Staff (Royal Air Force)

PERMANENT JOINT HEADQUARTERS (PJHQ)

The UK MoD established a Permanent Joint Headquarters (PJHQ) for joint military operations at Northwood in Middlesex on 1 April 1996. This headquarters brought together on a permanent basis, intelligence, planning, operational and logistics staffs. It contains elements of a rapidly deployable in-theatre Joint Force Headquarters that has the capability of commanding rapid deployment front line forces.

MoD officials have described the primary role of PJHQ as "Working proactively to anticipate crises and monitoring developments in areas of interest to the UK". The establishment of PJHQ has set in place a proper, clear and unambiguous connection between policy and the strategic direction and conduct of operations. Because it exists on a permanent basis rather than being established for a particular operation, PJHQ is involved from the very start of planning for possible operations. Where necessary, PJHQ then takes responsibility for the subsequent execution of these plans.

PJHQ, commanded by the Chief of Joint Operations (CJO), (currently a three star officer) occupies existing accommodation above and below ground at Northwood in Middlesex. PJHQ is responsible for planning all UK-led joint, potentially joint, combined and multinational operations and works in close partnership with MoD Head Office in the planning of operations and policy formulation, thus ensuring PJHQ is well placed to implement policy. Having planned the operation, and contributed advice to Ministers, PJHQ will then conduct such operations. Amongst its many tasks PJHQ is currently (mid 2007) engaged in planning and conducting UK military involvement in both Iraq and Afghanistan.

When another nation is in the lead, PJHQ exercises operational command of UK forces deployed on the operation.

Being a Permanent Joint Headquarters, PJHQ provides continuity of experience from the planning phase to the execution of the operation, and on to post-operation evaluation and learning of lessons.

Principal Additional Tasks of PJHQ Include:

- Monitoring designated areas of operational interest
- Preparing contingency plans
- Contributions to the UK MoD's decision making process
- Exercise of operational control of overseas commands (Falklands, Cyprus and Gibraltar)
- Managing its own budget
- Formulation of joint warfare doctrine at operational and tactical levels
- Conducting joint force exercises
- Focus for Joint Rapid Reaction Force planning and exercising

Overview of International Operations

From 1 Aug 1996 PJHQ assumed responsibility for military operations worldwide. Non-core functions, such as the day-to-day management of the Overseas Commands in Cyprus, Falkland Islands, and Gibraltar, are also delegated by MoD Head Office to the PJHQ. This allows MoD Head Office to concentrate in particular on policy formulation and strategic direction. As of early 2007 PJHQ has been involved with UK commitments in the following areas:

Afghanistan, Albania, Algeria, Angola, Bosnia, Burundi, East Timor, Eritrea, Honduras, Iraq (including operations during 2003), Kosovo, Montenegro, Montserrat, Mozambique, Sierra Leone, East Zaire, West Zaire (Democratic Republic of the Congo).

Operations for which PJHQ is not responsible include: UK Strategic Nuclear Deterrent; Defence of the UK Home Base; Defence of UK Territorial Waters and Airspace; Support to the Civil Power in Northern Ireland; Counter-terrorism in the UK and Operations in support of NATO (Article V General War).

PJHQ is commanded by the Chief of Joint Operations (CJO):

Lieutenant General J N R Houghton CBE (CJO)

Lieutenant General Nick Houghton was born in 1954 in Otley, West Yorkshire. He was educated at Woodhouse Grove School in Bradford, RMA Sandhurst and St Peter's College, Oxford, where he completed an in-service degree in Modern History.

Commissioned into the Green Howards in 1974, he had a variety of Regimental and Staff appointments before attending the Army Command and Staff Course at both Shrivenham and Camberley. Thereafter he was Military Assistant to the Chief of Staff British Army of the Rhine and a member of the Directing Staff at the Royal Military College of Science, Shrivenham. At Regimental Duty he was both a Company Commander in, and Commanding Officer of, 1st Battalion The Green Howards in the Mechanised and Airmobile roles, and in Northern Ireland.

More recently Lieutenant General Houghton was Deputy Assistant Chief of Staff, G3 (Operations & Deployment) in HQ Land Command 1994 – 1997 and attended the Higher Command and Staff Course in 1997. He commanded 39 Infantry Brigade in Northern Ireland from 1997 to 1999 and was the Director of Military Operations in the Ministry of Defence from December 1999 to July 2002. He was Chief of Staff of the Allied Rapid Reaction Corps from July 2002 to April 2004 before becoming the Assistant Chief of the Defence Staff

(Operations) from May 2004 to October 2005. He was the Senior British Military Representative Iraq and Deputy Commanding General of the Multi-National Force-Iraq from October 2005 until assuming his current appointment as Chief of Joint Operations at PJHQ (UK) in March 2006.

Lieutenant General J N R Houghton

PJHQ Structure

PJHQ brings together at Northwood some 400 civilian, specialist and tri-service military staff from across the MoD. The headquarters structure resembles the normal Divisional organisation, but staff operate within multidisciplinary groups which draw from across the headquarters. The headquarters must have the capability of supporting a number of operations simultaneously on behalf of the UK MoD.

PJHQ in the MoD Chain of Command

Defence and Overseas Policy Committee
(Chaired by Prime Minister)
|
Minister of Defence
|
Chief of the Defence Staff
(CDS)
|
Director of Operations
(D Ops)
|
Allied Operational —— **PJHQ** —— UK Commands
|
Joint Task Force Headquarters
(JTFHQ)

Note: The Defence and Overseas Policy Committee (DOPC) is responsible for the strategic direction of the UK Government's defence and overseas policy. The DOPC is chaired by the Prime Minister and members include the Secretary of State for Foreign and Commonwealth Affairs (Deputy Chair); Deputy Prime Minister and First Secretary of State; Chancellor of the Exchequer; Secretary of State for Defence; Secretary of State for the Home Department;

Secretary of State for International Development; Secretary of State for Trade and Industry. If necessary, other ministers, the Heads of the Intelligence Agencies and the Chief of Defence Staff may be invited to attend.

PJHQ Headquarters Structure

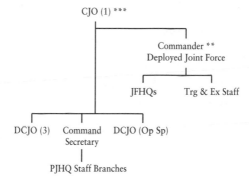

Notes:
(1) CJO – Chief of Joint Operations; (2) *** Denotes the rank of the incumbent (3) COS – Chief of Staff; (4) ACOS – Assistant Chief of Staff.

PJHQ Staff Branches/Departments

J1	Personnel and Admin
J2	Intelligence
J3	Operations (Sea-Air-Land)
J4	Logistics/Medical
J5	Policy and Crisis Planning
J6	Communications and Information Systems
J7	Joint Training
J8	Finance and Human Resources
J9	Legal
JFHQ	High Readiness Deployable Commander
JFLogCHQ	Standing Deployable Logistic Component Commander

The overall annual PJHQ budget is in the region of £606 million (for 2005/2006). Our estimate for the annual running costs of the Headquarters during 2004/2005 is approximately £52 million.

Included in the overall PJHQ budget are the costs of the UK forces in the Falkland Islands, Cyprus and Gibraltar. Major operations such as the Kosovo commitment, Afghanistan and Iraq are funded separately by way of a supplementary budget, and in almost all cases this requires government level approval. Small operations and the cost of reconnaissance parties are funded from the standard PJHQ budget.

JOINT RAPID REACTION FORCE (JRRF)

The JRRF is essentially the fighting force that PJHQ has immediately available. The JRRF provides a force for rapid deployment operations using a core operational group of the Army's 16th Air Assault Brigade and the Royal Navy's 3rd Commando Brigade, supported by a wide range of air and maritime assets including the Joint Force Harrier and the Joint Helicopter Command.

The force uses what the MoD has described as a 'golfbag' approach with a wide range of units available for specific operations. For example, if the operational situation demands assets such as heavy armour, long range artillery and attack helicopters, these assets can easily be assigned to the force. This approach means that the JRRF can be tailored for specific operations, ranging from support for a humanitarian crisis to missions including high intensity operations.

The 'reach' of the JRRF has been enhanced by the Royal Navy's new amphibious vessels HMS Albion and HMS Bulwark, currently entering service. Both of these ships will be able to carry 650 troops plus a range of armoured vehicles including main battle tanks. A flight deck will allow ship-to-shore helicopter operations.

Responsibility for providing units to the JRRF remains with the single service commands who ensure that units assigned are at an extremely high state of readiness. JRRF units remain committed to NATO.

Under normal circumstances, the Army would ensure that the the following land forces were available to the JRRF: a brigade sized grouping held at High Readiness and two Strategic Reserves—the Spearhead Land Element (SLE) held at Extremely High Readiness and the Airborne Task Force (ABTF) held at Very High Readiness. To command the JRRF a Joint Task Force HQ (JTFHQ) is maintained at 48 hours notice to move.

Since Operation Telic (Iraq) commenced the High Readiness Brigade has been routinely deployed to Iraq, and has therefore been unavailable to the JRRF. However, the SLE and ABTF have been maintained throughout.

The force commander is the CJRRFO (Chief of the Joint Rapid Reaction Force) who is responsible to the Chief of Joint Operations (CJO) at PJHQ. CJRRFO is supported by the Joint Force Operations Staff at PJHQ who provide a fully resourced Joint Task Force Headquarters (JTFHQ) at 48 hours notice to move anywhere in the world.

Joint Force Logistics Component

The Joint Force Logistics Component (JFLogC) provides a joint logistic headquarters with force logistics under the command of PJHQ. It delivers coordinated logistic support to the deployed Joint Force in accordance with the commander's priorities. The composition of the JFLogC will be determined by PJHQ during the mission planning stage. Two logistic brigades have been assigned to JFLogC.

DEFENCE EQUIPMENT AND SUPPORT

Following the establishment of PJHQ at Northwood it became important to combine the separate logistics functions of the three Armed Forces. As a result, in 2000 the three distinct separate service logistic functions were fused into one and the Defence Logistic Organisation was formed.

From 1 April 2007 the Defence Procurement Agency (DPA) and the Defence Logistic Organisation (DLO) were merged to form Defence Equipment and Support (DE&S). The first Chief of Defence Materiel is General Sir Kevin O'Donoghue who it is planned should be in post until late 2008.

The MoD plans for the DE&S to be the engine that delivers 'Through Life' equipment and logistic support, and making sure the whole factory to front line process is seamless and properly integrated.

Some of the DE&S responsibilities to Joint Operations include:

Logistics planning, resource management, contractual support and policy
Global fleet management and land-based equipment
Support of the naval fleet and all naval systems
Communication and Information Systems
Transport and movements
Food and ration packs
Ammunition
Fuel, Oil and Lubricants
Postal Services
Clothing and tentage
Storage for all equipment and materiel

With approximately 29,000 personnel, DE&S is one of the largest organisations within the MoD. With an annual budget of around £16 billion DE&S is at 65 locations and is represented at 150 specific sites.

THE UNITED KINGDOM DEFENCE BUDGET

> "You need three things to win a war,
> Money, money and more money".
>
> Trivulzio (1441–1518)

In general terms defence is related to money. Estimates for the world's top five defence budgets for 2006 (in billions of US$ and the latest year for which accurate figures are available) are as follows:

United States	US$ 535 billion
United Kingdom	US$ 55 billion
France	US$ 45 billion
Japan	US$ 41 billion
Germany	US$ 35 billion

For 2006 the Russian Defence Budget estimate is US$30 billion and the Chinese defence budget is estimated at being in the region of US$35 billion. The figures in the above table are figures derived from £ Sterling, Euro and Yen exchange rates in mid 2006.

In the 2006-2007 Financial Year (FY) the UK Government has allocated £28.6 billion on defence expenditure with £29.9 billion allocated for the FY 2007-2008. Actual expenditure in FY 2005-2006 represented about 2.3% of GDP. In 1985 UK defence expenditure represented about 5.2% of GDP.

The high unit costs of individual items of equipment illustrate the problems faced by defence planners when working out their annual budgets. At 2005 prices the following items cost:

Kinetic Energy Round for Challenger	£3,000 each
155 mm High Explosive Round	£900 each
Individual Weapon (IW)	£800 each (estimate)
5.56 mm round for IW	£1
One Rapier Missile	£60,000
One Challenger 2 MBT	£4.5 million (approx)
Combat High Boot	£95 per pair
Starstreak Missile	£100,000 each
Attack Helicopter	£42 million (region)
Eurofighter	£60 million (estimate)
Merlin Support Helicopter	£34 million

The costs of military operations in both Iraq and Afghanistan are included in Chapter 3 – International Commitments.

Under the early 1990s 'New Management Strategy' the UK defence budget was allocated to a series of 'Top Level Budget Holders' each of whom were allocated a budget with which to run their departments. The money allocated to these Top Level Budgets (TLBs) constitutes the building bricks upon which the whole of the defence budget is based.

Top Level Budgets FY2005-2006 (Departmental Expenditure Limits)
Naval Operational Areas (C-in-C Fleet)	£3,610 million
Army Operational Areas (C-in-C Land Command)	£5,829 million
General Officer Commanding (Northern Ireland)	£580 million
Air Force Operational Areas (AOC RAF Strike Command)	£4,071 million

Chief of Joint Operations	£605 million
Chief of Defence Logistics	£8,044 million
Second Sea Lord/Naval Home Command	£814 million
Adjutant General (Army) Personnel & Training Command	£1,971 million
RAF Personnel & Training Command	£1,058 million
Central	£2,625 million
Defence Procurement Agency	£2,885 million
Science, Information and Technology	£497 million
Defence Estates	£1,298 million

Defence Budgets – NATO Comparison (2006 Figures)

The nations of the North Atlantic Treaty Organisation (NATO) spent some US$761.6 billion on defence during 2006.

It is probably worth noting that Canada and the European members of NATO spent approximately US$226 billion, while the US spent some US$535 billion. Collectively, Canada and the European members of NATO spent 42% of the US total.

For ease of conversions from national currencies, amounts are shown in US$.

Country	2006 Budget (billions of US$)
Belgium	3.4
Bulgaria	0.7
Canada	14.1
Czech Republic	2.5
Denmark	3.4
Estonia	0.2
France	45.3
Germany	35.7
Greece	4.7
Hungary	1.3
Italy	15.5
Latvia	0.3
Lithuania	0.3
Luxembourg	0.2
Netherlands	9.9
Norway	4.8
Poland	5.8
Portugal	2.4
Romania	2.4
Spain	9.1
Slovakia	0.9
Slovenia	0.6
Turkey	8.0

United Kingdom	55.1
Other NATO	**226.6**
United States	535.0
Final Total	**761.6**

Note: Iceland has no military expenditure although it remains a member of NATO.

An interesting comparison is made by the total national defence budget divided by the total number of full time personnel in all three services. 2006 figures for the top five world defence spending nations are as follows:

Nation	2006 Defence Budget (US$)	Total Service Personnel	Cost per Serviceman
United States	535 billion	1,506,000	355,425
UK	55 billion	190,000	289,473
Japan	41 billion	240,000	170,833
France	45 billion	254,000	177,165
Germany	35 billion	245,000	142,857

BRITISH ARMY STATISTICS
Deployment of The Regular Army (As at 1 April 2006)

	Officers	Soldiers
Land Command		
Field Army	4,400	44,900
Joint Helicopter Command	1,400	10,800
Commander Regional Forces	1,400	11,100
Land Support	300	100
Adjutant General (Personnel & Training Command)		
Army Personnel Centre	1,400	2,300
ATRA	1,100	5,000
Army Programme	900	2,000
Chief of Staff	300	600
General Staff	600	600
Primary Health Care	100	100
Untrained Personnel	1,000	9,700
ATRA – Army Training and Recruitment Agency		
Northern Ireland	500	4,500
Defence Logistics Organisation		
Equipment Support (Land)	100	200

Service Personnel Deployed/Stationed outside the UK mainland (April 2006)

Germany	21,960
Balkans	30
Cyprus	3,040
Gibraltar	340
Sierra Leone	90
Iraq and the Gulf	7,500 (estimate)
Belize	30 (estimate)
Kenya	10 (estimate)
Canada	260
USA	410
Falkland Islands	1,270 (estimate)
Afghanistan	5,000 (estimate at mid 2006)
Brunei	800 (estimate)

Manning Figures (Including personnel under training)

Regular Army (As at 1 April 2007)

	2007	1995	1990
Trained Strength	101,800	104,600	137,200
Untrained Strength	11,300	7,200	15,600
	113,100	**11,800**	**152,800**

Note: Previous years figures are given for comparison purposes. Figures for 2007 include 3,090 trained Gurkhas.

Regular Army Reserves (As at 1 April 2006)

Regular Reserves	32,060
Individuals liable to recall	95,520
Territorial Army	32,150

Recruitment – Regular Army (During Financial Year 2006/2007)

	(2006/07)	(1980/81)
Officers	720	1,489
Soldiers	12,400	27,382
	13,120	**28,871**

Note: 1980/81 figures are given for comparison.
Outflow – Regular Army (During Financial Year 2006/2007)

	(2006/07)	(1990/91)	(1980/81)
Officers (Trained)	1,270 (1)	1,860	1,497
Soldiers	14,910 (2)	20,964	20,422
	16,180	**22,824**	**21,919**

(1)Includes 210 untrained officers   (2)Includes 4,480 untrained soldiers

Army Cadet Force

	(1 Apr 2006)	(1 Apr 1980)
Total Army Cadets	81,700	74,600

The Army Cadets are run and administered by the MoD. Figures include Combined Cadet Force and Army Cadet Force.

Full-time trained Strength of the Army (including FTRS*) at the beginning of 2007

	Strength
Staff	810
The Household Cavalry/ Royal Armoured Corps	5,560
Royal Regiment of Artillery	7,410
Corps of Royal Engineers	8,780
Royal Corps of Signals	8,640
The Infantry	24,520
Army Air Corps	1,980
Royal Army Chaplains Department	140
The Royal Logistics Corps	15,680
Royal Army Medical Corps	2,810
Royal Electrical and Mechanical Engineers	9,730
Adjutant General's Corps (Provost Branch)	2,010
Adjutant Generals Corps (Staff and Personnel Support Branch)	4,440
Adjutant Generals Corps (Educational and Training Services Branch)	340
Adjutant Generals Corps Royal (Army Legal Service)	100
Royal Army Veterinary Corps	190
Small Arms School Corps	150
Royal Army Dental Corps	370
Intelligence Corps	1,440
Army Physical Training Corps	440
Queen Alexandra's Royal Army Nursing Corps	840
Corps of Army Music	940
Long Service List	620
Unallocated	10
Total trained regular Army and FTRS	97,950
Gurkhas (trained and untrained)	3,360
Full-time trained Army	101,310

*FTRS (Full Time Reserve Service)

Over 100 Years Ago – Strength of the British Army at 1 Jan 1905

Regular Army	195,000
Colonial Troops or Native Indian Corps	14,000
Army Reserve	80,000
Militia	132,000
Yeomanry (Cavalry)	28,000

Note: Regular forces in India totalled 74,500

Three years previously Regular Army totals by Corps were:

Household Cavalry	1,390
Cavalry of the Line	20,200
Horse Artillery	3,483
Field Artillery	15,509
Mountain Artillery	1,200
Garrison Artillery	18,400
Royal Engineers	7,130
Foot Guards	5,873
Infantry of the Line	132,332
Colonial Corps	5,217
Army Service Corps	3,555
Ordnance Staff	920
Armourers	352
Medical Services	2,993
	218,554

The force reduction was due to the drawdown following the end of the war in South Africa.

CHAPTER 2 – ORGANISATIONS

The routine management of the Army is the responsibility of The Army Board the composition of which is shown in the next listing.

The Army Board

The Secretary of State for Defence
Minister of State for the Armed Forces
Minister of State for Defence Equipment and Support
Parliamentary Under-Secretary of State for Defence and Minister for Veterans
Chief of the General Staff
Second Permanent Under-Secretary of State
Adjutant General
Quartermaster General
Master General of the Ordnance
Commander in Chief (Land Command)
Assistant Chief of the General Staff

Executive Committee of the Army Board (ECAB)

Attended by senior UK Army commanders, ECAB dictates the policy required for the Army to function efficiently and meet the aims required by the Defence Council and government. The Chief of the General Staff is the chairman of the Executive Committee of the Army Board.

Army Board and ECAB decisions are acted upon by the military staff at the various headquarters worldwide.

CHIEF OF THE GENERAL STAFF

General Sir Richard Dannatt KCB CBE MC

General Sir Richard Dannatt

General Sir Richard Dannatt was commissioned into The Green Howards from Sandhurst in 1971 and has served with 1st Battalion The Green Howards in Northern Ireland, Cyprus and Germany. He commanded the Battalion in the Airmobile role from 1989 – 1991. In tours away from Regimental Duty he has been a Company instructor at Sandhurst, Chief of Staff of the 20th Armoured Brigade, Military Assistant to the Minister of State for the Armed Forces and Colonel Higher Command and Staff Course/Doctrine at the Staff College.

From 1994-1996 he commanded 4th Armoured Brigade. During this period he was deployed from Germany to Bosnia as Commander Sector South West in the final months of the United Nations Protection Force (UNPROFOR) and then commanding his Brigade at the start of the Implementation Force (IFOR) with Multinational Division (South West). From 1996-1998 he was Director of Defence Programmes in the Ministry of Defence. He took command of 3rd (United Kingdom) Division in January 1999, and served that year in Kosovo as Commander British Forces. In November 2000 he was appointed Deputy Commander Operations of the Stabilisation Force (SFOR) in Bosnia. He was the Assistant Chief of the General Staff in the UK Ministry of Defence from April 2001 to October 2002, and assumed the command of the Allied Rapid Reaction Corps on the 15th January 2003. In March 2005 he was appointed as the Commander-in-Chief Land Command and he assumed the appointment of Chief of the General Staff on 29 August 2006.

In addition to his current appointment, General Sir Richard Dannatt is Colonel Commandant of The King's Division, The Royal Military Police and Army Air Corps. He is President of the Army Rifle Association, and the Soldiers' and Airmen's Scripture Readers Association, and Vice-President of The Officers' Christian Union.

Note; General Sir Richard Dannatt's predecessor as CGS was General Sir Mike Jackson MBE CBE CB KCB DSO ADC Gen.

Chain-of-Command

The Army is commanded from the MoD via two subsidiary headquarters and a number of smaller headquarters worldwide. The Joint Headquarters (JHQ) at Northwood in Middlesex has an important input into this chain-of-command and it is almost certain that any operation with which the army is involved will be under the overall command of PJHQ. The following diagram illustrates this chain-of-command.

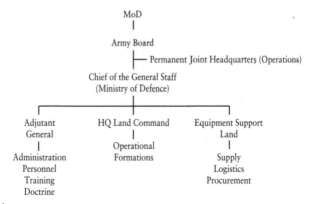

Staff Branches

The Staff Branches that you would expect to find at every military headquarters from the Ministry of Defence (MoD) down to Brigade level are as follows:

Commander	–	Usually a General (or Brigadier) who commands the formation.
Chief of Staff	–	The officer who runs the headquarters on a day-to-day basis and who often acts as a second-in-command. Generally known as the COS.
Gl Branch	–	Responsible for personnel matters including manning, discipline and personal services.
G2 Branch	–	Responsible for intelligence and security
G3 Branch	–	Responsible for operations including staff duties, exercise planning, training, operational requirements, combat development and tactical doctrine.
G4 Branch	–	Logistics and quartering.
G5 Branch	–	Civil and military co-operation

HQ Land Command

HQ Land Command is located at Erskine Barracks, Wilton near Salisbury and controls about 80% of the troops in the British Isles and almost 100% of its fighting capability.

Land Command's role is to deliver and sustain the Army's operational capability, whenever required throughout the world, and the Command comprises all operational troops in Great Britain, Germany, Nepal and Brunei, together with the Army Training Teams in Canada, Belize and Kenya.

Land Command has almost 75,000 trained Army personnel and the largest single Top Level Budget in Defence, with a budget of just over £5.6 billion annually. It contains all the Army's fighting equipment, including attack helicopters, Challenger 2 tanks, Warrior Infantry Fighting Vehicles, AS90 and the Multi-Launched Rocket System (MLRS).

Land Command is one of the three central commands in the British Army, the other two being the Adjutant General (with responsibility for administration, personnel and training) and Equipment Support (Land) responsible for supply and logistics. The Command is responsible for providing all the Army's fighting troops throughout the World. These are organised into eight formations and are commanded by Major Generals.

The Structure of Land Command

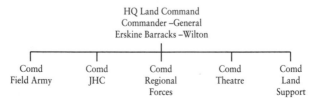

Future plans for HQ Land Command: Work to consider the benefits of rationalisation and collocation of the two main Army HQs – HQ Land Command (Wilton) and HQ Adjutant-General (Upavon) appears to be continuing. The Army is currently determining the possible size and structure of the new HQ organisation and, in parallel, assessing a number of local site options.

As of late 2006 there were 597 military and 759 civilian posts at HQ Land Command and with 325 military and 470 civilian posts at the Adjutant-General's headquarters in Upavon.

It would appear that Andover is the preferred site option for the new Headquarters Land Forces and subject to final decisions it is possible that from 1 April 2009, Headquarters Land Forces will be fully operational in its new location. This will provide the Army with a headquarters of about 1,750 military and civilian staff. Compared to current headquarters staffing levels this represents a reduction of about 240 civilian and 100 military posts and a probable significant reduction in running costs.

Field Army

The Commander Field Army has operational command of all Field Army Formations. This includes training designated forces for all types of military operations and providing appropriate military capability to Permanent Joint Headquarters and/or the Joint Rapid Reaction Forces as required.

Major units under the direct command of the Field Army include:

- 1 (UK) Division   (Ready Division)
- 3 (UK) Division   (Ready Division)
- Combat Service Support Group (United Kingdom)
- Combat Service Support Group (Germany)

Service personnel total for the Field Army at 1 April 2006 was 49,300 (including 4,400 officers).

Joint Helicopter Command (JHC)

The Joint Helicopter Command's primary role is to deliver and sustain effective Battlefield Helicopter and Air Assault assets, operationally capable under all environmental conditions, in order to support the UK's defence missions and tasks. JHC major formations are as follows:

- All Army Aviation Units
- RAF Support Helicopter Force
- Commando Helicopter Force
- Joint Helicopter Force (Northern Ireland)
- 16 Air Assault Brigade
- Combat Support Units
- Combat Service Support Units
- Joint Helicopter Command and Standards Wing

Service personnel total for the Joint Helicopter Command at 1 April 2006 was 12,300 (includes RAF and Royal Navy personnel and 1,400 officers).

Commander Regional Forces

The Commander Regional Forces maintains, and where possible, enhances the provision of the military capability and infrastructure support required to meet Land Command's operational requirements.

In addition, Commander Regional Forces at HQ LAND is the Inspector General of the Territorial Army, with additional responsibilities for Cadets and the University Officer Training Corps (UOTC).

Major units that assist Commander Regional Forces are amongst the following:

- 2 Division   (Regenerative Division)
- 4 Division   (Regenerative Division)
- 5 Division   (Regenerative Division)
- United Kingdom Support Command (Germany)
- London District
- Land Support Management Group

Service personnel total for the Commander Regional Forces at 1 April 2006 was 12,500 (including 1,400 officers).

Commander Land Support

The Defence Supply Chain provides a range of support functions to enable the British armed forces to carry out operations. These include storing and distributing all the supplies needed by the forces, such as equipment, mail, medical supplies, fuel, clothing, food and ammunition, as well as transporting personnel and freight anywhere in the world.

Personnel total for the Commander Land Support grouping at 1 April 2006 was 400 service and 800 civilian personnel.

Note: HQ Land also has responsibility for overseas detachments including Belize, Canada, Brunei, Nepal and Kenya. Troops in Northern Ireland, Cyprus and the Falkland Islands are commanded from the MoD via PJHQ. Overseas operations in Afghanistan, the Balkans, Iraq, and Sierra Leone are also the responsibility of PJHQ.

Theatre Troops

Commander Theatre Troops is responsible for the following:

- 1 Artillery Brigade
- 16 Regiment RA
- 1 Signal Brigade
- 2 (NC) Signal Brigade
- 11 Signal Brigade
- 8 Force Engineer Brigade
- 2 Medical Brigade

- ♦ 1 Reconnaissance Brigade
- ♦ 1 Military Intelligence Brigade
- ♦ 101 Logistic Brigade
- ♦ 102 Logistic Brigade
- ♦ 104 Logistic Brigade
- ♦ Equipment Support Theatre Troops
- ♦ HQ RLC TA

Ready Divisions

There are two 'Ready' Divisions: the 1st (UK) Armoured Division, based in Germany, and the 3rd (UK) Division in the United Kingdom. Both of these divisions are earmarked to form part of the Allied Command Europe Rapid Reaction Corps (ARRC), NATO's premier strategic formation; but they also have the flexibility to be employed on rapid reaction tasks or in support of other Defence Roles.

In addition to their operational roles, these divisions also command the Army units in specified geographic areas: in the case of the 1st Division, this area is made up of the garrisons in Germany where the Division's units are based; and in the case of some of the garrison areas in the 3rd Division's area of responsibility in the South West of England.

Regenerative Divisions

There are three Regenerative Divisions, based on old Districts in the United Kingdom. These are the 2nd Division with its Headquarters at Edinburgh, the 4th Division with its Headquarters at Aldershot, and the 5th Division with its Headquarters at Shrewsbury. These Regenerative Divisions are responsible for all non-deployable Army units within their boundaries, and could provide the core for three new divisions, should the Army be required to expand to meet a major international threat.

Districts

Two Districts remain: London District (although subordinated to 4th Division for budgetary purposes), and the United Kingdom Support Command (Germany).

London District is responsible for all Army units within the M25 boundary. The activity for which the Headquarters and the District is most well known is State Ceremonial and Public Duties in the Capital. The district insignia shows the Sword of St Paul representing the City of London and the Mural Crown representing the County of London. The District has its Headquarters in Horse Guards and is commanded by a Major General.

Between 500 and 600 troops are involved at any one time in MoD-sponsored equipment trials, demonstrations and exhibitions. Public Duties in London also take up two/three battalions at any one time. All troops not otherwise operationally committed are also available to provide Military Aid to the Civil Authorities in the United Kingdom.

The United Kingdom Support Command – Germany (UKSC(G)) with its Headquarters at Rheindahlen has about 3,600 personnel and provides essential support functions for 1 (UK) Armoured Division and the Headquarters of the ARRC.

HQ UKSC(G) also commands the only garrison west of the River Rhine, designated Rhine Garrison, which comprises mainly a signal brigade and logistic support units.

It also has administrative responsibility for the four other British Army Garrisons in Germany – at Osnabrück, Bergen-Hohne, Paderborn and Gütersloh.

There are two Combat Service Support (CSS) Groups:

Combat Service Support Group (United Kingdom) consists of a supply regiment, two transport regiments, general support medical regiment which has both Regular and Territorial Army squadrons, three field hospitals, and a field medical equipment depot. For operations, the group may have assigned to it two Territorial Army transport regiments, five Territorial Army field hospitals, and a Territorial Army Royal Electrical and Mechanical Engineers maintenance battalion.

Combat Service Support Group (Germany) consists of a supply regiment; two transport regiments, and a general support medical regiment which has both Regular and Territorial Army squadrons. For operations, the group may have assigned to it a Territorial Army transport regiment, six Territorial Army field hospitals, a Territorial Army field medical equipment depot, and a Territorial Army Royal Electrical and Mechanical Engineers maintenance battalion.

Other areas and tasks
Although Land Command is not responsible for running operations in Northern Ireland, the Former Yugoslavia, Afghanistan, Sierra Leone, Cyprus, the Falkland Islands and Iraq (a responsibility of PJHQ), it will provide the operational troops for these areas. Some 5,000 troops will be stationed in Northern Ireland from 2008; and a further 15,000 are deployed in Afghanistan, Cyprus, the Balkans, Sierra Leone, the Falkland Islands and Iraq.

Some 500 troops are involved at any one time in MoD -sponsored equipment trials, demonstrations and exhibitions. Public Duties in London take up two/three battalions at any one time. All troops not otherwise operationally committed are also available to provide Military Aid to the Civil Authorities (MACA) in the United Kingdom.

Land Command Divisional/District Summaries

Ready Divisions

1 (UK) Armoured Division and British Forces Germany (BFG)
The 1st Armoured Division was formed in 1940. Since World War II the Division has been re-titled three times and became the 1st (United Kingdom) Armoured Division in 1993, having successfully fought in the Gulf War of 1991. The Division has its headquarters at Herford in Germany and currently (2007) commands three Armoured Brigades situated throughout North West Germany and is the major component of British Forces Germany. By late 2008 we expect BFG to number approximately 21,800 personnel.

British Forces Germany (BFG) is the composite name given to the British Army, Royal Air Force and supporting civil elements stationed in Germany. The terms British Army of the

Rhine (BAOR) and Royal Air Force Germany (RAFG), until recently were the traditional names used to describe the two Service elements of the British Forces stationed in Germany.

For many years following World War II, and as a result of the confrontation between NATO and the former Warsaw Treaty Organisation, the UK Government had stationed four Army divisions and a considerable part of its Air Force at five airbases in the Federal Republic of Germany. On the whole this level of commitment was maintained until 1992 and although these forces appeared to be solely national, they were in fact closely integrated with the NATO Northern Army Group (NORTHAG) and the 2nd Allied Tactical Air Force (2 ATAF).

As a result of political changes in Europe and the UK Government's 'Options for Change' programme, the British Army's presence in Germany has been reduced to three armoured brigades and a divisional headquarters with logistical support. The majority of the RAF presence has been withdrawn.

Composition of 1(UK) Armoured Division

1 (UK) Armoured Division has its headquarters at Herford in Germany (about 50 kms from Hanover) and the three Armoured Brigades under command are located at Osnabruck, Bergen-Hohne and Paderborn.

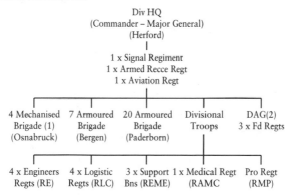

Note: (1) Under Future Army Structure proposals 4th Armoured Brigade became 4th Mechanised Brigade during 2006 and redeploys to Catterick (Yorkshire) in 2008–09, retaining a single Warrior Battalion. In general terms a Mechanised Brigade contains one Armoured Infantry Battalion equipped with Warrior. 1 (UK) Armoured Division will then consist of two Armoured Brigades.

(2) DAG (Divisional Artillery Group) This DAG could be reinforced by Rapier Air Defence and MLRS units from the UK as necessary. (3) Personnel total in Germany is approximately 21,800 with about 17,000 in 1 (UK) Armoured Division. During early 2008 this Division could probably provide the Headquarters (HQs) for up to six Battlegroups.

Estimate of Force Levels in 1 (UK) Armoured Division (1 Jan 2007)

Army Personnel	17,000
Challenger 2 MBT	150
Warrior AIFV	450
Other Tracked Vehicles	1,100
Helicopters (Army Aviation)	24
Artillery Guns	66
MLRS	0
AVLB	18

It is probable that in the event of hostilities (as was the case in recent operations in Iraq) considerable numbers of officers and soldiers from the Territorial Army (TA) would be used to reinforce this division. These reinforcements would consist of individuals, drafts of specialists, or by properly formed TA units varying in size from Mobile Bath Units of 20 men, to Major Units over 500 strong.

UKSC(G)

The United Kingdom Support Command (Germany) has responsibility for British Army Troops on the Continent of Europe that are not part of 1st (United Kingdom) Armoured Division. Its headquarters replaces that of the British Army of the Rhine, whose sign it has adopted. The headquarters of UKSC(G) is located at Rheindahlen and has about 3, 600 personnel under command.

Possible future changes in BFG Force Structure

In addition to the mid 2006 announcement of the move of 4 Armoured Brigade from Germany to the UK, the Secretary of State for Defence has announced the intention to make further adjustments to the structure of the British Forces in Germany. These include proposals for the possible return to the UK of Headquarters Allied Rapid Reaction Corps (HQ ARRC), 102 Logistic Brigade and 1 Signal Brigade, over the period 2008-2012, including identifying exactly where these units will be based in the UK.

A project team is being established to assess these proposals in greater detail, and to determine whether they are practicable and offer value for money. It is likely that the MoD will be in a position to announce a final decision late in 2007.

There are also plans for a series of minor moves within Germany which will lead to the closure of Osnabruck Station from early 2009. In the longer term there are proposals that may result in the closure of Munster Station and therefore Osnabruck Garrison as a whole. The current planning assumption is that this would not take place before 2010. The relocation of HQ ARRC (a NATO Headquarters), 102 Logistic Brigade and 1 Signal Brigade would allow the closure of Rhine Garrison in the period 2010-2012. This will result in the concentration of UK Germany-based forces in Hohne, Paderborn and Guttersloh garrisons.

Composition of 3 (UK) Mechanised Division

The 3rd (United Kingdom) Division is the only operational (Ready) Division in the UK. The Division has a mix of capabilities encompassing armoured and wheeled elements in its brigades.

In the diagram we have shown 16 Air Assault Brigade as being part of 3 (UK) Division purely as an example of how this formation might be deployed. 16 Air Assault Brigade is under the command of the Joint Helicopter Command (JHC). However, the JHC is not an Operational Headquarters and for operations, 16 Air Assault Brigade will probably be detached to under command of HQ Allied Rapid Reaction Corps, PJHQ, HQ 1 (UK) Division or HQ 3 (UK) Division.

```
                          HQ 3 (UK)
                           (Bulford)
                   Commander-Major General
    ┌──────────────────────┬──────────────────────┐
1 Mech Bde (1)        19 Light Bde (2)        12 Mech Bde
  (Tidworth)            (Catterick)            (Aldershot)
    │                      │                      │
   DAG                 52 Inf Bde          16 Air Assault Brigade
   (3)                 (Edinburgh)             (Colchester)        Divisional
                                                                    Troops
    ┌──────────────┬──────────────┬──────────────────┐
  Signal      Force Recce      Aviation         2 x Engr Regt
  Regt           Regt          Regt(4)
    ┌──────────────┬──────────────┬──────────────────┬──────────┐
Gen Sp Regt  Close Sp Regt     Sp Bn           Cs Med Bn      Pro Coy
  (RLC)         (RLC)          (REME)            (RAMC)         (RMP)
                                 │
                            3 x Fd Wksps
```

Note: (1) 1 Mechanised Brigade; (2) 19 Brigade has re-roled to become a light brigade and is now ready for deployment in this role, where it serves as the contingent NATO response force. From 2008 onward, the Headquarters of 19 Light Brigade will probably be in Scotland with some units in Northern Ireland; (3) Divisional Artillery Group Artillery Regiment with Multi Launch Rocket System (if allocated), UAVs, Close Support Artillery plus Rapier and HVM air defence systems when required ; (4) Army Air Corps Regiment with Lynx & Gazelle (from Joint Helicopter Command as required); The composition of this division allows the UK MoD to retain a balanced force for out of NATO area operations.
3 Commando Brigade (a Royal Naval formation) is available to support 3 (UK) Division if necessary. Details of the organisation of 3 Commando Brigade are given in the Miscellaneous Chapter.

REGENERATIVE DIVISIONS

There are three Regenerative Divisions, based on older UK military districts. These are the 2nd Division with its Headquarters at Edinburgh, the 4th Division with its Headquarters at Aldershot, and the 5th Division with its Headquarters at Shrewsbury. These Regenerative Divisions are responsible for all army units within their boundaries and could provide the core for three new divisions, should the Army be required to expand to meet a major international threat. From 1 April 2007 the composition of these three Regenerative Divisions has been as follows:

2nd Division

The 2nd Division has responsibility for the whole of Scotland and Northern England. The Divisional Headquarters is in Edinburgh. The 2nd Division comprises four brigades and a garrison:

- 15 (North East) Brigade, with its HQ in York, responsible for units in the North East of England

- 38 (Irish) Brigade with HQ in Lisburn

- 51 (Scottish) Brigade, with its HQ in Stirling, responsible for all units north of Stirling including Shetland and the Western Isles

- Catterick Garrison, including units in Ripon, Topcliffe and Dishforth. Currently (2007) Catterick Garrison also hosts 19 Light Brigade (until 2008) which is under operational command of 3rd (UK) Division.

4th Division

The 4th Division has military responsibility for South East England, including Bedfordshire, Essex and Hertfordshire and its Headquarters is in Aldershot. The division consists of the following:

- 2 Brigade based in Shorncliffe. This is a light role infantry brigade with battalions based in various locations.

- 43 (Wessex) Brigade in Exeter

- 145 (Home Counties) Brigade in Aldershot

- 16 Air Assault Brigade is based in Colchester. The Brigade is administered by 4th Division but under the operational command of HQ Land Command and the Joint Helicopter Command.

5th Division

The 5th Division has responsibility for military units and establishments in Wales, the West Midlands and the South West. The Division has its Headquarters in Shrewsbury and the divisional area of responsibility covers about one third of Great Britain. The following brigades are under command:

- 42 (North West) Brigade, with its HQ in Preston, responsible for units in the North West of England
- 49 (East) Brigade in Chilwell
- 143 (West Midlands) Brigade based at Shrewsbury
- 160 (Wales) Brigade based at Brecon

ARMY BRIGADES

Under the Future Army Structure (FAS) proposals the UK Armed Forces will have the following combat brigades available for deployment once restructuring is complete:

Armoured Brigades: 7 Armoured Brigade; 20 Armoured Brigade
Mechanised Brigades: 1 Mechanised Brigade; 4 Mechanised Brigade; 12 Mechanised Brigade
Light Brigades: 16 Air Assault Brigade; 19 Light Brigade; 3 Commando Brigade (Royal Marines)

Armoured Brigade Organisation

The following diagram illustrates the possible composition of an Armoured Brigade in 1(UK) Armd Div on operations.

Totals:
      58 x Challenger MBT (Possibly)
      145 x Warrior AIFV
      320 x AFV 432/Spartan Armoured Vehicles
      24 x AS 90 SP Gun
      Approx 5,000 personnel

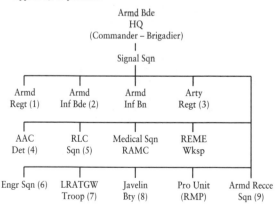

Notes: (1) Armoured Regiment with approx 58 x Challenger MBT; (2) Armoured Infantry Battalion with approx 52 x Warrior (with rifle coys) and approx 40 x FV432; (3) Artillery

Regiment with 24 x AS90 SP Guns; (4) Army Air Corps Detachment (possibly Lynx and Gazelle); (5) Transport Squadron RLC with approximately 60 -70 trucks; (6) Engineer Squadron with about 68 vehicles but size of squadron depending upon the task; (7) Long Range Anti-Tank Guided Weapon Troop (Swingfire) but due to be replaced in the longer term; (8) RA Bty with possibly 36 x HVM AD missiles; (9) Armoured Recce Squadron; (10) This Brigade could provide the HQs for three Battlegroups.

Mechanised Brigade Organisation

The following is an example of the possible Mechanised Brigade organisation (dependent on task).

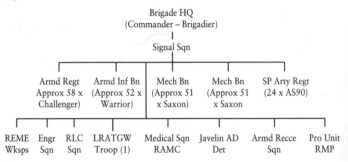

Note: Where appropriate Army Air Corps assets may be allocated plus Long Range Anti-Tank Guided Weapons.

16 Air Assault Brigade

Nearly 10,000 personnel form the personnel component of 16 Air Assault Brigade. Using everything from the latest Apache helicopter to air-mobile artillery equipment and high velocity air defence missiles, this Brigade has marked a considerable leap forward in Britain's defence capability.

The following diagram shows a possible configuration for 16 Air Assault Brigade during significant operations:

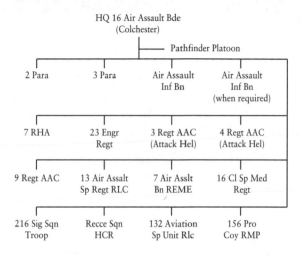

HQ 16 Air Assault Bde
(Colchester)

Pathfinder Platoon

| 2 Para | 3 Para | Air Assault Inf Bn | Air Assault Inf Bn (when required) |

| 7 RHA | 23 Engr Regt | 3 Regt AAC (Attack Hel) | 4 Regt AAC (Attack Hel) |

| 9 Regt AAC | 13 Air Assalt Sp Regt RLC | 7 Air Asslt Bn REME | 16 Cl Sp Med Regt |

| 216 Sig Sqn Troop | Recce Sqn HCR | 132 Aviation Sp Unit Rlc | 156 Pro Coy RMP |

The Brigade capitalises on the combat capabilities of the former 24 Airmobile Brigade and 5 Airborne Brigade, including two parachute battalions with an increase in combat service support. The introduction of the Apache Attack Helicopter has provided a new generation of weapons systems bringing major improvements in military capability. This brigade is under the command of the JHC (Joint Helicopter Command) and would be detached to other formations for operations.

Support helicopters are provided by the RAF (from the Joint Helicopter Command) and the Brigade would normally expect to operate with 18 x Chinook and 18 x Puma. An air assault infantry battalion can be moved by 20 x Chinook equivalents lifts. Each air assault infantry battalion has a personnel strength of 687 and a battalion has 12 x Milan firing posts.

19 Light Brigade
On operations 19 Light Brigade could have the following configuration:

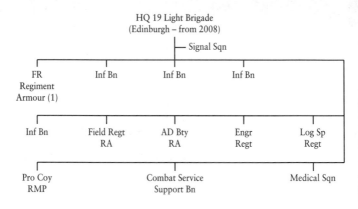

HQ 19 Light Brigade
(Edinburgh – from 2008)

— Signal Sqn

| FR Regiment Armour (1) | Inf Bn | Inf Bn | Inf Bn |

| Inf Bn | Field Regt RA | AD Bty RA | Engr Regt | Log Sp Regt |

| Pro Coy RMP | Combat Service Support Bn | Medical Sqn |

Note: (1) Formation Reconnaissance with Scimitar.

Logistics Brigades
There are three Logistic Brigades – 101 Logistic Brigade, 102 Logistic Brigade and 104 Logistic Brigade.

The operational role of a Logistic Brigade is to receive both troops and equipment into the theatre of operations, and be responsible for movement to the forward areas, ensuring that the combat formations have the combat supplies necessary to achieve their aim. 102 Logistics Brigade is also responsible for the establishment of Field Hospitals and the evacuation of casualties to the UK.

In general terms a logistic brigade might consist of the following:

Supply Regiment RLC
2 x Transport Regiment RLC
General Support Medical Regiment RAMC
Regiment RMP
Military Dog Support Unit RAVC
Signals Squadron R Signals

The Battlegroup
A division usually consists of two or three brigades.These brigades are further sub-divided into smaller formations known as battlegroups. The battlegroup is the basic building brick of the fighting formations.

A battlegroup is commanded by a Lieutenant Colonel and the infantry battalion or armoured regiment that he commands, provides the command and staff element of the formation. The battlegroup is then structured according to task, with the correct mix of infantry, armour and supporting arms.

The battlegroup organisation is very flexible and the units assigned can be quickly regrouped to cope with a change in the threat. A typical battlegroup fighting a defensive battle on the FEBA (Forward Edge of the Battle Area), and based upon an organisation of one armoured squadron and two mechanised companies, could contain about 600 men, 16 tanks and about 80 armoured personnel carriers.

The number of battlegroups in a division and a brigade could vary according to the task the formation has been given. As a general rule you could expect a division to have as many as 12 battlegroups and a brigade to have up to three or four. The following diagram shows a possible organisation for an armoured battlegroup in either 1(UK) Armd Div or 3(UK) Div.

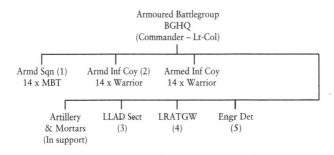

Notes:
(1) Armoured Squadron; (2) Armoured Company (in a Mechanised Company the vehicles will be Saxon); (3) LLAD-Low Level Air Defence – HVM; (4) LRATGW – Long Range Anti Tank Guided Weapon; (5) Engineer Detachment.

Company Groups/Task Group
Each battlegroup will operate with smaller organisations called task groups or company groups. These groups which are commanded by a Major will be allocated tanks, armoured personnel carriers and supporting elements depending upon the aim of the formation. Supporting elements such as air defence, anti-tank missiles, fire support and engineer expertise ensure that the combat team is a balanced all arms grouping, tailored specifically for the task. In general a battlegroup similar to the one in the previous diagram could be expected to form three company groups.

A possible Company Group/Task Group organisation could resemble the following diagram:

```
                            Task Group HQ
                        (Commander – Major)
                            2 x Warrior
                            1 x 1 Tonne
┌──────────┬──────────┬──────────┬──────────┬──────────┐
Tank Tp    Tank Tp    Inf Pl     Inf Pl     FOO
4 x MBT    4 x MBT    4 x Warrior 4 x Warrior Party (1)
                                             & MFC

┌──────────┬──────────┬──────────┬──────────┬──────────┐
Engr       LRATGW     LLAD       Close Recce HQ Sec
Sec        Det (2)    Det (3)    Sec (4)     Supply
                                             Recovery
                                             Medical
```

Notes: (1) Forward Observation Officer (FOO – usually a Captain) with his party from the Royal Artillery. This FOO will be in direct communication with a battery of six/eight guns and the Artillery Fire Direction Centre. The MFC is usually a sergeant from an infantry battalion mortar platoon who may have up to six mortar tubes on call. In most Combat Teams both the FOO and MFC will travel in close proximity to the Combat Team Commander; (2) Possibly 2 x Striker with Swingfire; (3) Possibly 2 x Spartan with HVM; (4) Possibly 2 x Scimitar.

Special Forces

Although the exact detail is highly classified the UK Special Forces Group (UKSF) is under the command of the Director Special Forces (DSF). Units known to be part of the UK Special Forces Group include:

22nd Special Air Service Regiment (Army)	22 SAS
Special Boat Service (Royal Marines)	SBS
Special Forces Support Group	SFSG
Special Reconnaissance Regiment	SRR
Reserve Components	

Special Forces Reserve (SF-R) – The two reserve SAS Regiments (21 and 23 SAS) together with 63 SAS Signal Squadron and the SBS Reserve have evolved into the Reserve Component of the UKSF Group.

Special Forces Support Group

Based around a core group from the 1st Battalion The Parachute Regiment, The Special Forces Support Group (SFSG) is a new unit within the UK Special Forces, which was set up on 3 April 2006. SFSG directly supports Special Forces operations worldwide and also provides an additional counter-terrorist capability. Personnel for the SGSG also come from the Royal

Marines, and the Royal Air Force Regiment. Members of the Special Forces Support Group (SFSG) will retain the cap badges of their parent units but also wear the SFSG insignia. All SFSG personnel have passed either the Royal Marines Commando course, the Airborne Forces Selection course run by the Parachute Regiment or the RAF Pre-Parachute Selection course. Quaified personnel are then equipped and provided with additional training to fit their specific specialist role on joining the SFSG.

The UK MoD has described the main role of the SFSG as "Providing direct support to UK Special Forces intervention operations around the world. They will be prepared to operate in war-fighting, counter-insurgency and counter-terrorism operations at short notice. Their roles may include provision of supporting or diversionary attacks, cordons, fire support, force protection and supporting training tasks. Prior to the creation of the SFSG, these tasks have been carried out by other units on an ad hoc basis".

Special Reconnaissance Regiment
The Special Reconnaissance Regiment (SRR) was formed in April 2005 to meet a growing worldwide demand a for special reconnaissance capability. The term 'special reconnaissance' covers a wide range of highly classified specialist skills and activities related to covert surveillance.

The SRR draws its personnel from existing units and can recruit new volunteers from serving members of the Armed Forces where necessary.
Other sub-units provide combat and service support.

Northern Ireland
On 1 Aug 2007 Op BANNER, the military support to the civilian police in Northern Ireland ends and the future shape of the garrison is becoming clearer.

The MoD envisaged a peacetime garrison of no more than 5,000 Service personnel in about 14 core sites based around existing facilities at Aldergrove, Antrim, Ballykinler, Ballykinler Training Camp, Coleraine (subject to a review of adventurous training provision), Divis Key Point (on Divis Mountain), Duke of Connaught Unit, Holywood, Kinnegar, Lisburn and Magilligan. It is expected that there will be closures at facilities such as Shackleton Barracks, Ballykelly (April 2008), St Lucia Barracks, Omagh (31 July 2007) and St Patrick's Barracks, Ballymena (31March 2008). In addition, it is probable that the garrison of about 5,000 personnel will be supported by about 2,000 civilian staff.

Military units in Northern Ireland will include those under command of 19 Light Brigade that are expected to relocate to Northern Ireland in 2007 and 2008, a new and non-deployable regional brigade headquarters 38 (Irish) Brigade that will form at Thiepval Barracks, Lisburn in August 2007.

The worst year for terrorist violence was in 1972 when 131 service personnel were killed and 578 injured. At one stage in 1972 there were over 30,000 service personnel in the Province supported by another 10,000 police. Overall 763 members of the armed forces and 303 members of the security forces lost their lives as a result of the violence in Northern Ireland.

CHAPTER 3 – INTERNATIONAL COMMITMENTS

NATO Command Structure

The United Kingdom is a member of NATO (North Atlantic Treaty Organisation) and the majority of military operations are conducted in concert with the forces of NATO allies. In 1993, NATO was reorganised from three into two major Commands with a further reorganisation of these two commands in 2003. The first is ACT (Allied Command Transformation) with headquarters at Norfolk, Virginia (USA) and the second is ACO (Allied Command Operations), with its headquarters at Mons in Belgium.

NATO operations in which the United Kingdom was a participant would almost certainly be as part of a NATO force under the command and control of Allied Command Operations (ACO). The current Supreme Allied Commander is General John Craddock.

SACEUR – General John Craddock

General John Craddock graduated from West Virginia University and was commissioned as an Armour Officer. A tour of duty with the 3rd Armoured Division in Germany was followed by a tour at Fort Knox Kentucky with the US Army Armour and Engineer Board. Completion of the Armour Officer Advanced Course saw his return to 3rd Armoured Division as a tank company commander.

In 1981, Craddock was reassigned to the Office of the Programme Manager, Abrams Tank System first as a systems analyst, later as executive officer. Graduation from the Command and General Staff College preceded a return to Germany, this time with the 8th Infantry Division (Mechanised).

In 1989, Craddock assumed command of the 4th Battalion, 64th Armour 24th Infantry Division (Mechanised) at Fort Stewart, Georgia. It was during this posting that he deployed to Operations Desert Shield and Desert Storm. After a period as Assistant Chief of Staff

General John Craddock

(Operations) for the 24th Division, General Craddock attended the US Army War College, assuming command of the 194th Separate Armoured Brigade upon his graduation, before becoming Assistant Chief of Staff (Operations) for III Corps at Fort Hood, Texas.

1996 saw General Craddock move to the Joint Staff at the Pentagon as Assistant Deputy Director (Plans and Policy), J5. Two years later he moved back to Germany as the Assistant Divisional Commander for Manoeuvre of 1st Infantry Division (Mechanised). It was during this time that he was designated Commander US forces for the initial phase of operations in Kosovo. He went on to be the Commanding General of the 7th Army Training Command, US Army Europe then assumed command of 1st Infantry Division (Mechanised). A tour as the Senior Military Assistant to the Secretary of Defence preceded the post of Combatant Commander US Southern Command. General Craddock led the US Southern Command from 2004 until 2006.

General Craddock holds a Masters degree in Military Arts and Sciences.

There are two major NATO Commands:

♦ Allied Command Operations (ACO)
♦ Allied Command Transformation (ACT)

ALLIED COMMAND OPERATIONS (ACO)

Allied Command Operations, with its headquarters, SHAPE, near Mons, Belgium, is responsible for all Alliance operations. The levels beneath SHAPE have been significantly streamlined, with a reduction in the number of headquarters. The operational level consists of two standing Joint Force Commands (JFCs) one in Brunssum, the Netherlands, and one in Naples, Italy – which can conduct operations from their static locations or provide a land-based Combined Joint Task Force (CJTF) headquarters, and a robust but more limited standing Joint Headquarters (JHQ), in Lisbon, Portugal, from which a deployable sea-based CJTF HQ capability can be drawn. The current organisation of Allied Command Operations is as follows:

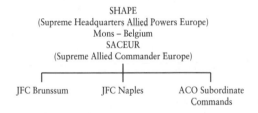

SHAPE
(Supreme Headquarters Allied Powers Europe)
Mons – Belgium
SACEUR
(Supreme Allied Commander Europe)

| JFC Brunssum | JFC Naples | ACO Subordinate Commands |

Component Headquarters at the tactical level

The component or tactical level will consist of six Joint Force Component Commands (JFCCs), which will provide service-specific land, maritime, or air expertise to the operational level. Although these component commands will be available for use in any operation, they will be subordinated to one of the Joint Force Commanders.

Joint Forces Command – Brunssum

HQ JFC Brunssum

| JFCC Air | JFCC Maritime | JFCC Land |
| Ramstein – Germany | Northwood – UK | Heidelberg – Germany |

Joint Forces Command – Naples

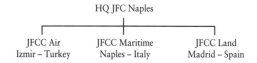

HQ JFC Naples

JFCC Air	JFCC Maritime	JFCC Land
Izmir – Turkey	Naples – Italy	Madrid – Spain

Static Air Operations Centres (CAOC)

In addition to the above component commands there will be four static Combined Air Operations Centres with two more deployable as follows:

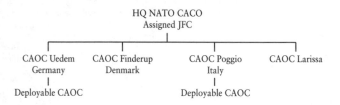

HQ NATO CACO
Assigned JFC

CAOC Uedem	CAOC Finderup	CAOC Poggio	CAOC Larissa
Germany	Denmark	Italy	
Deployable CAOC		Deployable CAOC	

As the deployable CAOCs will need to exercise their capability to mobilise and deploy, the current facilities at Torrejon Air Base in Spain will probably be the primary site for training and exercising in that region. A small NATO air facility support staff would be stationed at Torrejon to support this capability.

Deployable Immediate Reaction Forces (IRF) available:

Immediate Reaction Forces (Maritime) – There are three Maritime Immediate Reaction Forces that provide NATO with a continuous naval presence and can be deployed NATO-wide, when required.

ACE Rapid Reaction Corps (ARRC) – The ARRC is prepared for deployment throughout Allied Command Europe in order to augment or reinforce local forces whenever necessary. The Headquarters of the ARRC are located in Rheindahlen, Germany.

NATO Airborne Early Warning Force (NAEWF) – The NATO Airborne Early Warning Force provides air surveillance and command and control for all NATO commands. It is based in Geilenkirchen, Germany, and Waddington, United Kingdom.

NATO Programming Centre (NPC) – The NATO Programming Centre maintains NATO Air Command and Control Software and provides system expertise to nations and NATO agencies and headquarters. It is located in Glons, Belgium.

Allied Command Transformation (ACT)

In the future, Allied Command Transformation, with its headquarters in Norfolk, US, will oversee the transformation of NATO's military capabilities. In doing so, it will enhance training, improve capabilities, test and develop doctrines and conduct experiments to assess new concepts. It will also facilitate the dissemination and introduction of new concepts and promote interoperability. There will be an ACT Staff Element in Belgium primarily for resource and defence planning issues.

ACT will command the Joint Warfare Centre in Norway, a new Joint Force Training Centre in Poland and the Joint Analysis and Lessons Learned Centre in Portugal. ACT Headquarters will also supervise the Undersea Research Centre in La Spezia, Italy. There will be direct linkages between ACT, Alliance schools and NATO agencies, as well as the US Joint Forces Command. A NATO Maritime Interdiction Operational Training Centre in Greece, associated with ACT, is also envisaged. In addition, a number of nationally or multinationally-sponsored Centres of Excellence focused on transformation in specific military fields will support the command.

The Latest NATO concept

Under the 2003 concept, NATO forces should be able to rapidly deploy to crisis areas and remain sustainable, be it within or outside NATO's territory, in support of both Article 5 and Non-Article 5 operations. The successful deployments of the Allied Command Europe Rapid Reaction Corps (ARRC) to two NATO-led Balkan operations (the Implementation Force (IFOR) to Bosnia Herzegovina in 1995 and Kosovo Force (KFOR) to Kosovo in 1999) are early examples of non-Article 5 crisis response operations outside NATO territory.

The new concept will have its largest impact on land forces. Maritime and air forces are by nature already highly mobile and deployable and often have a high state of readiness. Most of NATO's land based assets, however, have been rather static and have had limited (strategic) mobility. In the new structure, land forces should also become highly deployable and should have tactical and strategic mobility. The mobility requirements will have great impact on the Alliance's transport and logistic resources (sea, land and air based). The need for quick reaction requires a certain amount of highly trained forces that are readily available. Further, interoperability (the possibility of forces to co-operate together with other units) and sustainability (the possibility to continue an operation for an extended period of time) are essential in the new force structure.

High Readiness Forces and Forces of Lower Readiness

There will be forces of two different kinds of readiness posture. First, forces with a higher state of readiness and availability, the so-called High Readiness Forces (HRF) to react on short notice. Second, forces with a lower state of readiness (FLR) to reinforce and sustain. Graduated Readiness Headquarters will be developed to provide these forces with command and control facilities.

High Readiness Forces (Land) Headquarters candidates available:

The Allied Command Europe Rapid Reaction Corps (ARRC) HQ in Rheindalen (Germany) with the United Kingdom as framework nation;

The Rapid Deployable German-Netherlands Corps HQ, based on the 1st German-Netherlands Corps HQ in Munster (Germany);

The Rapid Deployable Italian Corps HQ based on the Italian Rapid Reaction Corps HQ in Solbiate Olona close to Milan (Italy);

The Rapid Deployable Spanish Corps HQ based on the Spanish Corps HQ in Valencia (Spain);

The Rapid Deployable Turkish Corps HQ based on the 3rd Turkish Corps HQ near Istanbul (Turkey);

The Eurocorps HQ in Strasbourg (France) sponsored by Belgium, France, Germany, Luxembourg and Spain.

Note: The Eurocorps Headquarters which has a different international military status based on the Strasbourg Treaty has signed a technical arrangement with SACEUR and can also be committed to NATO missions.

Forces of Lower Readiness (Land) Headquarters candidates:
The Multinational Corps HQ North-East in Szczecin (Poland) sponsored by Denmark, Germany and Poland;

The Greek "C" Corps HQ near Thessaloniki (Greece).

High Readiness Forces (Maritime) Headquarters:
Headquarters Commander Italian Maritime Forces on board of the Italian Naval Vessel GARIBALDI

Headquarters Commander Spanish Maritime Forces (HQ COMSPMARFOR) on board of LPD CASTILLA

Headquarters Commander United Kingdom Maritime Forces (HQ COMUKMARFOR) onboard a UK Aircraft Carrier

THE ALLIED RAPID REACTION CORPS (ARRC)
The concept of the Allied Rapid Reaction Corps was initiated by the NATO Defence Planning Committee in May 1991. The concept called for the creation of Rapid Reaction Forces to meet the requirements of future challenges within the alliance. The ARRC provides the Supreme Allied Commander Europe with a multinational corps sized grouping in which forward elements can be ready to deploy within 14 days (lead elements and recce parties at very short notice).

As stated by SHAPE the mission of the ARRC is: "HQ ARRC, as a High Readiness Force (Land) HQ, is prepared to deploy under NATO, EU or coalition auspices to a designated area, to undertake combined and joint operations across the operational spectrum as:

♦ A Corps HQ

♦ A Land Component HQ

♦ A Land Component HQ in command of the NATO Response Force

♦ A Joint Task Force HQ for Land-centric operations

These formations will enable support crisis support management options or the sustainment of ongoing operations."

As NATO's first and most experienced High Readiness Force (Land) Headquarters the ARRC is actively engaged in the NATO Response Force (NRF) transformation initiative. Currently the ARRC trains for missions across the spectrum of operations from deterrence and crisis management to regional conflict.

Headquarters ARRC is located in Rheindahlen, Germany with a peace time establishment of about 400 personnel. It comprises staff from all the contributing nations. A French liaison officer is officially accredited to the Headquarters. As the Framework Nation, the UK provides the infrastructure, administrative support, communications and 60% of the staff.

The Commander (COMARRC) and Chief of Staff are UK 3 Star and 2 Star generals and the Deputy Commander is an Italian 2 Star general. The other appointments, as with the training and exercise costs, are shared among the contributing nations.

During early 1996, HQ ARRC deployed to Sarajevo in the Former Yugoslavia to command the NATO Implementation Force (IFOR). In 1999 HQ ARRC was responsible for operations in Kosovo and Macedonia and in 2002 and 2006 in Afghanistan.

Command Posts and Deployment: Due to the need to be able to respond flexibly to the whole range of potential operations, HQ ARRC has been developing the capability for rapidly deployable and modular HQs. Deployment will begin with the despatch of a Forward Liaison and Reconnaissance Group (FLRG) within 48 hours of the order being given which can then be quickly followed up.

Within four days the key enablers from 1 (UK) Signal Brigade would be within theatre and three days later HQ ARRC Forward and HQ Rear Support Command (RSC) Forward – as required – could be established. The forward-deployed HQs are light, mobile and C-130 transportable. While there is a standard 'default' setting for personnel numbers, the actual staff composition is 'tailored' to the task and can vary from approximately 50 to 150 staff, depending on the requirement. The 'in-theatre' task would then be supported by the remainder of the staff, using sophisticated 'Reachback' techniques and equipment.

The Early Entry HQs are capable of sustained independent operations if required but can also be used as enablers if it is decided to deploy the full HQ ARRC. This deployment concept has been tested and evaluated on several exercises and has proven its worth. In parallel, HQ ARRC is continuously looking to make all of its HQs lighter and more survivable.

Outline Composition of the ARRC (ACE Rapid Reaction Corps)

For operations HQ ARRC might have some of the following formations under command:

```
                        HQ ARRC
                           |
                      Corps Troops
             (including 1st (UK) Signal Brigade
              Corps Combat Support Cell
```

Air Defence	Aviation	Artillery	Engineers
1 (US) Armd Div (1)	1(UK)Armd Div(2)	3(UK) Div(3)	3(IT) Mech Div(4)
7(GE) Armd Div(5)	2(GR) Mech Div(6)	1 (TU) Div(7)	Spanish Rapid Reaction Div (Sp RRD)

Notes: (1) United States (2) Resident in Germany (3) Resident in the UK (4) IT – Italy (5) GE – Germany (6) GR – Greece (7) TU – Turkish.

The operational organisation, composition and size of the ARRC would depend on the type of crisis, area of crisis, its political significance, and the capabilities and availability of lift assets, the distances to be covered and the infrastructure capabilities of the nation receiving assistance. It is considered that a four-division ARRC would be the maximum employment structure.

The main British contribution to the ARRC is 1 (UK) Armoured Division. This division is stationed in Germany and there are also a considerable number of British personnel in both the ARRC Corps HQ and Corps Troops. In addition, in times of tension 3 (UK) Mechanised Division and 16 Air Assault Brigade could, if required, move to the operational area to take their place in the ARRC's order of battle. In total, we believe that if the need arose some 40,000 British soldiers could be assigned to the ARRC together with substantial numbers of Regular Army Reservists and formed TA Units.

EUROPEAN UNION

The position of the UK Government (June 2007) is that NATO is the cornerstone of UK national defence, but that the EU can accomplish many tasks that are complementary to NATO.

The European Union (EU) consists of

Austria; Belgium; Bulgaria; Cyprus (Greek part); Czech Republic; Denmark; Estonia; Finland; France; Germany; Greece; Hungary; Ireland; Italy; Latvia; Lithuania; Luxembourg; Malta; Netherlands; Poland; Portugal; Romania; Slovakia; Slovenia; Spain; Sweden; United Kingdom.

EUROPEAN DEFENCE AGENCY

The European Defence Agency (EDA) was established on 12 July 2004 following a unanimous decision by European Heads of State and Government. It was established under the Council Joint Action 2004/5 51/CFSP on the basis of Article 14 of the treaty on the European Union (Maastricht).

The purpose of the European Defence Agency is to support the Member States and the Council of Europe in order to improve European defence capabilities in the field of crisis management, and to sustain and develop the European Security and Defence Policy.

The EDA has the following tasks:

- ◆ To improve the EU's defence capabilities in the field of crisis management.
- ◆ To promote European armaments cooperation.
- ◆ To strengthen the European defence industrial and technological base and create a competitive European defence equipment market, in consultation with the Commission.
- ◆ To promote research, in liaison with Community research activities, with a view to strengthening Europe's industrial and technological potential in the defence field.

In the longer term the EDA will achieve its goals by:

- ◆ Encouraging EU Governments to spend defence budgets on meeting tomorrow's challenges and not, in their words, yesterday's threats.
- ◆ Helping EU Governments to identify common needs and promoting collaboration to provide common solutions.
- ◆ The EDA is an agency of the European Union and therefore under the direction and authority of the European Council, which issues guidelines to, and receives reports from High Representative Janvier Solana (March 2007) as Head of the Agency. Detailed control and guidance, however, is the responsibility of the Steering Committee.

EDA Organisation

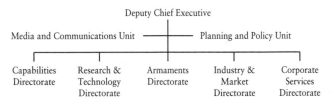

Steering Committee

Chief Executive

Deputy Chief Executive

Media and Communications Unit —— Planning and Policy Unit

| Capabilities Directorate | Research & Technology Directorate | Armaments Directorate | Industry & Market Directorate | Corporate Services Directorate |

Janvier Solana chairs the Steering Committee, the principal decision-making body of the Agency, made up of Defence Ministers from participating Member States (all EU members except Denmark) and a member of the European Commission. In addition to ministerial meetings at least twice a year, the Steering Committee also meets at the level of national armaments directors, national research directors, national capability planners and policy directors.

Budget: The Agency has a budget of 22.1 million (£14.8 million) for 2007 with around 5 million allocated to operations. The United Kingdom will pay around 17.5 % of the budget and this UK contribution will be paid from the budget of the UK MoD.

For 2009 the budget is projected to be around 28 million (£18.7 million) of which 10 million should be allocated to operations. During 2005 the EDA had a budget to employ 80 staff. The EDA's chief executive is Nick Witney, a former UK Ministry of Defence civil servant.

EU Helsinki Headline Goal 2010

The European Union (EU) has adopted the following illustrative scenarios which form the basis for force planning to meet the EU Helsinki Headline Goal 2010:

- Stabilisation, reconstruction and military advice to third world countries
- Separation of parties by force
- Assistance to humanitarian operations
- Conflict Prevention
- Evacuation Operation in a non-permissive environment

UK Commitment to the European Helsinki Goal 2010

In early 2005 the UK MoD confirmed a declaration of up to 12,500 troops towards the Helsinki Headline Goal on a voluntary case-by-case basis. Of this figure about 35% are infantry troops.

The UK currently offers three brigades which allows the UK to provide either an Armoured Brigade (based on Warrior Armoured Fighting Vehicles and Challenger 2 Main Battle Tanks), a Mechanised Brigade (based on Saxon Infantry Fighting Vehicles and Challenger 2 Main Battle Tanks) or an Air Assault Brigade consisting of lightly equipped infantry in the Air Manoeuvre role. An Amphibious Brigade (3 Commando Brigade) from the Royal Navy may also be available. Up to 18 UK warships and 72 UK combat aircraft are also available for EU operations.

However, these national forces are made available for EU operations on a voluntary, case-by-case basis, as for NATO or UN operations. UK contributions to such operations are provided from within existing forces.

As yet (early 2007) there is no standing European Rapid Reaction Force nor any EU agreement to create one. What has sometimes been referred to as a 'European Rapid Reaction Force' is, in fact, a catalogue of forces which member states could make available to the EU should they choose to participate in a particular EU-led operation. Any contribution to a particular EU-led operation would depend on the operation's requirements, the availability of forces at the time and the willingness of EU members to participate.

EU Military Plans

In the immediate future, the EU plans to be able to provide at least one coherent Battle Group package, to undertake single Battle Group-sized operations in support of the EU Helsinki Headline Goals.

Full Operational Capability (FOC) will be reached at the end of 2007 when all Battle Groups will be available. The EU should then have the capacity to undertake at least two concurrent single Battle Group-size rapid response operations, including the ability to launch both such operations nearly simultaneously.

EU Member States have indicated that they will commit to Battle Groups, formed as follows by late 2007:

1	United Kingdom
2	France and Belgium
3	Italy
4	Spain
5	France, Germany, Belgium, Luxembourg and Spain
6	Germany, the Netherlands and Finland
7	Germany, Austria and Czech Republic
8	Italy, Hungary and Slovenia
9	Italy, Spain, Greece and Portugal
10	Poland, Germany, Slovakia, Latvia and Lithuania

EU MILITARY STRUCTURES

The following table sets out the main multilateral military structures outside NATO which include European Union members. A number of these also include non-EU countries. In addition, there are many other bilateral military agreements between individual EU member states.

The UK is a party to military agreements in respect of four of the structures listed in the following table. Military agreements between other EU members are a matter for those member states' governments.

Structure	EU participants
EAG – European Air Group	Belgium, France, Germany, Italy, Spain, UK
European Airlift Centre	Belgium, France, Germany, Italy, Netherlands, Spain, UK
Sealift Coordination Centre (Eindhoven)	Netherlands, UK
European Amphibious Initiative (including the UK/Netherlands Amphibious Force)	France, Italy, Netherlands, Spain, UK
SHIRBRIG – Stand-by High Readiness Brigade	Austria, Denmark, Finland, Ireland, Italy, Lithuania, Netherlands, Norway, Poland, Portugal, Slovenia, Spain, Sweden. (Observers: Czech Republic, Hungary)
SEEBRIG – South-Eastern Europe Brigade	Greece, Italy, Slovenia
NORDCAPS – Nordic Coordinated Arrangement for Military Peace Support	Finland, Sweden, Denmark
EUROCORPS	Germany, Belgium, Spain, France, Luxembourg
EUROFOR	France, Italy, Portugal, Spain
EUROMARFOR	France, Italy, Portugal, Spain

EUROCORPS

The Eurocorps was created in 1992 and comprises military contributions from its five framework nations: Belgium, France, Germany, Luxembourg and Spain. The Headquarters is located in Strasbourg (France). Austria, Canada, Greece, Italy, Poland and Turkey have military liaison staff co-located at Eurocorps HQ.

The Common Committee, composed of the political directors of the foreign ministries and the chiefs of defence staffs of the nations providing Eurocorps contingents is the highest level of command for the Eurocorps. The Common Committee meets once a year.

For coordination and day-to-day control, the Common Committee has established the POLMIL Group, which includes representatives at the military/political level from the framework nations' Ministries of Defence.

The Commander Eurocorps (COMEC) is a lieutenant general (3 stars). The Deputy Commander (DCOM) is a major general (2 stars). The staff is directed by the Chief of Staff (COS), also a major general and he is supported by two Deputy Chiefs of Staff (DCOS) for Operations and Support, both of whom are brigadier generals (1 star).

The posts of Commanding General, DCOM and the other general officers as well as some key functions are filled by EC framework nations on a rotational basis. COMEC, DCOM and COS are always of different nationalities. Their tour of duty generally lasts for two years.

The Eurocorps consists of formations under direct operational control and formations earmarked for assignment during an emergency:

Under direct operational control:

♦ Franco German Brigade (GE-FR Bde)

♦ Multinational Command Support Brigade (MNCS Bde)

Formations earmarked for assignment during an emergency:

French Contribution
Etat-Major de Force numéro 3 (EMF3) in Marseille (equivalent to a divisional HQ) composed of:

1 x Armoured Brigade

1 x Mechanised Infantry Brigade

Specialised support units

German Contribution
The 10th Armoured Division, with its HQ in Sigmaringen, composed of:

    12th Armoured Brigade in Amberg

    30th Mechanised Brigade in Ellwangen

    Support units

Belgian Contribution
Belgian Operational Command Land, with its HQ in Evere, composed of:

    1st Mechanised Brigade in Leopoldsburg

    7th Mechanised Brigade in Marche-en-Fammene

    Support units

Spanish Contribution

1st Mechanised Division with its HQ in Burgos, composed of:

> 10th Mechanised Brigade in Cordoba
>
> 11th Mechanised Brigade in Badajoz
>
> 12th Armoured Brigade in Madrid

Luxembourg Contribution

Luxembourg assigns a reconnaissance company composed of about 180 personnel. During operations this unit would be integrated into the Belgian contingent.

During the past decade the Eurocorps has been involved in operations as follows:

> SFOR (Bosnia) 1999-2000
>
> KFOR III (Kosovo) 2000
>
> ISAF IV (Afghanistan) 2004-2005

Note: If all earmarked national contributions were committed to operations, the Eurocorps would number approximately 60,000 personnel.

IRAQ (OPERATION TELIC)

British Forces are serving in Iraq as part of the Coalition Force authorised under United Nations Security Council Resolution 1546. This mandate will expire upon the completion of the political process or if requested by the Government of Iraq.

The UK Government has stated that it is committed to Iraq for as long as the Iraqi Government judge that the coalition is required to provide security and assist in the development of the Iraqi Security Forces. UK military forces are mainly located around the area of Basrah in Southern Iraq and military operations are conducted under the Codename of Operation Telic.

During February 2007 the UK MoD announced a reduction in UK troop levels from 7,100 to 5,500 by late summer 2007. Remaining troops will stay into 2008, to give back-up to the Iraqi security forces if required.

The majority of United Kingdom troops deployed to Iraq spend six months in the theatre of operations and are in units commanded by the Multinational Division (South-East).

The ongoing tasks for UK Forces in Iraq include:

- Training and support to Iraqi forces
- Operations in support of the Iraqi Department of Border Enforcement, including integrity of the Iraqi-Iranian border
- Protection of Coalition supply routes and key Iraqi strategic infrastructure
- Targeted Strike operations in the pursuit of a secure environment.

Since early 2003 UK force levels in Iraq have been as follows:

- Peak during Major Combat Operations (March/April 2003): 46,000
- At the end of May 2003: 18,000
- At the end of May 2004: 8,600
- At the end of May 2005: 8,500
- At the end of May 2006: 7,200
- At the end of May 2007: 7,000 (approximately)

Other Coalition force levels in Iraq during early 2007 were approximately:

US	146,000
South Korea	2,300
Poland	900
Georgia	800
Australia	900
Romania	600
Denmark	450
El Salvadore	380
Bulgaria	150

Multinational Division (South-East) MND(SE)

The Headquarters of the MND(SE) is located at Basrah Air Base in Southern Iraq. This is a composite multinational headquarters with the majority of the personnel and infrastructure being provided by the UK. MND(SE) covers four provinces in Iraq.

The primary activities of MND(SE) are:

- Supporting the ongoing political process in Iraq
- Security Sector Reform – Training the new Iraqi security Forces with partnership operations where MND(SE) forces back-up, assisting and monitoring these Iraqi Security Forces
- Normalisation – Helping to get society on its feet again by assisting in the restoration of water, power, health, education, judiciary, oil industry and heritage and encouraging commercial markets and the economy.

During mid 2007 the following UK units were under the command of MND (SE):

- HQ 1 Mechanised Brigade
- 215 Signal Squadron Royal Signals
- 2 x Squadrons from the Household Cavalry Regiment
- The Kings Royal Hussars

- 2 x Squadrons from the 2nd Royal Tank Regiment
- 1st Battalion Irish Guards
- 1 x Company from 1st Battalion The Royal Welsh
- 2nd Battalion The Royal Welsh
- 4th Battalion The Rifles
- 1st Regiment Royal Horse Artillery
- 22 Engineer Regiment
- 1 x Squadron from 23 Pioneer Regiment Royal Logistic Corps
- 3 Logistic Support Regiment Royal Logistic Corps
- 1x Company from 6 Battalion Royal Electrical & Mechanical Engineers
- Close Medical Support Squadron, 3 Close Support Medical Regiment Royal Army Medical Corps
- 158 Provost Company 3rd Regiment Royal Military Police
- 22 Battery, 32 Regiment Royal Artillery
- 34 Field Hospital Royal Army Medical Corps

Approximately 260 members of the reserve forces are believed to have been deployed in support of the above units.

A very high readiness reserve battalion (VHRR) is held in the UK at 10 days' readiness to deploy to Iraq.

In addition to the UK personnel, in early 2007 MND(SE) had approximately 2,000 troops from countries that include: Australia, Denmark, South Korea and Romania.

AFGHANISTAN (OPERATION HERRICK)
Following deployments in Helmand Province by 16 Air Assault Brigade and 3 Commando Brigade in mid 2007, UK Forces in Afghanistan were drawn mainly from 12 Mechanised Brigade. In addition, following the UK handover of command of the International Security Assistance Force (ISAF) in February 2007 some 150 personnel remain deployed with the ISAF Headquarters in Kabul.

This will mean that towards late summer 2007 the number of UK personnel in Southern Afghanistan should settle at around 5,800.

The UK MoD has also decided to maintain until April 2009 some capabilities already deployed in Afghanistan, including the Harrier GR7/GR9s, the Apache Attack Helicopters, Viking all-terrain vehicles, and Royal Engineers to support reconstruction activities.

The principal units deployed in mid 2007 were:

- HQ 12 Mechanised Brigade
- Brigade Headquarters and Signal Squadron
- The Light Dragoons
- 1st Battalion The Grenadier Guards
- 1st Battalion The Royal Anglian Regiment
- 1st Battalion The Worcestershire and Sherwood Foresters
- 26 Engineer Regiment Royal Engineers
- 19 Regiment Royal Artillery
- 2 Signal Regiment
- 4 Logistic Support Regiment
- 4 General Support Medical Regiment

Elements of other units are also deploying to provide niche capabilities. These included:

- Armoured Support Group of the Royal Marines
- 2nd Royal Tank Regiment
- 3 Regiment, Army Air Corps
- 9 Regiment, Army Air Corps

RAF support is provided by:

- 1 (Fighter), IV (Army Co-Operation) Squadron
- Elements of 18, 24, 27, 30, 47 and 70 Squadrons
- Elements of 3, 5 and 7 Force Protection Wing Headquarters
- Elements of 2, 51 and 15 Squadrons of the Royal Air Force Regiment.

As with previous deployments to operational areas there will be a requirement to deploy reservists to Afghanistan. Early 2007 plans suggest that approximately 420 reservists will be required to support 12 Mechanised Brigade.

THE INTERNATIONAL SECURITY ASSISTANCE FORCE (ISAF)
The International Security Assistance Force (ISAF) is mandated under Chapter VII of the United Nations (UN) Charter (Peace Enforcing) by a number of UN Security Resolutions. ISAF exists to help the Afghan people, not to govern them. Additionally, under the UN mandate, the role of ISAF is to assist in the maintenance of security to help the Islamic Republic of Afghanistan and the UN in those areas it is responsible for.

NATO assumed command and control of the ISAF mission on 11 August 2003.

More than 35,000 troops make up ISAF, with contributions from 37 nations with national contingent strengths changing on a regular basis. Major contributors include:

- United States   2,000
- United Kingdom   5,800
- Germany   2,800
- Netherlands   2,300
- Canada   2,300
- Italy   1,300
- France   1,000
- Australia   1,000
- Spain   572

There are another 12,000 US troops in Afghanistan deployed outside ISAF command under the terms of the US Operation Enduring Freedom.

COSTS – IRAQ AND AFGHANISTAN

The Ministry of Defence figures set out below identify the costs of operations in terms of the net additional costs they have incurred. The costs that the department would have incurred regardless of the operation taking place, such as wages and salaries, are not included. Savings on activities that have not occurred because of the operation; training exercises, for example, are taken into account in arriving at the net figures. All of these costs are met, by convention, from the Treasury's reserves.

Costs – Iraq

2002-03

Operations in Iraq	£629 million
Expenditure on capital equipment	£218 million
Total	£874 million

2003-04

Operations in Iraq	£1,051 million
Expenditure on capital equipment	£260 million
Total	£1,311 million

2004-05

Operations in Iraq	£747 million
Expenditure on capital equipment	£163 million
Total	£910 million

2005-06

Operations in Iraq	£798 million

| Expenditure on capital, equipment | £160 million |
| Total | £958 million |

This gives a grand total of £4,026 million and the current (early 2007) estimated cost of operations in Iraq for 2006-07 is in the region of £860 million.

Costs – Afghanistan

Operations in Afghanistan	£187 million
Expenditure on capital equipment	£34 million
Total	£221 million

2002-03

Operations in Afghanistan	£236 million
Expenditure on capital equipment	£75 million
Total	£311 million

2003-04

Operations in Afghanistan	£36 million
Expenditure on capital equipment	£10 million
Total	£46 million

2004-05

Operations in Afghanistan	£58 million
Expenditure on capital equipment	£9 million
Total	£67 million

2005-06

Operations in Afghanistan	£148 million
Expenditure on capital equipment	£51 million
Total	£199 million

This gives a grand total of £844 million and the cost of operations in Afghanistan for 2006-07 is estimated to be in the region of £540 million (early 2007 figures).

CHAPTER 4 – THE HOUSEHOLD CAVALRY AND THE ROYAL ARMOURED CORPS

OVERVIEW

The Household Cavalry (HCav) and The Royal Armoured Corps (RAC) have traditionally provided the tank force and armoured reconnaissance component of the British Army. More recently the RAC have also become responsible for providing the Army element of the Joint NBC Regiment.

Armour has provided battle winning shock action and firepower since the earliest tanks helped to break the stalemate of the Western Front during the First World War. In the same way, armoured reconnaissance, with the ability to penetrate the enemy's forward defences and gain information by using stealth and firepower, has shaped the way in which armour has been used to its best advantage.

Defence represents the best use of ground features in conjunction with engineering and concealed firepower. The ability of armour to overwhelm all but the heaviest defences and deliver a group of highly capable armoured fighting platforms into the combat area remains a battle winning capability embraced by all major armies.

The modern main battle tank weighs between 50 and 70 tonnes, can move at up to 60 kph and can virtually always guarantee a first round hit with its main armament out to 2000 m. Last tested in combat in the Gulf War of 2003, UK armoured forces demonstrated the advantages of armour in a desert landscape. Amongst these was the ability to cover rough terrain quickly and by the use of superior concentrated firepower, create operational level, rather than simple local tactical, advantage. These tanks used the most up to date information systems and state of the art imaging and sighting systems to locate, close with and destroy the enemy. The 2003 Gulf War experience underlined the need for all elements of manoeuvre forces to be able to move swiftly and securely with protection and firepower to maintain a high 'operational tempo'. This includes infantry, artillery and of course the massive logistic supply required.

However, since the earliest discovery of the power of the tank, military planners and scientists have sought ways of negating its power and defeating its protection to reduce its advantage. To counter these enhancements, in turn the tank has repeatedly been adapted and improved to maintain its advantage. Thermal imaging sights enable the tank to acquire a target and identify it by day or by night and in conditions of much reduced visibility. The tank's organic armour protection can be supplemented with explosive reactive armour packs that detonate on contact with an incoming round, disrupting its destructive power. More sophisticated anti-tank weapons, mines, missiles and indeed helicopters, have created a new battlefield environment of sensing and counter-sensing while trying to manoeuvre to exercise firepower advantage.

The UK's Armoured Regiments are equipped with 'Challenger 2' built by Vickers whereas the Formation Reconnaissance Regiments are equipped with the 'Scimitar' tracked reconnaissance vehicles built by Alvis. The planned replacement of these systems is integrated into future UK defence planning. The replacement for Scimitar will be the new reconnaissance vehicle which will be provided by one of the variants of the Future Rapid Effect System (FRES) which will be introduced around the turn of the decade. Challenger 2, which was fully fielded into service in January 2002, will not be due for replacement until around 2030. Future enhancements to Challenger 2 are likely to be those that enhance its protection in the face of more capable and accurate detectors and weapons, while maintaining its ability to strike at the enemy. What is most likely is the application of improvement through a number of technological 'insertion packages' which will be designed to enhance both battlefield survivability but also its essential lethality. The replacement reconnaissance vehicle will embody as many interim capability enhancements as possible and experience in this field will to some extent shape the ultimate replacement for the tank itself.

While the future design of the MBT may be affected by new technologies such as surveillance from space, Unmanned Aerial Vehicles and attack from complex unseen helicopter mounted or seeker weapons, the military will continue to require a mechanism to verify and occupy territory. This force, however small or specialised will require personnel who will need the protection, lethality and mobility which we have come to look upon as the role of the cavalry in both attack and reconnaissance. This assumption until history proves it wrong, suggests that the spirit and élan we have come to expect of the Armoured Corps will still have a major role in the Army of the 21st Century.

Ongoing operations in Iraq and Afghanistan, where a requirement for battlefield effect, that falls between that provided by heavy armour and basic force reconnaissance, has resulted in a tactic that provides a new relationship between armour, infantry and the 21st century battlefield. Known as 'Medium Armour' this tactic is about delivering effect on the enemy with the use of automatic gun and cannon. Combining the tracked vehicle's agility, the tank-mind set and the use of a troop of three or four CVR(T)s at the points of contact on the ground, the Medium Armour concept makes for very effective support for the infantry. Some RAC Regiments equipped with Challenger MBT now include a Medium Armour Squadron equipped with Scimitar CVR(T).

Organisation

The RAC is composed of 12 regular regiments (including the two regiments of the Household Cavalry, discussed below) and four reserve Yeomanry Regiments in the TA. Apart from the Royal Tank Regiment, which was formed in the First World War with the specific task of fighting in armoured vehicles, the regular element of the RAC is provided by those regiments which formed the mounted units of the pre-mechanised era. The Yeomanry Regiments are tasked with providing individual War Establishment Reinforcements to the regular regiments in each of the roles of Armour, Reconnaissance, NBC and Armour Replacement.

Although very much part of the RAC, as an 'Arm' the Household Cavalry (HCav) is a discrete corps consisting of two regiments. The Household Cavalry Mounted Regiment (HCMR), which is permanently stationed in London, has the task of providing mounted troops for state ceremonial functions. The Household Cavalry Regiment (HCR) is stationed in Windsor and is a Force Reconnaissance (FR) Regiment that plays a full role in operational and training activity within the Field Army. Officers and soldiers from the Household Cavalry are posted between the two regiments as needs dictate. (For general purposes, in this publication, the term RAC includes the HCav).

Following recent Future Army Structure changes we believe that by late 2008 the 11 regular field force units of the RAC will be deployed as follows:

<u>In Germany</u>.   Three Armoured Regiments and one FR Regiment.

<u>In the UK</u>.   Two Armoured Regiments, four FR Regiments and the Joint NBC Regiment.

Note: The Household Cavalry Mounted Regiment is permanently stationed in London.

During early 2007 the personnel strength of the RAC and Household Cavalry was 5,560 officers and soldiers.

Under Future Army Structure plans the RAC TA is being increased in size from 1,312 to 1,750 (about 33 per cent) and will be able to provide more support to the Regular RAC units. A number of additional Yeomanry Detachments will be formed to allow TA Yeomanry Squadrons to recruit enough volunteers. In general terms TA squadrons will increase in size from about 50-60 personnel to 80-90 personnel.

FORMATION RECONNAISSANCE REGIMENT
Following the FAS proposals, Formation Reconnaissance was re-organised to provide five regular regiments. Four of these regiments have three sabre squadrons and a command and support squadron, whereas the HCR has a fourth squadron which is specifically affiliated to 16 Air Assault Brigade.

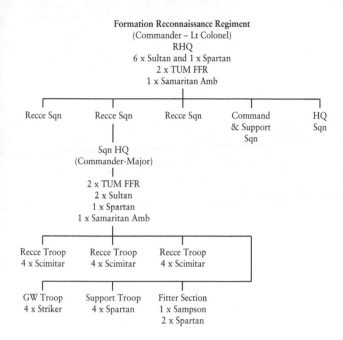

Formation Reconnaissance Regiment
(Commander – Lt Colonel)
RHQ
6 x Sultan and 1 x Spartan
2 x TUM FFR
1 x Samaritan Amb

| Recce Sqn | Recce Sqn | Recce Sqn | Command & Support Sqn | HQ Sqn |

Sqn HQ
(Commander-Major)

2 x TUM FFR
2 x Sultan
1 x Spartan
1 x Samaritan Amb

| Recce Troop | Recce Troop | Recce Troop |
| 4 x Scimitar | 4 x Scimitar | 4 x Scimitar |

GW Troop	Support Troop	Fitter Section
4 x Striker	4 x Spartan	1 x Sampson
		2 x Spartan

Notes:

(1) In war, each Formation Reconnaissance Regiment receives a fourth squadron.

(2) Full wartime establishment is approximately 600 all ranks.

(3) The Command and Support Squadron includes a Ground Surveillance Troop. Expect this squadron to have a TACP/FAC party, surveillance troop and an NBC protection troop.

Formation Reconnaissance regiments are usually under the direct command of a divisional headquarters. Their more usual task in a defensive scenario is to identify the direction and strength of the enemy thrusts, impose maximum delay and damage to the enemy's reconnaissance forces while allowing main forces to manoeuvre to combat the threat. They would be assisted in such a task by using their own organic long range anti-tank guided weapons (the Swingfire missile on CVR(T) Striker) and other assets that might be attached such as anti-tank helicopters (Lynx with TOW and perhaps Apache Longbow (WAH64D) in the future). In support would be the indirect fire guns (AS90) and Multiple Launch Rocket

System (MLRS) of the divisional artillery, and an air defended area (ADA) maintained by Rapier and Stormer HVM air defence missiles.

The basic task of Formation Reconnaissance is to obtain accurate information about the enemy and develop an intelligence picture in their areas of responsibility for their superior commanders in the chain-of-command, as quickly as possible. However, Formation Reconnaissance Regiments are now capable of providing 'Medium Armour Support' to infantry on operations in Iraq and Afghanistan.

Armoured Regiment
The following diagram shows the current structure of an Armoured Regiment equipped with Challenger 2. Three Regiments equipped with Challenger 2 (CR2) have three 'Sabre' Squadrons and one Interim Medium Armour Squadron (with 12 x CVRT(T) Scimitar). A Challenger 2 Regiment with four Squadrons of main battle tanks would have an all up total of 58 tanks when deployed for war. In some regiments, one of the main battle tank squadrons has been replaced by a Medium Armour Squadron.

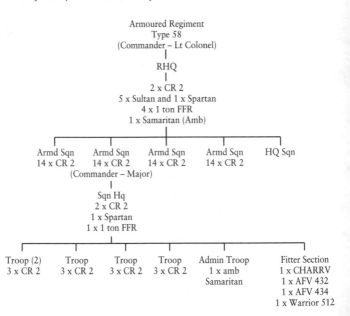

Armoured Regiment
Type 58
(Commander – Lt Colonel)
|
RHQ
|
2 x CR 2
5 x Sultan and 1 x Spartan
4 x 1 ton FFR
1 x Samaritan (Amb)

| Armd Sqn
14 x CR 2
(Commander – Major) | Armd Sqn
14 x CR 2 | Armd Sqn
14 x CR 2 | Armd Sqn
14 x CR 2 | HQ Sqn |

Sqn Hq
2 x CR 2
1 x Spartan
1 x 1 ton FFR

| Troop (2)
3 x CR 2 | Troop
3 x CR 2 | Troop
3 x CR 2 | Troop
3 x CR 2 | Admin Troop
1 x amb
Samaritan | Fitter Section
1 x CHARRV
1 x AFV 432
1 x AFV 434
1 x Warrior 512 |

Notes:

(1) HQ Sqn has a Reconnaissance Troop with 8 x Scimitar which is under direct control of the CO in the field.

(2) Tank Troop commanded by 2Lt/Lt with Troop Sergeant as 2ic in own tank. The third tank is commanded by a Corporal.

(3) Totals: 58 x CR2, 8 x SCIMITAR, 4 x CHARRV. Total strength for war is approx 550.

(4) A Challenger 2 has a crew of 4 – Commander, Driver, Gunner and Loader/Operator.

JOINT NUCLEAR, BIOLOGICAL AND CHEMICAL REGIMENT (JT NBC REGT)

Following the Strategic Defence Review, the Jt NBC Regt was created and is based at RAF Honington, Suffolk. The Regiment is composed of two squadrons from 1 RTR and 27 Sqn RAF Regiment plus supporting staff from other army units. The Jt NBC Regt fields specialist NBC defence equipment, specifically the Fuchs nuclear and chemical reconnaissance and survey vehicle, the Integrated Biological Detection System (IBDS) and the Multi-Purpose Decontamination System (MPDS). The Regiment is an essential element for any joint force operation where there is an NBC threat, enhancing the integral NBC defence capabilities of the remainder of the force. Not only does the Regiment support Army formations but also other vital assets such as air bases, logistic areas and key lines of communication.

Joint NBC Regiment

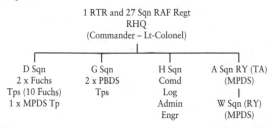

1 RTR and 27 Sqn RAF Regt
RHQ
(Commander – Lt-Colonel)

D Sqn	G Sqn	H Sqn	A Sqn RY (TA)
2 x Fuchs	2 x PBDS	Comd	(MPDS)
Tps (10 Fuchs)	Tps	Log	
1 x MPDS Tp		Admin	W Sqn (RY)
		Engr	(MPDS)

Note:
Where appropriate the Direct Application Decontamination System (DADS) is available.

In peace the Army may be asked to provide Military Assistance to the Civil Authorities. In these circumstances, the Joint NBC Regiment may be called on to deal with radiological, biological or chemical hazards. The Joint NBC Regiment offers a challenging role to the Royal Armoured Corps, requiring new skills, innovative ideas and a significant intellectual challenge. The Regiment provides a firm basis on which to develop the Joint NBC defence capability in the future.

Challenger 2

(345 available). Crew 4; Length Gun Forward 11.55 m; Height 2.5 m; Width 4.2 m with appliqué armour; Ground Clearance 0.51 m; Combat Weight 62.5 tonnes- MLC 76; Main Armament 1 x 120 mm L30 CHARM Gun; Ammunition Carried max 50 rounds stowed – APFSDS, HESH and Smoke; Secondary Armament Co-axial 7.62 mm Chain Gun; Loaders pintle mounted 7.62 mm GPMG; Ammunition Carried 4000 rounds 7.62 mm; Engine CV12 12 cylinder – Auxiliary Power Unit 4 – stroke diesel; Gearbox TN54 epicyclic – 6 forward gears and 2 reverse; Road Speed 59 kph; Cross-Country Speed 40 kph; Fuel Capacity 1,592 litres usable internal plus 2 x 175 litre external fuel drums.

Challenger 2 was manufactured by Vickers Defence Systems and production was undertaken at their factories in Newcastle-Upon-Tyne and Leeds. At 1999 prices Challenger 2 is believed to cost £4 million per vehicle.

Although the hull and automotive parts of the Challenger 2 are based upon that of its predecessor Challenger 1, the new tank incorporates over 150 improvements which have achieved substantially increased reliability and ease of maintenance. The Challenger 2 turret is, however, of a totally new design. The vehicle has a crew of four – commander, gunner, loader/signaller and driver and is equipped with a 120 mm rifled Royal Ordnance L30 gun firing all current tank ammunition natures plus the new depleted uranium (DU) round with a stick charge propellant system.

The design of the turret incorporates several of the significant features that Vickers had developed for its Mk 7 MBT (a Vickers turret on a Leopard 2 chassis). The central feature is an entirely new fire control system based on the Ballistic Control System developed by Computing Devices Company (Canada) for the US Army's M1A1 MBT. This second generation computer incorporates dual 32-bit processors with a MIL STD1553B databus and has sufficient growth potential to accept Battlefield Information Control System (BICS) functions and navigation aids (a GPS satnav system). The armour is an uprated version of Challenger 1's Chobham armour.

Challenger Repair and Recovery Vehicle (CHARRV)

(80 in Service) Crew 3; Length 9.59 m; Operating Width 3.62 m; Height 3.005 m; Ground Clearance 0.5 m; Combat Weight 62,000 kg; Max Road Speed 59 kph; Cross Country Speed 35 kph; Fording 1.07 m; Trench Crossing 2.3 m; Crane – Max Lift 6,500 kg at 4.9 m reach; Engine Perkins CV12 TCA 1200 26.1 V-12 direct injection 4-stroke diesel.

Between 1988 and 1990 the British Army ordered 80 Challenger CHARRV in two batches and the contract was completed with the last vehicles accepted into service during 1983. A

'Type 58' tank Challenger 2 Regiment has 5 x CHARRV, one with each sabre squadron and one with the REME Light Aid Detachment (LAD).

The vehicle has a crew of three plus additional space in a separate compartment for another two REME fitters. The vehicle is fitted with two winches (main and auxiliary) plus an Atlas hydraulically operated crane capable of lifting a complete Challenger 2 powerpack. The front dozer blade can be used as a stabiliser blade for the crane or as a simple earth anchor.

Fv 107 Scimitar

(Approx 320 available) Armament 1 x 30 mm Rarden L21 Gun; 1 x 7.62 mm Machine Gun; 2 x 4 barrel smoke dischargers; Engine BTA 5.9 Cummins diesel; Fuel Capacity 423 litres; Max Road Speed 80 kph; Combat Weight 8,000 kg; Length 4.9 m; Height 2.096 m; Width 2.2 m; Ground Clearance 0.35 m; Road Range 644 km; Crew 3; Ammunition Capacity 30 mm – 160 rounds; 7.62 mm – 3,000 rounds; Main Armament Elevation – 10 degrees to + 35 degrees.

CVR(T) Scimitar is the mainstay reconnaissance vehicle with which all Formation Reconnaissance regiments are equipped as well as all Close Reconnaissance troops and platoons of Armoured and Mechanised Battlegroups. The Scimitar is an ideal reconnaissance vehicle, mobile and fast with good communications and excellent viewing equipment. The vehicle's small size and low ground pressure make it extremely useful where the terrain is hostile and movement difficult.

Fv 102 CVR(T) Striker

(Approx 48 available) Crew 3; Armament 10 x Swingfire Missiles: 1 x 7.62 mm Machine Gun: 2 x 4 barrel smoke dischargers. Engine: B6 Cummins diesel. Fuel Capacity 350 litres: Max Road Speed 80 kph: Road Range 483 km: Length 4.8 m: Height 2.2 m: Width 2.4 m: Combat Weight 8,100 kg; Ground Clearance 0.35 m: Ammunition Capacity 3,000 rounds of 7.62 mm: Main Armament Traverse 53 degrees left, 55 degrees right.

Striker is one of the family of the CVR(T) vehicles (Combat Vehicle Reconnaissance Tracked) which includes Scimitar, Spartan, Sultan, Samson and Samaritan. Striker carries 10 Swingfire anti-tank missiles with a range of up to 4,000 metres. Five of these missiles are carried in bins on top of the vehicle, which can be lowered when the system is not expected to be in action. There is also a separated sight available which enables the launch vehicle to be hidden in dead ground, and the operator to fire and control the flight of the missile from a position up to 100 m away from the launch vehicle.

The striker system enables a fast, hard hitting anti-tank missile launch platform to keep up with the latest MBTs. Striker is to be found in the Formation Reconnaissance regiment which has a troop of four vehicles in each of its three reconnaissance squadrons. Striker is likely to be replaced by the Future Rapid Effect System (FRES) variant.

Swingfire Data
Type – Anti Tank Guided Missile; Wire Guided; Command to line of sight; Length of Missile 1.06 m; Body Diameter 37.3 cm; Warhead Hollow Charge HE; Propellant Solid Fuel; Weight of Missile 37 kg; Minimum Range 150 m; Maximum Range 4,000 m.

A Swingfire missile has an estimated in-service life of about 17 years and the missile is believed to be in the process of being replaced by Javelin ATGW.

Fuchs
(11 available) Road Range 800 kms; Crew 2; Operational Weight 17,000 kg; Length 6.83 m; Width 2.98 m; Height 2.30 m; Road Speed 105 kph; Engine Mercedes-Benz Model OM-402A V-8 liquid cooled diesel; Armament 1 x 7.62 mm MG; 6 x Smoke Dischargers.

Manufactured by the German company Thyssen-Henschel, Fuchs can detect radiation and identify either surface deposits of chemical agents or chemical vapour. The vehicle is equipped with a Global Positioning System (GPS) and provides the crew with integral collective protection.

Panther Command and Liaison Vehicle (Panther CLV)
The UK MoD announced in July 2003 that the BAE Systems Land Systems (formerly Alvis) Multi-role Light Vehicle (MLV) had been selected as the British Army's Future Command and Liaison Vehicle (FCLV). The first procurement contract was signed in November 2003 for an initial 401 vehicles, with an option for up to 400 more. The vehicle has been named the Panther Command and Liaison Vehicle (CLV). In June 2004, Thales Defence Optronics was selected to provide the Driver's Vision Enhancer (DVE) for the Panther CLV. Thales' DVE driver's sight is based on an uncooled thermal imager.

Panther CLV is based on a design by Iveco Defence Vehicles Division of Italy and the vehicles will be manufactured during the period 2006 to 2010. A Development and Demonstration contract covers the build and test of seven vehicles by 2005, with a planned in-service date of 2007. Acquisition cost for some 400 vehicles is £193 million spread over five years. The first batch of 50 vehicles is to be delivered in late 2007.

The current gross vehicle weight of a Panther CLV is 7.1 tonnes. The vehicle is to be air transportable, underslung beneath a Chinook helicopter or carried inside C130, C17 and A400M aircraft.

Panther CLV will replace a range of vehicles which are reaching the end of their operational lives, for example some types of Land Rover, Saxon, some FV432 and a number of Combat Vehicle (Reconnaissance) Tracked. The vehicles will also enter service with the Royal Air Force Regiment.

Multi-Purpose Decontamination System (MPDS)

MPDS is a diesel driven, high pressure cleaning and decontamination system. It consists of two KARCHER water pumps, capable of spraying water at various temperatures, ranging from cold through to steam, and a 9000 litre water tank mounted on a DROPS flatrack. The system is capable of drawing water (including seawater) from either an open source or Service sources such as bulk water carriers. The system is operated in conjunction with decontaminants. It can be operated mounted on DROPS or dismounted.

Integrated Biological Detection System (IBDS)

IBDS has recently replaced the Prototype Biological Detection System (PBDS) in service with the UK Joint NBC Regiment. This modern system provides an enhanced and automated NBC detection system. Major IBDS elements include:

- A detection suite, including equipment for atmospheric sampling
- Meteorological station and GPS
- NBC filtration and environmental control for use in all climates
- Chemical agent detection
- Independent power supply
- Cameras for 360 degree surveillance

IBDS is installed in a container which can be mounted on a vehicle (standard 4 ton) or ground dumped and can be transported by either fixed wing aircraft or helicopters. IBDS provides the commander in the field with early warning of a chemical or biological warfare attack.

SA-80 Carbine

During late 2006 RAC personnel were equipped with a smaller version of the 5.56 mm SA80 rifle, designed specifically to fit into tight spaces. The weapons will replace the 9 mm pistols previously issued to armoured vehicle crewmen.

Future Rapid Effect System (FRES)

The FRES Programme is the UK Ministry of Defence (MoD) forward plan to provide the British Army with a family of medium-weight, network-enabled, air-deployable armoured vehicles to meet a variety of (possibly 16) battlespace roles.

The FRES requirement is for a family of fighting vehicle platforms (including a range of Ground Manoeuvre Reconnaissance roles), which only when integrated with a variety of other capabilities produces a complete system of systems. It will seek to make full use of any intelligence-gathering capabilities that are, or become, available. However, the project is still in the Assessment Phase and therefore the precise nature of the interface with other capabilities is not yet determined.

Following acceptance into service it is expected that there will be three FRES-equipped brigades and this will enable the UK to deploy armoured forces more rapidly in support of national and alliance interests. The exact number of FRES type vehicles to be procured has not yet been determined but it is expected to be at least 3,000 if the current fleet of CVR(T), Saxon and FV432 series vehicles are to be replaced.

A major FRES requirement is that it should be able to be transported in a C-130 Hercules aircraft which will place severe constraints on the platform weight and eventual design. However, experience in Iraq and Afghanistan has underlined the vulnerability of existing vehicles to attack by roadside bombs and rocket-propelled grenades, causing the Ministry of Defence to demand that FRES is better armoured. As a result, planned weight of the vehicles has risen from about 17 tons to between 20 tons and 27 tons which raises questions over whether they will be too heavy for the RAF's new A400M transport aircraft. As yet there does not appear to have been a decision as to whether FRES will be tracked or wheeled.

The programme will comprise three families of vehicles: Utility, Heavy and Reconnaissance with the MoD planning to deliver the Utility vehicle first. The MoD has set four key requirements of the FRES Utility vehicle: 'survivability' through the integration of armour; 'deployability' by the A400M aircraft; a 'networked-enabled capability' through the integration of digital communication technology, and through-life upgrade potential throughout its anticipated 30 year service life.

FRES vehicle 'family groups' are based around the following requirements:

Group 1 FRES utility vehicles are expected to include protected mobility, light armoured support, command-and-control, medical, equipment support and a driver-training vehicle.

Group 2 FRES vehicles will cover intelligence, surveillance, target acquisition and reconnaissance (ISTAR) and fire control. This group will include vehicles that also improve indirect fire support, direct-fire support, indirect fire control, engineer reconnaissance, ground-based surveillance, scout, anti-tank guided weapon and an enhanced protected mobility vehicle.

Group 3 FRES vehicles will include the formation communications variants (Falcon) and electronic warfare versions (Soothsayer). Variants of the former are expected to include Bowman gateway and a variety of Falcon and Wasp capable platforms.

Group 4 FRES vehicles will be formation force protection and manoeuvre support and will include an armoured vehicle launched bridge, armoured vehicle engineer, armoured engineer tractor and CBRN reconnaissance and survey.

Group 5 FRES vehicles currently consists of a remotely delivered mine system to replace the current Shielder, based on a Stormer chassis.

It appears that Ministers have still to set a date for FRES to enter service. The MoD has acknowledged that the original service date of 2009 had slipped to 'the early part of the next decade'. As a result, if the FRES programme goes ahead we would expect to see the first vehicles accepted into service around 2012-2014.

THE FUTURE

The argument that 'the days of the tank are over' has been around for many years and certainly since the appearance of the man-portable guided missile in large numbers such as during the Yom Kippur war. The advent of the highly capable Attack Helicopter and long-range, smart top-attack precision munitions has only added to this debate. However, tanks remain in the world in large numbers – at least 100,000 by current estimates – and in a surprisingly large number of countries. Whilst the supremacy of armour on the modern battlefield will continue to be challenged by ever more sophisticated anti-armour systems, the requirement for highly mobile, protected direct firepower that can operate in all conditions and climates will remain an enduring requirement to support the infantry. It is this 'endurance' characteristic and the ability to operate in all circumstances which is unique and is not shared by helicopters and aircraft.

What is certain to change is the shape and size of future tanks. The key is that new technology will allow protection to be delivered in quite different ways. Traditionally, protection has been provided through ballistic armour which, because of its weight, has to be optimised over a relatively narrow frontal arc, with reduced protection on the sides, top rear and belly. Thus full protection is only possible on a small proportion of the total surface area. In the future a more holistic approach is likely to incorporate a wide range of 'survivability' characteristics in view of the three-dimensional and all round threat. These measures include: signature reduction in all aspects – acoustic, visual, thermal, radar cross-section etc; suites of active and passive defensive aids and electro-optic countermeasures; and inherent redundancy in vehicle design and crew i.e. the ability to sustain considerable damage yet be able to continue fighting. The concept is based on a theory of 'don't be detected – if detected, don't be acquired – if acquired, don't be hit – if hit, don't be penetrated – if penetrated, don't be killed'. Such an approach is likely to see future tanks of much smaller design and of significantly lesser weight. In turn, reduced weight and size will improve mobility and enable armour to be deployed more rapidly, strategically if necessary, whilst also reducing the very considerable mobility and logistic support that the heavy 60-70 tonne MBTs of today require.

In terms of firepower, smart, extended range munitions such as fire and forget Gun Launched Anti-tank Guided Missiles, pre-programmable ammunition and other novel natures are all likely to increase the potency of armour. In coming to a balanced view on the future of the tank, the heavy modern tank of today has as much in common with the Mark V tank of 1916 as it will have with its successor in 2030.

Digitisation of the future battlefield has been identified as essential, but base architecture programmes essential for the target data transmission through battlefield management systems is currently running some ten to fifteen years behind schedule. This time lag may enable the tank in its present form to survive for much longer than many analysts had previously predicted.

As we enter the 21st Century, we see the major defence orientated countries of the world undergoing a major doctrinal and conceptual rethink based on the information age, embracing new IT and digital technology capabilities. The future, however, always has its roots in the present and while the large fleets of tanks we now have may be more visible from space, and more difficult to protect from remotely fired missiles and guns, the armies who have them will continue to explore and exploit armoured 'stretch' technologies to ensure their armoured capability is credible until successor technologies appear in service.

In terms of NBC defence, there will be an increasing requirement to provide a detection capability, coupled with the rapid passage of NBC hazard information. Such assets should be capable of matching the performance of other reconnaissance troops. Whilst detection may remain a core reconnaissance skill, in depth identification and analysis will be required, provided by a range of vehicles across the joint battlespace. The need to conduct rapid and efficient decontamination will remain. These capabilities must be supported by a robust suite of other NBC defensive measures designed to minimise casualties whilst maximising operational efficiency.

CHAPTER 5 – INFANTRY

REGIMENTS AND BATTALIONS

The British Infantry is based on the well tried and tested Regimental System, which has proved to be repeatedly successful on operations over the years. It is based on Regiments, most of which have one or more regular Battalion and all have associated TA Battalions. The esprit de corps of the Regimental system is maintained in the names and titles of British Infantry Regiments handed down through history, with a tradition of courage in battle. The repeated changing size of the British Army, dictated by history and politics, is reflected in the fact that many of the most illustrious Regiments still have a number of Regular and Territorial Reserve Battalions. For manning purposes, in a number of cases Infantry Regiments are grouped within administrative 'Divisions'. These 'Divisions' are no longer field formations but represent original historical groupings based on recruiting geography.

The 'Division' of Infantry is an organisation that is responsible for all aspects of military administration, from recruiting, manning and promotions for individuals in the Regiments under its wing, to the longer term planning required to ensure continuity and cohesion. Divisions of Infantry have no operational command over their regiments, and should not be confused with the remaining operational divisions, such as 1(UK) Armoured Division and 3 (UK) Division.

Under the terms of the December 2004 Future Army Structure (FAS) the infantry has been restructured as follows:

a. The number of Regular Line Infantry Battalions is reducing by four (from 40 to 36 by April 2008), with the manpower and structure of one of the four being used as the core of a new 'special reconnaissance' battalion.

b. A new Regimental system and structure will be adopted over the coming years. This will be based on large, Multi Battalion Regiments.

c. Arms Plotting will cease, limited relocations will occur for Battalions in particular roles/locations.

d. There will be an increase from 19 (48%) to 23 (64%) of Infantry battalions in All Arms Brigades.

e. The 9th platoon in Armoured Infantry Battalions will be decaderised.

f. Enhancements will be made to reconnaissance platoons.

g. Fire Support platoons will be established with a mix of AGL and GPMG.

At the beginning of 2008 we believe that the infantry will be located as follows:

United Kingdom	29 battalions (3 Resident in Northern Ireland)
Germany	6 battalions
Iraq	2 or 3 battalions on detachment
Afghanistan	3 battalions on detachment
Cyprus	2 battalions

Falkland Islands	1 company group on detachment
Brunei	1 battalion (Gurkha)

INFANTRY STRUCTURE IN LATE 2007

By late 2007 we expect the Administrative 'Divisions' of Infantry to be structured as follows:

The Guards Division	5 regular battalions
The Scottish Division	5 regular battalions
The Queen's Division	6 regular battalions
The King's Division	5 regular battalions
The Prince of Wales Division	5 regular battalions

Not administered by 'Divisions' of Infantry but operating under their own similar administrative arrangements were the following:

The Parachute Regiment	3 regular battalions
The Brigade of Gurkhas	2 regular battalions
The Royal Irish Regiment	1 regular battalion
The Rifles	5 regular battalions

Note: 1st Bn The Parachute Regiment form the core element of the Special Forces Support Group and are not counted in the infantry battalion total.

TA battalions were under the administrative command of the following:

The Guards Division	1 TA battalion
The Scottish Division	2 TA battalions
The Queen's Division	3 TA battalions
The King's Division	2 TA battalions
The Prince of Wales Division	2 TA battalions
The Rifles	2 TA battalions
The Parachute Regiment	1 TA battalion
The Royal Irish Regiment	1 TA battalion
The Royal Gibraltar Regiment	1 composite battalion

In total the British Army has 36 regular battalions available for service and this total combined with the 14 TA battalions (excluding the Royal Gibraltar Regiment) could provide mobilisation strength of 50 infantry battalions.

Outside the above listed Regiments are three companies of guardsmen each of 110 men, who are provided to supplement the Household Division Regiments while on public duties in London. This allows Regiments of the Foot Guards to continue to carry out normal training on roulement from guard duties. Gibraltar also has its own single battalion of the Royal Gibraltar Regiment comprising one regular and two volunteer companies.

The following listing shows the infantry structure from late 2007.

THE GUARDS DIVISION

REGULAR BNS

1st Bn Grenadier Guards	1 GREN GDS
1st Bn Coldstream Guards	1 COLDM GDS
1st Bn Scots Guards	1SG
1st Bn Irish Guards	1 IG
1st Bn Welsh Guards	1 WG

TERRITORIAL ARMY BN

The London Regiment	LONDONS

THE SCOTTISH DIVISION

REGULAR BNS

The Royal Scots Borderers, 1st Bn The Royal Regiment of Scotland	1 SCOTS
The Royal Highland Fusiliers, 2nd Bn The Royal Regiment of Scotland	2 SCOTS
The Black Watch, 3rd Bn The Royal Regiment of Scotland	3 SCOTS
The Highlanders, 4th Bn The Royal Regiment of Scotland	4 SCOTS
The Argyll and Sutherland Highlanders, 5th Bn The Royal Regiment of Scotland	5 SCOTS

TERRITORIAL ARMY BNS

52nd Lowland, 6th Bn The Royal Regiment of Scotland	6 SCOTS
51st Highland, 7th Bn The Royal Regiment of Scotland	7 SCOTS

THE QUEEN'S DIVISION

The Princess of Wales's Royal Regiment (Queen's and Royal Hampshires)

REGULAR BNS

1st Bn The Princess of Wales's Royal Regiment (Queen's and Royal Hampshires)	1 PWRR
2nd Bn The Princess of Wales's Royal Regiment (Queen's and Royal Hampshires)	2 PWRR

TERRITORIAL ARMY BN

3rd Bn The Princess of Wales's Royal Regiment (Queen's and Royal Hampshires)	3 PWRR

The Royal Regiment of Fusiliers

REGULAR BNS

1st Bn The Royal Regiment of Fusiliers	1 RRF
2nd Bn The Royal Regiment of Fusiliers	2 RRF

TERRITORIAL ARMY BN

5th Bn The Royal Regiment of Fusiliers	5 RRF

The Royal Anglian Regiment

1st Bn The Royal Anglian Regiment	1 R ANGLIAN
2nd Bn The Royal Anglian Regiment	2 R ANGLIAN

TERRITORIAL ARMY BN

3rd Bn The Royal Anglian Regiment	3 R ANGLIAN

THE KING'S DIVISION

The Duke of Lancaster's Regiment (King's, Lancashire and Border)

REGULAR BNS

1st Bn The Duke of Lancaster's Regiment (King's, Lancashire and Border)	1 LANCS
2nd Bn The Duke of Lancaster's Regiment (King's, Lancashire and Border)	2 LANCS

TERRITORIAL ARMY BN

4th Bn The Duke of Lancaster's Regiment (King's, Lancashire and Border)	3 LANCS

The Yorkshire Regiment

REGULAR BNS

1st Bn The Yorkshire Regiment (Prince Of Wales's Own)	1 YORKS
2nd Bn The Yorkshire Regiment (Green Howards)	2 YORKS
3rd Bn The Yorkshire Regiment (Duke of Wellington's)	3 YORKS

TERRITORIAL ARMY BN

4th Bn The Yorkshire Regiment	4 YORKS

THE PRINCE OF WALES'S DIVISION

The Mercian Regiment (from August 2007)

REGULAR BNS

1st Bn The Mercian Regiment (Cheshire)	1 MERCIAN
2nd Bn The Mercian Regiment (Worcesters and Foresters)	2 MERCIAN
3rd Bn The Mercian Regiment (Staffords)	3 MERCIAN

TERRITORIAL ARMY BN

4th Bn The Mercian Regiment	4 MERCIAN

The Royal Welsh

REGULAR BNS

1st Bn The Royal Welsh (The Royal Welsh Fusiliers)	1 R WELSH
2nd Bn The Royal Welsh (The Royal Regiment of Wales)	2 R WELSH

TERRITORIAL ARMY BN

3rd Bn The Royal Welsh	3 R WELSH

THE RIFLES

REGULAR BNS

1st Bn The Rifles	1 RIFLES
2nd Bn The Rifles	2 RIFLES
3rd Bn The Rifles	3 RIFLES
4th Bn The Rifles	4 RIFLES
5th Bn The Rifles	5 RIFLES

TERRITORIAL ARMY BNS

6th Bn The Rifles	6 RIFLES
7th Bn The Rifles	7 RIFLES

THE ROYAL IRISH REGIMENT

REGULAR BN

1st Bn The Royal Irish Regiment	1 R IRISH

TERRITORIAL ARMY BN

The Royal Irish Rangers	RANGERS

THE PARACHUTE REGIMENT

REGULAR BNS

1st Bn The Parachute Regiment	1 PARA
2nd Bn The Parachute Regiment	2 PARA
3rd Bn The Parachute Regiment	3 PARA

TERRITORIAL ARMY BN

4th Bn The Parachute Regiment	4 PARA

Note: 1 PARA have formed the core element of the new Special Forces Support Group and as such have been removed from the formal Infantry structure

REGULAR BNS

1st Bn The Royal Gurkha Rifles	1 RGR
2nd Bn The Royal Gurkha Rifles	2 RGR

Recent overall infantry liability and actual strengths are as follows:

Regular Army Infantry Liability/Strength at 1 April 2006

	Regular Army Infantry Liability	Infantry Strength
2001	26,740	25,690
2002	26,740	25,640
2003	26,200	25,480
2004	26,360	25,870
2005	24,420	25,060
2006	24,450	24,080

Note: Figures are for all infantry trained officers and soldiers (excluding Colonels and above) regardless of where they are serving. Figures exclude Gurkhas and figures have been rounded to the nearest 10.

Infantry Recruiting Figures 2001-2006

Financial Year	Infantry recruiting target	Infantry enlistment achievement
2001-02	5,160	4,490
2002-03	4,270	4,950
2003-04	4,460	4,620
2004-05	4,150	3,410
2005-06	4,150	3,450

Infantry entry 2006 – 2009

These next tables show the UK MoD figures for the number of trained officers and soldiers expected to join the infantry over the next three years.

Officers		Financial year	
Method of entry	2006–07	2007–08	2008–09
Direct entry	165	165	165
Late entry	28	28	28
Total	193	193	193

Note: Direct entry relates to those who enter the Royal Military Academy Sandhurst direct from education or civilian life. Late entry refers to those who apply for a commission through the ranks.

Soldiers		Financial year	
Category	2006–07	2007–08	2008–09
Foot Guards	418	430	430

Line Regiments	2,134	2,036	2,036
Parachute Regiment	221	234	234
Total	2,780	2,700	2,700

Force Operations and Readiness Mechanism (FORM)

Under the Future Army Structure there is a strategy to deliver both training and commitments known as the Force Operations and Readiness Mechanism (FORM); a replacement for the Formation Readiness Cycle. All Army units, including Infantry Battalions, will programme their training and operational commitment activities according to the principles of FORM. This system should enable the Army to meet its outputs (force elements ready for both programmed operations and contingent operations/emergency deployments) from within the force structure. The sequence of activity for any one force element, such as an Infantry Battalion, is in five separate six month phases:

Phase 1 – Recuperation

Phase 2 – Unit and battle group training

Phase 3 – Formation training

Phase 4 – High readiness

Phase 5 – An operational deployment

Operational units

As explained in Chapter 3, it would be unusual for the Infantry to fight as battalion units especially in armoured or mechanised formations. If the task is appropriate, the HQ of an infantry battalion will become the HQ of a 'battle group', and be provided with armour, artillery, engineers and possibly aviation to enable it to become a balanced Infantry Battle Group. Similarly Infantry Companies can be detached to HQs of Armoured Regiments to make up Armoured Battle Groups.

In the pages that follow, the groupings are based on Unit Establishment figures for peace support operations. For Warfighting a pairing mechanism operates which provides augmentation which allows a unit to meet its role. For example, an Armoured Infantry Regiment will receive additional Manoeuvre Support assets and another Rifle Company to reach its Warfighting Establishment (WFE) of 4 x Companies, 9 x Mortars and 18 x Medium Range Anti-Tank Guided Weapons (ATGW).

Types of Infantry Battalions

Infantry Battalion Armoured	- Equipped with Warrior AFV.
Infantry Battalion Mechanised	- Equipped with Saxon APC.
Infantry Battalion Light Role	- Equipped for General Service.
Infantry Battalion Air Assault	- Equipped for Air Mobile Operations

Armoured Infantry Battalion

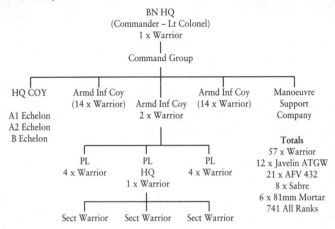

BN HQ
(Commander – Lt Colonel)
1 x Warrior

Command Group

HQ COY

A1 Echelon
A2 Echelon
B Echelon

Armd Inf Coy
(14 x Warrior)

Armd Inf Coy
2 x Warrior

Armd Inf Coy
(14 x Warrior)

Manoeuvre
Support
Company

PL
4 x Warrior

PL
HQ
1 x Warrior

PL
4 x Warrior

Sect Warrior   Sect Warrior   Sect Warrior

Totals
57 x Warrior
12 x Javelin ATGW
21 x AFV 432
8 x Sabre
6 x 81mm Mortar
741 All Ranks

Armoured Infantry Battalion – Manoeuvre Support Company

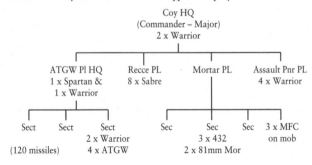

Coy HQ
(Commander – Major)
2 x Warrior

ATGW Pl HQ
1 x Spartan &
1 x Warrior

Recce PL
8 x Sabre

Mortar PL

Assault Pnr PL
4 x Warrior

Sect   Sect   Sect
2 x Warrior
4 x ATGW
(120 missiles)

Sec   Sec   Sec
3 x 432
2 x 81mm Mor

3 x MFC
on mob

86

Mechanised Infantry Battalion

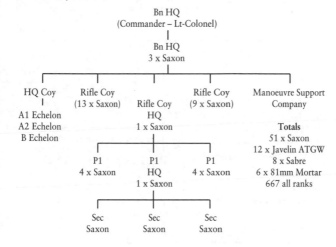

Mechanised Infantry Battalion – Manoeuvre Support Company

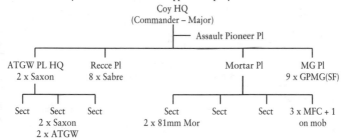

Light Role Infantry Battalion

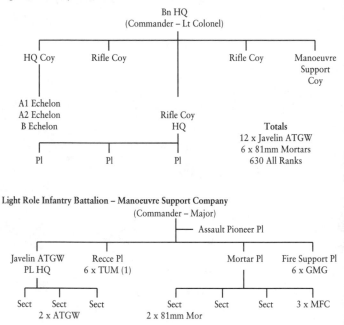

Bn HQ
(Commander – Lt Colonel)

HQ Coy   Rifle Coy   Rifle Coy   Manoeuvre Support Coy

A1 Echelon
A2 Echelon
B Echelon

Rifle Coy HQ

Pl   Pl   Pl

Totals
12 x Javelin ATGW
6 x 81mm Mortars
630 All Ranks

Light Role Infantry Battalion – Manoeuvre Support Company
(Commander – Major)

Assault Pioneer Pl

Javelin ATGW PL HQ   Recce Pl 6 x TUM (1)   Mortar Pl   Fire Support Pl 6 x GMG

Sect   Sect   Sect
2 x ATGW

Sect   Sect   Sect   3 x MFC
2 x 81mm Mor

Notes: (1) TUM is the abbreviation for Truck-Utility-Medium; (2) Air Assault Bns have an HMG Pl with 6 x .50 Calibre Machine Guns mounted on TUM.

Platoon Organisation

The basic building bricks of the Infantry Battalion are the platoon and the section.

Under normal circumstances, the whole platoon with the exception of the LMG (Light Machine Gun) gunners are armed with IW – SA80 (Individual Weapon).

In an armoured or mechanised battalion, the platoon vehicles could be either Warrior or AFV 432.

Under normal circumstances expect a British infantry platoon to resemble the organisation in the following diagram:

```
                Armoured or Mechanised Infantry Platoon
                   Platoon Commander (2/Lt or Lt)
                        Platoon Sergeant
                        Radio Operator
                     51 mm Mortar Operator
                               |
            Mounted in Warrior or APV 432 AIFV/APC
```

Section	Section	Section
AIFV/APC	AIFV/APC	AIFV/APC
|	|	|
Fire Team	Fire Team	Fire Team
|	|	|
Sec Comd (Cpl)	Sec Comd	Sec Comd
Rifleman	Rifleman	Rifleman
Rifleman	Rifleman	Rifleman
LMG Gunner	LMG Gunner	LMG Gunner
|	|	|
Fire Team	Fire Team	Fire Team
|	|	|
Sec 2i/c	Sec 2i/c	Sec 2i/c (Lcpl)
Rifleman	Rifleman	Rifleman
Rifleman	Rifleman	Rifleman
LMG Gunner	LMG Gunner	LMG Gunner

TA Infantry

The new TA Infantry structure has been organised to support and complement the regular regimental structure, thereby restoring a true sense of identity at TA battalion level. There are 14 TA infantry battalions. These provide reinforcement of the regular infantry for up to 14 unit HQs or, where necessary individual or smaller unit reinforcements.

In addition the new TA Infantry Structure can provide the manpower to include up to seven Defence Troops for Armoured and Formation Reconnaissance Regiments committed to operations. Restructuring for TA infantry battalions has been conducted on the basis of a minimum of approximately 400 soldiers per battalion.

AFV 432 and Bulldog

(Approx 1,492 in service of which 811 are base line vehicles – models include command vehicles, ambulances, and 81 mm mortar carriers). Crew 2 (Commander and Driver); Weight loaded 15,280kg; Length 5.25 m; Width 2.8 m; Height 2.28 m; Ground Pressure 0.78 kg km squared; Armament 1 x 7.62 Machine Gun; 2 x 3 barrel smoke dischargers; Engine Rolls Royce K60 No 4 Mark 1-4; Engine Power 240 bhp; Fuel Capacity 454 litres; Max Road Speed 52 kph; Road Range 580 km; Vertical Obstacle 0.9 m; Trench Crossing 2.05 m; Gradient 60 degrees; Carries up to 10 men; Armour 12.7 mm max.

The vehicle is NBC proof and when necessary can be converted for swimming when it has a water speed of 6 kph (if required). Properly maintained it is a rugged and reliable vehicle with a good cross-country performance.

In July 2006 the UK Mod announced the provision, for Iraq, of around 70 uparmoured and upgraded FV430 troop carriers (Bulldog), in addition to the 54 already on contract. Deliveries started in late 2006.

For counter-insurgency operations the up-armoured FV430 will provide a similar level of protection to Warrior and the vehicle will be able to carry out many of the same tasks as Warrior, thereby relieving the pressure on heavily committed Warrior vehicles in armoured infantry battle groups.

MCV – 80 Fv 510 (Warrior)

(793 available) Weight loaded 24,500 kg; length 6.34 m; Height to turret top 2.78 m; Width 3.0 m; Ground Clearance 0.5 m; Max Road Speed 75 kph; Road Range 500 km; Engine Rolls Royce CV8 diesel; Horsepower 550 hp; Crew 2 (carries 8 infantry soldiers); Armament L21 30 mm Rarden Cannon; Coaxial EX-34 7.62 mm Hughes Helicopter Chain Gun; Smoke Dischargers Royal Ordnance Visual and Infra Red Screening Smoke (VIRSS).

Warrior is an Armoured Infantry Fighting Vehicle (AIFV) that replaced the AFV 432 in the armoured infantry battalions. The original buy of Warrior was reduced to 789 units. Of this total the vast majority had been delivered by early 1995 and the vehicle is in service with three armoured infantry battalions in the UK with 3 (UK) Div and six armoured infantry battalions in Germany with 1 (UK) Armd Div.

Warrior armed with the 30 mm Rarden cannon gives the crew a good chance of destroying enemy APCs at ranges of up to 1,500 m and the vehicle carries a crew of three and seven dismounted infantry.

The vehicle is NBC proof, and a full range of night vision equipment is included as standard.

The vehicle has seen successful operational service in the Gulf (1991), with British troops serving in the Balkans and more recently in Iraq. The vehicle has proven protection against mines, and there is dramatic BBC TV footage of a Warrior running over a Serbian anti-tank mine with little or no serious damage to the vehicle or crew.

The hull and mechanical components of Warrior are exceptional and few other vehicles in the world can match it for reliability and performance. The Warrior armament fire control system and electronics require upgrading if the vehicle is to remain in service to 2025 as intended.

A Warrior Mid-Life Improvement Programme is due to be implemented between 2007 and 2012. This should provide a new power pack, vehtronics enhancement, a digital fire control system (FCS) and a modern medium calibre cannon system. This extension of capability for Warrior will provide the necessary lead time for the introduction of future advanced capability systems vehicles to replace both Challenger 2 and Warrior.

The future digitisation programme in-service date (ISD) has slid to around 2017. Current thinking suggests that the British Army may replace existing rifle platoon Warrior with the improved Warrior 2000. This would release existing Warrior to be refitted to fulfil roles currently carried out by ageing and obsolescent FV 432s. This plan would create a new Battalion Assault Support Vehicle (BASV) which could carry Manoeuvre Support elements, principally 81 mm mortars, at the same pace as the Warrior fighting vehicles.

Numbers in UK service are believed to include 482 x Warrior Basic; 59 x Warrior RA; 126 x Warrior Rec and Repair. The Kuwait MoD has signed a contract for the purchase of 230 Warrior vehicles some of which are Recce vehicles armed with a 90 mm Cockerill gun.

AFV 103 Spartan
(478 in service) Crew 3; Weight 8,172 kg; Length 5.12 m; Height 2.26 m; Width 2.26 m; Ground Clearance 0.35 m; Max Road Speed 80 kph; Road Range 483 kms; Engine Jaguar J60 No.1 Mark 100B; Engine Power 190 bhp; Fuel Capacity 386 litres; Ammunition Carried 3,000 rounds of 7.62 mm; Armament 1 x 7.62 Machine Gun.

Spartan is the APC of the Combat Vehicle Reconnaissance Tracked (CVRT) series of vehicles, which include Fv 101 Scorpion, Fv 102 Striker, Fv 104 Samaritan, Fv 105 Sultan, Fv 106 Sampson and Fv 107 Scimitar. Spartan is a very small APC that can only carry four men in addition to the crew of three. It is therefore used to carry small specialised groups such as the reconnaissance teams, air defence sections, mortar fire controllers and ambush parties.

Samaritan, Sultan and Sampson are also APC type vehicles, Samaritan is the CVRT ambulance vehicle, Sultan is the armoured command vehicle and Sampson is an armoured recovery vehicle.

Spartan, like FV 432 is likely to be replaced in some roles in the future.

Spartan is in service with the following nations: Belgium – 266: Oman – 6: Philippines – 7.

Sabre
(136 in service) Crew 3; Height 2.17 m; Width 2.24 m; Length 4.7 m; Combat weight 8,100 kg; Armament 1 x 30 mm L21 Rarden cannon and 1 x 7.62 mm chain gun; Ammunition 160 x 30 mm APEP and HE plus 3,000 x 7.62 mm rounds; Engine Cummins BTA 5.9 diesel; Maximum Speed 80kph.

Essentially Sabre consists of the older Scorpion (light tank) chassis fitted with the turret of a wheeled Fox reconnaissance vehicle. We believe that about 136 Sabre vehicles are in service and the vehicle is in service with the Reconnaissance Platoons of Armoured and Mechanised Infantry Battalions. The vehicle has a similar profile to that of Scimitar but with the turret roof slightly lower and a co-axial chain gun instead of the GPMG.

AT – 105 Saxon
(622 available of which 482 are baseline vehicles) Weight 10,670 kg; Length 5.16 m; Width 2.48 m; Height 2.63 m; Ground Clearance (axles) 0.33 m; Max Road Speed 96 kph; Max Road Range 510 km; Fuel Capacity 160 litres; Fording 1.12 m; Gradient 60 degrees; Engine Bedford 600 6-cylinder diesel developing 164 bhp at 2,800 rpm; Armour proof against 7.62 rounds fired at point blank range; Crew 2 + 10 max.

The Saxon was manufactured by GKN Defence and the first units for the British Army were delivered in late 1983. The vehicle, which can be best described as a battlefield taxi is designed around truck parts and does not require the same level of maintenance of track and running gear normally associated with APC/AIFVs.

Each vehicle cost over £100,000 at 1984 prices and they are on issue to Mechanised Infantry Battalions assigned to 3 (UK) Division.

The Army holds a number of Saxon IS (Patrol) vehicles for service in counter insurgency operations. The IS (Internal Security) equipped vehicle has a Cummins BT 5.1 engine instead of the Bedford 6-cylinder installed on the APC version and other enhancements for internal security operations such as roof-mounted searchlights, improved armour, a barricade removal device and an anti-wire device.

Saxon is in operational service with British forces in both Iraq and Afghanistan.

Mastiff Force Protection Vehicle (FPV)
(108 available) Height 2.64 m; Width 2,53 m; Length 7.08 m; Top speed 90 kph; All up weight 23,500 kg; Payload 6,350 kg.

Mastiff is a heavily armoured, wheeled armoured vehicle suitable for road patrols and convoys and is the newest delivery in a range of protected patrol vehicles being used for operations.

Manufactured by the US Company Force Protection Inc (where it is named Cougar) Mastiff is a 6 x 6 wheel-drive patrol vehicle which carries six people, plus two crew. It has a maximum speed of 90 kph and can be armed with a machine gun, 50 mm canon or 40 mm automatic grenade launcher

The UK MoD purchased some 108 vehicles in an order worth approximately US$70.1 million (£35 million).

Javelin LF ATGW
Launch Unit: Weight 6.4 kg; Sight magnification x 4; Missile: Range 2,500 m; Weight 11.8 kg; Length 1.08 m; Seeker – Imaging infra-red; Guidance – Lock on before launch, automatic self-guidance; Missile – Two stage solid propellant with a tandem shaped charge; Weight of Launch unit and missile 22 kg.

Javelin will equip Light Forces, Mechanised and Armoured Infantry, and Formation Reconnaissance units. The UK version of the US Javelin ATGW system, is a more sophisticated guided weapon with a range of some 2,500 m. A production contract was signed in early 2003 worth over £300 million. Industry sources suggest that up to 5,000 missiles and 300 firing posts have been ordered. First deliveries to the UK have been made and the system has replaced Milan. In UK service Javelin has a number of modifications which include an enhanced Command Launch Unit (CLU) with a wider field of view, and the ability to recognise targets at longer ranges.

Although Javelin has been developed mainly to engage armoured fighting vehicles, the system can also be used to neutralise bunkers, buildings, and low-flying helicopters. Javelin's top-attack tandem warhead is claimed to defeat all known armour systems.

The US Army and Marine Corps have been using Javelin for some years and the system is either in service, or has been selected by Australia, Ireland, Jordan, Lithuania, New Zealand, and Taiwan. Over 7,000 Javelin launchers have been manufactured since 1995. Javelin is planned to be in UK service until 2025.

LAW 80

Effective Range up to 500 m; Armour Penetration up to 650 mm; Impact Sensor – Scrub and Foliage Proof; Launcher Length (Firing Mode) 1.5m; Launcher Length (Carrying Mode) 1 m; Carrying Weight 10 kg; Projectile Diameter 94 mm; Temperature Range -46 to +65 degrees C; Rear Danger Area 20 m.

LAW 80 replaced the 84 mm Carl Gustav and the US 66 mm in service with the British Army, and infantry units in armoured and mechanised battalions were equipped down to section level with this weapon that is capable of destroying main battle tanks at ranges of up to 500 m.

MBT LAW

MBT LAW (formerly NLAW) is a man-portable, short-range anti-armour weapon. It will provide a capability out to a range of 600 m, against main battle tanks and light armoured vehicles; have the ability to be fired from enclosed spaces and defensive positions and be a means of attack against personnel in structures.

The MBT LAW prime contractor is SAAB Bofors Dynamics of Sweden, with Thales Air Defence Ltd as the main UK sub-contractor, the Demonstration and Manufacture contract having been placed in June 2002. The final cost of the MBT LAW contract is in the order of £400M. The system is planned to enter service in late 2007 and will replace LAW 80 and the interim ILAW (Bofors AT-4).

The MBT LAW system is being developed in a collaborative programme with Sweden.

81 mm L16 Mortar

(450 in service including 100 SP) Max Range HE 5,650 m; Elevation 45 degrees to 80 degrees; Muzzle Velocity 255 m/s; Length of barrel 1280 mm; Weight of barrel 12.7 kg; Weight of base plate 11.6 kg; In action Weight 35.3 kg; Bomb Weight HE L3682 4.2 kg; Rate of Fire 15 rpm; Calibre 81 mm.

The 81mm Mortar is on issue to all infantry battalions, with each battalion having a mortar platoon with three or four sections; and each section deploying two mortars. These mortars are the battalion's organic Manoeuvre Support Firepower and can be used to put a heavy weight of fire down on an objective in an extremely short period. Mortar fire is particularly lethal to infantry in the open and in addition is very useful for neutralising dug-in strong points or forcing armour to close down.

The fire of each mortar section is controlled by the MFC (Mortar Fire Controller) who is usually an NCO and generally positioned well forward with the troops being supported. Most MFCs will find themselves either very close to or co-located with a Task Group Commander.

The MFC informs the base plate (mortar position) by radio of the location of the target and then corrects the fall of the bombs, directing them onto the target.

Mortar fire can be used to suppress enemy positions until assaulting troops arrive within 200-300 m of the position. The mortar fire then lifts onto enemy counter attack and supporting positions while the assault goes in. The 81 mm Mortar can also assist with smoke and illuminating rounds.

The mortar is carried in an AFV432 or a Truck (Utility Light or Medium) and if necessary can be carried in two, man portable loads of 11.35 kg and one 12.28 kg respectively. In the past, infantry companies working in close country have carried one 81 mm round per man when operating in areas such as Borneo where wheeled or tracked transport was not available. For Air Mobile and Air Assault operations mortar rounds are issued in twin packs of two rounds per man on initial deployment. These are used as initial ammunition resources until further ammunition loads can be flown in.

The L16A2 81 mm Mortar has undergone a mid life upgrade (MLU) to embrace recent technological developments. The inclusion of the new SPGR (Specialised Personal GPS Receiver) and the LH40C (Laser) combine to make the new TLE (Target Locating Equipment). This generates a significant enhancement in first round accuracy and the ease, and speed with which accurate fire missions can be executed. Additionally, the equipment reduces the number of adjustment rounds which will be used and lead to greater dispersal of mortar barrels, thus increasing protection for the mortar crew soldiers. Plans continue to develop further synergies with The Royal Artillery to improve the existing levels of co-ordination between Artillery and Mortars in fighting the indirect fire battle.

Improved performance ammunition with greater lethality against buildings, armour and equipment is expected to be in service within the next two years.

51 mm Light Mortar
(About 2,000 available) Range 750 m; Bomb Weight 800 gms (illum), 900 gms (smk), 920 gms (HE); Rapid Rate of Fire 8 rpm; Length of barrel 750 mm; Weight Complete 6.275 kg; Calibre 51.25 mm

The 51 mm Light Mortar is a weapon that can be carried and fired by one man, and is found in the HQ of an infantry platoon. The mortar is used to fire smoke, illuminating and HE rounds out to a range of approximately 750 m; a short range insert device enables the weapon to be used in close quarter battle situations with some accuracy. The 51 mm Light Mortar has replaced the older l940s 2' mortar.

Currently (mid 2007) the weapon is approaching its planned out of service date across the armed forces. The capability provided by the 51 mm mortar will be replaced by a combination of systems including the 40 mm Underslung Grenade Launcher and rocket hand-fired illumination and smoke rounds. In Afghanistan, the 51 mm capability is being augmented by a purchase of a more modern 60 mm mortar.

5.56 mm Individual Weapon (IW) (SA 80 and SA 80A2)

Effective Range 400m; Muzzle Velocity 940 m/s; Rate of Fire from 610-775 rpm; Weight 4.98 kg (with 30 round magazine); Length Overall 785 mm; Barrel Length 518 mm; Trigger Pull 3.12-4.5 kg.

Designed to fire the standard NATO 5.56 mm x 45 mm round, the SA 80 was fitted with an x4 telescopic (SUSAT) sight as standard. The total buy for SA 80 was for 332,092 weapons. Issues of the weapon are believed to have been made as follows:

Royal Navy	7,864
Royal Marines	8,350
Royal Air Force	42,221
MoD Police	1,878
Army	271,779

At 1991/92 prices the total cost of the SA 80 contract was in the order of £384.16 million. By late 1994 some 10,000 SA 80 Night Sights and 3rd Generation Image Intensifier Tubes for use with SA80 had been delivered.

The SA 80 had a mixed press and following some severe criticism of the weapons mechanical reliability the improved SA 80A2 was introduced into service during late 2001.

SA 80A2: Some 13 changes were made to the weapon's breech block, gas regulation, firing-pin, cartridge extractor, recoil springs, cylinder and gas plug, hammer, magazine and barrel. Since modification the weapon has been extensively trialled.

Mean time before failure (MTBF) figures from the firing trials for stoppages, following rounds fired are as follow:

	SA 80A2	LSW
UK (temperate)	31,500	16,000
Brunei (hot/wet)	31,500	9,600
Kuwait (hot/dry)	7,875	8,728
Alaska (cold/dry)	31,500	43,200

The first SA 80A2 were in operational service during early 2002 and these weapons were in service across the army by late 2004. The cost of the programme was £92 million and some 200,000 weapons were modified by the time the programme ended in May 2006.

5.56mm Light Machine Gun (Minimi)

Effective range 800 m; Calibre 5.56 mm; Weight 7.1 kg; Length 914 mm; Feed 100-round disintegrating belt; Cyclic rate of fire 700 to 1000 rounds per minute.

FN Herstal's Minimi belt fed 5.56mm Light Machine Gun (LMG), has entered service on a scale of one per four-man fire team. The Minimi has been used operationally by British troops in Afghanistan and Iraq and the UK MoD is buying 2,472 weapons. The contract which will boost the firepower within infantry sections was believed to have been completed in late 2007.

The Minimi is in service with Australia, Canada and New Zealand as well as the US Armed Forces.

7.62 mm General Purpose Machine Gun (GPMG)

Range 800 (Light Role) l,800 m (Sustained Fire Role); Muzzle Velocity 538 m/s; Length 1.23 m; Weight loaded 13.85 kg (gun + 50 rounds); Belt Fed; Rate of Fire up to 750 rpm; Rate of Fire Light Role 100 rpm; Rate of Fire Sustained Fire Role 200 rpm.

An infantry machine gun which has been in service since the early 1960s, the GPMG can be used in the light role fired from a bipod or can be fitted to a tripod for use in the sustained fire role. The gun is also found pintle-mounted on many armoured vehicles. Used on a tripod the gun is effective out to 1,800 m although it is difficult to spot strike at this range because the tracer rounds in the ammunition belt burns out at 1,100 m.

Machine Gun platoons in air assault battalions remain equipped with the GPMG in the sustained fire role. GPMG performance has recently been enhanced by the issue of a Maxi Kite night image intensification sight giving excellent visibility out to 600 m. There are 11,300 in service and the weapon is to be withdrawn from service in 2015.

12.7 mm Heavy Machine Gun (HMG)

Effective range – up to 2000 m; Calibre 12.7 mm; Weight 38.15 kg (gun only); Length: 1,656 mm; Barrel Length 1,143 mm; Muzzle Velocity 915 m/s; Cyclic rate of fire – 485 – 635 rounds per minute.

The 12.7 mm Heavy Machine Gun (HMG) is an updated version of the Browning M2 'Fifty-cal' – generally recognised as one of the best heavy machine guns ever developed. Currently, the HMG provides integral close-range support from a ground mount tripod or fitted to a Land Rover TUM using a Weapon Mount Installation Kit (WMIK) and a variety of sighting systems. The performance of the HMG has recently been enhanced with a new 'soft mount' (to limit recoil and improve accuracy) and a quick change barrel.

Long Range Rifle (LRR)

The SA 80 is designed to shoot accurately out to 300 m and be easily handled in combat situations. With the disappearance of the .303 the skill of shooting accurately above 400 m has largely died away. The 7.62 Sniper Rifle filled the gap for a while but the vulnerability of the round to wind deflection over longer ranges made it desirable to come up with a weapon which could be fired with some precision in all phases of modern warfare.

The result has been the development by Accuracy International UK of the 6.8 mm (.338) Long Range Large Calibre Rifle. Capable of shooting accurately out to 1100 m, the LRR came into service in early 2000. The weapon has been issued to JRRF (Joint Rapid Reaction Force) units on the basis of 14 per battalion, with one per platoon and a small pool for snipers in the battalion recce platoons.

Infantry battalion strength against liability as at 1 November 2006
(includes personnel on full time reserve service (FTRS))

	Strength	*Liability*
Guards Division	2,540	2,920
1 Grenadier Guards	540	570
1 Coldstream Guards	540	570
1 Scots Guards	470	640
1 Irish Guards	490	570
1 Welsh Guards	500	570
Scottish Division	2,790	2,930
1 Royal Regiment of Scotland	700	570
2 Royal Regiment of Scotland	500	570
3 Royal Regiment of Scotland	560	570
4 Royal Regiment of Scotland	550	640
5 Royal Regiment of Scotland	480	590
Queen's Division	3,140	3,560
1 Princess of Wales's Royal Regiment	490	640
2 Princess of Wales's Royal Regiment	520	570
1 Royal Regiment of Fusiliers	550	640
2 Royal Regiment of Fusiliers	480	570
1 Royal Anglian Regiment	580	600
2 Royal Anglian Regiment	530	560
King's Division	2,960	3,500
1 Yorkshire Regiment	510	570
2 Yorkshire Regiment	470	570
3 Yorkshire Regiment	510	600
1 Duke of Lancaster's Regiment	500	590
2 Duke of Lancaster's Regiment	590	620
3 Duke of Lancaster's Regiment	400	560
Prince of Wales Division	2,360	2,970

1 Cheshire Regiment	460	570
1 Royal Welsh Regiment	460	570
2 Royal Welsh Regiment	470	640
1 Worcestershire and Sherwood Foresters Regiment	490	560
1 Staffordshire Regiment	480	640
Light Div (Now The Rifles)	**3,060**	**3,510**
1 Devonshire and Dorset Regiment, Light Infantry	490	590
1 Royal Gloucestershire, Berkshire and Wiltshire Regiment, Light Infantry	450	560
1 Light Infantry	570	640
2 Light Infantry	520	570
1 Royal Green Jackets	490	570
2 Royal Green Jackets	530	600
Parachute Regiment	**1,460**	**1,760**
1 Parachute Regiment	460	580
2 Parachute Regiment	480	590
3 Parachute Regiment	520	590
Royal Irish Regiment		
1 Royal Irish Regiment	450	590

Note:
(1) The establishment figures refer to the number of posts within a battalion that may be filled by Infantry personnel (officers and soldiers). It excludes posts that are filled by attached personnel of other Arms and Services such as cooks, clerks, etc. Establishments will also vary depending on the particular role of a battalion; for example, Armoured Infantry battalions have larger establishments than light role Infantry battalions.
(2) The Guards Division strengths and establishments exclude the Public Duty Companies.
(3) Figures do not include Gurkhas.

CHAPTER 6 – ARTILLERY

BACKGROUND

The Royal Regiment of Artillery (RA) provides the battlefield fire support and air defence for the British Army in the field. Its various regiments are equipped for conventional fire support using field guns, for area and point air defence using air defence missiles and for specialised artillery locating tasks.

The RA remains one of the larger organisations in the British Army with 15 Regiments included in its regular Order of Battle. Late 2006 personnel figures suggest that the RA had a personnel figure of 7,300 officers and soldiers representing 97% of its establishment strength.

Following restructuring, by late 2007 the RA should have the following structure in both the UK and Germany.

	UK	Germany
Field Regiments (AS 90 SP Guns)	2	3
Field Regiments (Light Gun)	3 (1)	-
Depth Fire Regiments (MLRS)	1 (2)	–
Air Defence Regiments (Rapier)	1	–
Air Defence Regiment (HVM)	2	–
Surveillance & Target Acquisition Regiment	1	–
UAV Regiment	1	–
Training Regiment (School Assets Regt)	1	–
The Kings Troop (Ceremonial)	1	–

Note:
(1) Of these three Regiments, one is a Commando Regiment (29 Cdo Regt) and another is an Air Assault Regiment (7 PARA RHA). Either of these Regiments can be called upon to provide Manoeuvre Support Artillery to the AMF (Allied Command Europe Military Force).
(2) A second MLRS Regiment is now a TA Regt with 12 Launch vehicles in peace uprateable to 18 in war.
(3) Although the artillery is organised into Regiments, much of the 'Gunner's' loyalty is directed towards the battery in which they serve. The guns represent the Regimental Colours of the Artillery and it is around the batteries where the guns are held that history has gathered. A Regiment will generally have three or four gun batteries under command.
(4) The Schools Asset Regiment is not included in the totals given for artillery in Chapter 1.

The Royal Horse Artillery (RHA) is also part of the Royal Regiment of Artillery and its regiments have been included in the totals above. There is considerable cross posting of officers and soldiers from the RA to the RHA, and some consider service with the RHA to be a career advancement.

Future Army Structure

Under the terms of the recent Future Army Structure (FAS) programme the following changes have taken place.

a. One AS90 Regiment (40 Regt RA) has re-roled as a Light Gun Regiment in support of 19 Light Brigade.

b. The Gun Groups of three AS90 batteries will be cut.

c. An additional UAV battery, a rocket battery and a STA battery are being established. Providing direct support for the activities of the Field Army will be a new surveillance and target acquisition (STA) battery equipped with the MAMBA (Ericsson ARTHUR) weapon locating radar to be formed by redeploying personnel from a ground air defence regiment (22 Regiment RA – now disbanded). Other personnel from 22 Regiment are to be used to form an additional unmanned aerial vehicle (UAV) battery, while the remaining third will be re-allocated to allow the formation of a multiple rocket launcher battery.

d. There will be an overall reduction in Ground Based Air Defence but the UK Rapier capability will be owned and operated by the RA.

e. Tactical Groups for Formation Reconnaissance Regiments and the 4th Light Role Battalion in 16 Air Assault Brigade will be established, and there will be enhancements to the current Aviation Tactical Group to provide better support for the Attack Helicopter Regiments.

f. The FAS documentation also noted the investment being made in HUMINT (Human Intelligence) for fire-support purposes. For this role the Honourable Artillery Company (HAC – a reserve regiment) is devoted to surveillance and target (STA) acquisition patrolling. The HAC provides a number of battery level patrol groupings.

CURRENT ORGANISATION

In late 2007 the Regular Regiments of the Royal Artillery were as follows:

United Kingdom

1 Regiment RHA	155 mm AS 90
3 Regiment RHA	155 mm AS 90
4 Regiment RA	155 mm AS 90
5 Regiment RA	STA & Special Ops (1)
7 Parachute Regiment RHA	105 mm Lt Gun
12 Regiment RA	HVM
14 Regiment RA	All School Equipments
16 Regiment RA	Rapier
19 Regiment RA	155 mm AS 90
26 Regiment RA	155 mm AS 90
29 Commando Regiment RA	105 mm Light Gun (2)
32 Regiment RA	UAVs

39 Regiment RA	MLRS
40 Regiment RA	105 mm Light Gun
47 Regiment RA	HVM
The King's Troop RHA	13-Pounders (Ceremonial)

Notes:
(1) STA – Surveillance and target acquistion.
(2) The Regimental HQ of 29 Commando Regiment with one battery is at Plymouth. The other two batteries are at Arbroath and Poole. Those at Poole provide the amphibious warfare Naval Gunfire Support Officers (NGSFO).
(3) All Regiments equipped mainly with 155 mm AS 90 now have the ability to deploy on operations using the 105 mm Light Gun.

TA Artillery Regiments

Under the TA Restructuring plans announced in March 2006 the 7x Royal Artillery TA Regiments will be restructured as follows:

1 x Observation Post Regiment
1 x STA/MLRS Regiment
1 x Unmanned Air Vehicle/General Support Regiment
1 x Ground Based Air Defence Regiment (HVM)
3 x Close Support Regiments (105 mm Light Gun)

This grouping will evolve from the TA Artillery grouping prior to restructuring which was:

HAC	London	STA and Special Ops
100 Regt RA (V)	Luton	Light Gun
101 Regt RA (V)	Newcastle	STA/ MLRS
103 Regt RA (V)	Liverpool	Light Gun
104 Regt RA (V)	Newport	HVM
105 Regt RA (V)	Edinburgh	HVM
106 Regt RA (V)	London	HVM

1 Artillery Brigade

1 Artillery Brigade commands the MLRS related Surveillance and Target Acquisition (STA) and artillery support and logistics units. The Brigade commander is a Colonel. 1 Artillery Brigade has the following major units under command:

5 Regiment	Catterick	(STA).
32 Regiment	Larkhill	(Phoenix UAV).
39 Regiment	Newcastle	(MLRS).
Honourable Artillery Company,	London	(Special Ops TA).
101 Regiment (V)	Newcastle	(MLRS).

Training

Artillery recruits spend the first period of recruit training (Phase 1 Training, Common Military Syllabus) at the Army Training Regiment – Pirbright, the Army Training Regiment – Bassingbourn or the Army Foundation College – Harrogate.

Artillery training (Phase 2) is carried out at the Royal School of Artillery (RSA) at Larkhill in Wiltshire. During Phase 2 intensive training is given in gunnery, air defence, surveillance or signals. Soldiers also undergo driver training on a variety of different vehicles. After Phase 2 training officers and gunners will be posted to RA units worldwide, but almost all of them will return to the RSA for frequent career and (Phase 3) employment courses.

ARTILLERY FIRE SUPPORT

The Royal Artillery provides the modern British formation with a protective covering on the battlefield. The close air defence assets cover the immediate airspace above and around the formation, with the artillery assets reaching out to over 50 kms in front, and 60 kms across the flanks of the formation being supported. An armoured formation that moves out of this protective covering is open to immediate destruction by an intelligent enemy.

An armoured or mechanised division has it own artillery under command. This artillery usually consists of three Close Support Regiments, with a number of units detached from the Corps Artillery and could include TA reinforcements from the UK. In war the composition of the DAG will vary from division to division according to the task. The following is a reasonable example of the possible organisation for a DAG.

Armoured Divisional Artillery Group (DAG) – Organisation for War

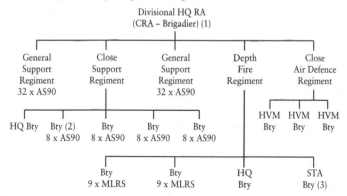

Notes:

(1) This is a diagram of the artillery support which may typically be available to an Armd Div deployed with the ARRC. Expect each brigade in the division to have one Close Support

Regiment with AS 90. Artillery regiments are commanded by a Lieutenant Colonel and a battery is commanded by a Major.

(2) The number of batteries and guns per battery in an AS 90 Close Support Regiment has changed post SDR 1999 at four batteries of six guns per battery in the UK Regiments, and three batteries of six in the Regiments stationed in Germany Regiments. In war all batteries will have eight guns each. AS 90 Regiments now train with 105 mm Light Guns prior to deployment on operations in Iraq or Afghanistan.

(3) The locating Battery in the Depth Fire Regiment may have a metrological troop with BMETS, a radar troop with Cobra and a UAV troop with Phoenix.

(4) Area Air Defence (AAD) is provided by Rapier.

(5) The staff of an armoured or mechanised division includes a Brigadier of Artillery known as the Commander Royal Artillery (CRA). The CRA acts as the Offensive Support Advisor to the Divisional Commander, and could normally assign one of his Close Support Regiments to support each of the Brigades in the division. These regiments would be situated in positions that would allow all of their batteries to fire across the complete divisional front. Therefore, in the very best case, a battlegroup under extreme threat could be supported by the fire of more than 128 guns.

The term Offensive Support Group is the term used when units other than artillery provide fire support:

Offensive Support Group (OSG)

An example of an OSG was illustrated in a late 2006 exercise involving the OSG of 1 Armoured Division. Taking part in the exercise which was commanded by Brigadier Bill Kingdon, Commander Royal Artillery 1 (UK) Armoured Division were C Battery, D Battery and J Battery from 3 RHA and 17 Battery from 26 Regiment RA firing 155 mm AS 90. In Addition 97 and 88 Battery from 4 Regiment RA were firing 106 mm Light Guns, prior to deployment on operations and 12 Regiment Royal Artillery deployed high velocity missiles (HVM) to carry out force-on-force training with the UK and German Air Forces.

The 81 mm mortars of 1 Scots Guards Mortars supported the fire planning with live 81 mm mortar fire. 1 Regiment Army Air Corps provided aviation support, 100 Squadron RAF flew Hawk aircraft in support, 12 Logistic Support Regiment provided logistic support, 2 Battalion Royal Electrical & Mechanical Engineers (REME) equipment support and 1 CSMR medical support.

Also taking part were the Danish artillery 'tac' groups who were required to fire UK artillery tasks in preparation for their future operational deployment with UK Forces.

Artillery Fire Missions

A square brigade (of two infantry battalions and two armoured regiments) will probably have a Close Support Regiment of four batteries in support, and the CO of this regiment will act as the Offensive Support Advisor to the Brigade Commander.

It would be usual to expect that each of the four Battlegroups in the brigade would have a Battery Commander acting as the Offensive Support Advisor to the Battlegroup Commander. Squadron/Company Groups in the Battlegroup would each be provided with a Forward

Observation Officer (FOO), who is responsible for fire planning and directing the fire of the guns onto the target. The FOO and his party travel in equivalent vehicles to the supported troops to enable them to keep up with the formation being supported and are usually in contact with:

(a) The Gun Positions
(b) The Battery Commander at BGHQ
(c) The Regimental Fire Direction Centre
(d) The Company Group being supported.

Having identified and applied prioritisation of targets, the FOO will call for fire from the guns, and he will then adjust the fall of shot to cover the target area. The FOO will be assisted in this task by the use of a Warrior FCLV OP vehicle containing the computerised fire control equipment which provides accurate data of the target location.

Given a vehicle with its surveillance and target acquisition suite the FOO can almost instantly obtain the correct grid of the target and without calling for corrections, order 'one round fire for effect'.

FIELD ARTILLERY

AS 90
(146 available): Crew 5; Length 9.07 m; Width 3.3 m; Height 3.0 m overall; Ground Clearance 0.41 m; Turret Ring Diameter 2.7 m; Armour 17 mm; Calibre 155 mm; Range (39 cal) 24.7 kms (52 cal) 30 kms; Recoil Length 780 mm; Rate of Fire 3 rounds in 10 secs (burst) 6 rounds per minute (intense) 2 rounds per minute (sustained); Secondary Armament 7.62 mm MG; Traverse 6,400 mills; Elevation -89/+1.244 mills; Ammunition Carried 48 x 155 mm projectiles and charges (31 turret & 17 hull); Engine Cumminis VTA903T turbo-charged V8 diesel 660 hp; Max Speed 53 kph; Gradient 60%; Vertical Obstacle 0.75 m; Trench Crossing 2.8 m; Fording Depth 1.5 m; Road Range 420 kms.

AS 90 was manufactured by Vickers Shipbuilding and Engineering (VSEL) at Barrow in Furness. 179 Guns were delivered under a fixed price contract for £300 million. These 179 guns completely equipped six field regiments replacing the older 120 mm Abbot and 155 mm M109 in British service. At the beginning of 2005 three of these Regiments were under the command of 1(UK) Armoured Division in Germany and three under the command of 3 (UK) Div in the United Kingdom.

AS 90 equipped with a 39 calibre gun fires the NATO L15 unassisted projectile out to a range of 24.7 kms (Base Bleed ERA range is 30 kms). Funding is available for the re-barreling of 96 x AS 90 with a 52 calibre gun with ranges of 30 kms (unassisted) and 60 to 80 kms with improved accuracy and long range ERA ammunition. However, due to the current inability of the selected bi-modular charge system to meet the requirement for insensitive munitions this programme is on hold.

AS 90 has been fitted with an autonomous navigation and gunlaying system (AGLS), enabling it to work independently of external sighting references. Central to the system is an inertial dynamic reference unit (DRU) taken from the US Army's MAPS (Modular Azimuth Positioning System). The bulk of the turret electronics are housed in the Turret Control Computer (TCC) which controls the main turret functions, including gunlaying, magazine control, loading systems control, power distribution and testing.

Artillery has always been a cost effective way of destroying or neutralising targets. When the cost of a battery of guns, (approx £20 million) is compared with the cost of a close air support aircraft, (£40 million) and the cost of training each pilot, (£4 million +) the way ahead for governments with less and less to spend on defence is clear.

227 mm MLRS
(63 launchers available – 54 operational) Crew 3; Weight loaded 24,756 kg; Weight Unloaded 19,573 kg; Length 7.167 m; Width 2.97 m; Height (stowed) 2.57 m; Height (max elevation) 5.92 m; Ground Clearance 0.43 m; Max Road Speed 64 kph; Road Range 480 km; Fuel Capacity 617 litres; Fording 1.02 m; Vertical Obstacle 0.76 m; Engine Cummings VTA-903 turbo-charged 8 cylinder diesel developing 500 bhp at 2,300 rpm; Rocket Diameter 227 mm; Rocket Length 3.93 m; M77 Bomblet Rocket Weight 302.5 kg; AT2 SCATMIN Rocket Weight 254.46 kg; M77 Bomblet Range 11.5 –32 kms; AT2 SCATMIN Rocket Range 39 kms; One round 'Fire for Effect' equals one launcher firing 12 rockets; Ammunition Carried 12 rounds (ready to fire).

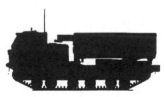

The MLRS is based on the US M2 Bradley chassis and the system is self loaded with 2 x rocket pod containers, each containing 6 x rockets. The whole loading sequence is power assisted and loading takes between 20 and 40 minutes. There is no manual procedure.

A single round 'Fire for Effect' (12 rockets) delivers 644 bomblets or 336 scatterable mines and the coverage achieved is considered sufficient to neutralise a 500 m x 500 m target or produce a minefield of a similar size. Currently the weapon system accuracy is range dependent and therefore more rounds will be required to guarantee the effect as the range to the target increases. Future smart warhead sub munitions currently under development will enable pinpoint accuracy to considerably extended ranges. Ammunition for the MLRS is carried on the DROPS vehicle which is a Medium Mobility Load Carrier. Each DROPS vehicle with a trailer can carry 8 x Rocket Pod Containers and there are 15 x DROPS vehicles supporting the 9 x M270 Launcher vehicles within each MLRS battery.

The handling of MLRS is almost a military 'art form' and is an excellent example of the dependence of modern artillery on high technology. Getting the best out of the system is more than just parking the tubes and firing in the direction of the enemy. MLRS is the final link in a chain that includes almost everything available on the modern battlefield, from high speed communications, collation of intelligence, logistics and a multitude of high technology artillery skills and drills. Unmanned aerial vehicles (UAVs) can be used to acquire targets, real time TV and data links are used to move information from target areas to formation commanders and onward to the firing positions. Helicopters can be used to dump ammunition and in some cases to move firing platforms. The refining of this capability is an interesting and dynamic future development area in which available technologies are currently being harnessed and applied.

MLRS is deployed as independent launcher units, using 'shoot-and-scoot' techniques. A battery of nine launchers will be given a battery manoeuvre area (BMA), within which are allocated three Troop Manoeuvre Areas (TMA). These TMAs will contain close hides, survey points and reload points. In a typical engagement, a single launcher will be given its fire mission orders using burst data transmission.

An important initial piece of information received is the 'drive on angle'; the crew will drive the launcher out of the hide (usually less than 100 m) and align it with this angle. Using the navigation equipment, its location is fed into the ballistic computer which already has the full fire mission details. The launcher is then elevated and fired and the process can take as little as a few minutes to complete.

As soon as possible after firing, the vehicle will leave the firing location and go to a reload point where it will unload the empty rocket pods and pick up full ones; this can be done in less than five minutes. It will then go to a new hide within the TMA via a survey point to check the accuracy of the navigation system (upon which the accuracy of fire is entirely dependent). The whole of this cycle is coordinated centrally, and details of the new hide and reload point are received as part of the fire mission orders. The complete cycle from firing to being in a new hide ready for action might take half an hour.

In a typical day, a battery could move once or twice to a new BMA but this could impose a strain upon the re-supply system unless well planned (bearing in mind the need for the ammunition to be in position before the launcher vehicle arrives in a new BMA). The frequent moves are a result of security problems inherent in MLRS's use. In addition to attack by radar-controlled counterbattery fire, its effectiveness as an interdiction weapon makes it a valuable target for enemy special forces units. Although MLRS will be hidden amongst friendly forces up to 15 km behind the FEBA, its firing signature and small crew (three) will force it to move continually to avoid an actual confrontation with enemy troops.

There is currently (early 2007) one Regular and one TA MLRS Regiment. The Regular Regiment operates 18 launcher vehicles and the TA Regiment 12 in peace and 18 in war. The US Army is currently operating 857 MLRS, the French have 58, the West Germans 154 and the Italians 21.

LIMAWS (R)

LIMAWS (R) or the LIMAWS rocket system is capable of supporting rapid intervention and manoeuvre support forces. It fires the latest (GMLRS) guided munitions in order to defeat both area and precision targets at long-range.

The system, that can be transported by the C-130 Hercules, Chinook helicopter, assault landing craft and the future A400M transport aircraft will give the UK light forces a major advantage on the battlefield. The LIMAWS platform is based on a six-wheeled, four-wheel drive Supacat vehicle and a self-loading launcher mechanism manufactured by Lockheed Martin.

GMLRS rockets contain Global Positioning System (GPS) elements and the latest advanced computer technology giving them accuracy out to a range of over 60 kms. Armed with a 200 lb (90 kg) high explosive warhead which carries a payload of 404 Dual Purpose Improved Conventional Munition (DPICM) submunitions, the improved missile can engage more targets with a lower risk of collateral damage and with a smaller logistical burden.

The overall programme is worth over £250 million and will see the UK take delivery of several thousand rockets by the end of the decade. The GMLRS rocket has been developed by a five-nation collaboration of the UK, France, Germany, Italy and the US.

Following a series of successful trials the Guided Multiple Rocket Launch System (GMLRS) was declared fit for deployment with UK troops in Afghanistan in 2007.

LIMAWS (G)

The Light Mobile Artillery Weapon System (LIMAWS(G)) 155 mm Ultralight Field Howitzer (UFH) is a new equipment to provide an increased capability for the Royal Artillery, supplementing the AS90 and the Light Gun. The provisional in-service date is 2009.

The probable UK system is a development of the US M777 which is entering service with the US Army and US Marine Corps. BAE Systems has developed a mobile version of the gun (M777 Portee) which is mounted on a customised 8 x 6 Supacat platform.

The M777A1 is usually operated by a crew of eight. If necessary the gun can be operated with a detachment of five.

It is expected that the weapon selected to meet the LIMAWS(G) requirement will enter service later this decade (possibly 2009) and up to 32 systems will be required. The total acquisition **costs** for the LIMAWS systems is £750 million.

105 mm Light Gun

(Approximately 136 available) Crew 6; Weight 1,858 kg; Length 8.8 m; Width 1.78 m; Height 21.3 m; Ammunition HE, HEAT, WP, Smoke, Illuminating, Target Marking; Maximum Range (HE) 17.2 kms; Anti Tank Range 800 m; Muzzle Velocity 709m/s; Shell Weight HE 15.1 kg; Rate of Fire 6 rounds per minute.

The 105 mm Light Gun has been in service with the Royal Artillery for 25 years, and has just received its first and only major upgrade in that time. The enhancement is an Auto Pointing System (APS) which performs the same function as the DRU on the AS 90. The APS is based on an inertial navigation system which enables it to be unhooked and into action in 30 seconds. The APS replaces the traditional dial sight and takes into account trunion tilt without the requirement to level any spirit level bubbles as before.

A touch screen display tells the gun controller when his gun is laid onto the correct target data provided. This enhancement improves the accuracy of the fall of shot to a greater degree of accuracy than possible with the dial sight.

The Light Gun is in service with three Artillery Regiments as a go-anywhere, airportable weapon which can be carried around the battlefield underslung on a Puma or Chinook. In addition artillery units deployed to both Iraq and Afghanistan can be equipped with the Light Gun.

The gun was first delivered to the British Army in 1975 when it replaced the 105 mm Pack Howitzer. A robust, reliable system, the Light Gun proved its worth in the Falklands, where guns were sometimes firing up to 400 rounds per day. Since then the gun has seen operational service in Kuwait, Bosnia, Afghanistan and Iraq.

During March 2005 the UK MoD placed a contract for an advanced and more effective light artillery shell. This contract for 105 mm Improved Ammunition awarded to BAE Systems led to an initial buy of 50,000 High Explosive shells, and was worth around £17 million.

The new High Explosive munitions will be more effective against a range of targets than current shells and will incorporate the latest Insensitive Munitions (IM) technology, making them even safer to transport and handle. Under the programme, planned deliveries commenced late in 2006 and will be spread over three years, with possible future buys until 2017.

The Light Gun has been extremely successful in the international market with sales to Australia (59), Botswana (6), Brunei (6), Ireland (12), Kenya (40), Malawi (12), Malaysia (20),

Morocco (36), New Zealand (34), Oman (39), Switzerland (6), UAE (50), United States (548) and Zimbabwe (12).

AIR DEFENCE

Starstreak HVM

84 Fire Units on Stormer and 145 on Light Mobile Launcher; Missile Length 1.39 m; Missile Diameter 0.27m; Missile Speed Mach 3+; Maximum Range 5.5 kms.

Short Missile Systems of Belfast were the prime contractors for the HVM (High Velocity Missile) which continues along the development path of both Blowpipe and Javelin. The system can be shoulder launched by mounting on the LML (lightweight multiple launcher) or vehicle borne on the Alvis Stormer APC. The Stormer APC has an eight round launcher and 12 reload missiles can be carried inside the vehicle.

HVM has been optimised to counter threats from fast pop-up type strikes by attack helicopters and low flying aircraft. The missile employs a system of three dart type projectiles which can make multiple hits on the target. Each of these darts has an explosive warhead. It is believed that the HVM has an SSK (single shot to kill) probability of over 95%.

Under a £72 million contract the HVM Thermal Sighting System (TSS) has been procured to enable the HVM to have the capability to operate at night, through cloud or in poor visibility. Some 84 x TSS are believed to be entering service with first units having been equipped at late 2006.

12 Regiment RA and 47 Regiment RA stationed at Thorney Island in West Sussex are equipped with HVM and there is 1 x TA Artillery Regiment similarly equipped. There are three TA HVM regiments. On Mobilisation, 12 and 47 Regiment is believed to be configured as follows:

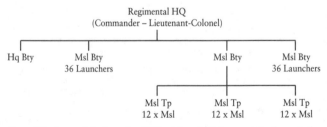

Note: On mobilisation, each Regiment has 108 launchers divided amongst the three missile batteries. An HVM detachment of four is carried in a Stormer armoured vehicle and in each vehicle there are four personnel. Inside the vehicle there are twelve ready to use missiles with a further eight stored inside as reloads.

Rapier (FS'C')
(57 fire units available – possibly 24 in service) Guidance Semi Automatic to Line of Sight (SACLOS); Missile Diameter 13.3 cm; Missile Length 2.35 m; Rocket Solid Fuelled; Warhead High Explosive; Launch Weight 42 kg; Speed Mach 2+; Ceiling 3,000 m; Maximum Range 6,800 m; Fire Unit Height 2.13 m; Fire Unit Weight 1,227 kg; Radar Height (in action) 3.37 m; Radar Weight 1,186 kg; Optical Tracker Height 1.54 m; Optical Tracker Weight 119 kg; Generator Weight 243 kg; Generator Height 0.91 m.

The Rapier system provides area 24 hour through cloud, Low Level Air Defence (LLAD) over the battlefield. The two forms of Rapier in service are as follows:-

Rapier Field standard C (FSC) incorporates a range of technological improvements over its predecessor including an advanced three dimensional radar tracker acquisition system designed by Plessey. The towed system launcher mounts eight missiles (able to fire two simultaneously) which are manufactured in two warhead versions. One of these is a proximity explosive round and the other a kinetic energy round. The total cost of the Rapier (FSC) programme is £1,886 million.

The UK's future Rapier air defence capability will be 16 Regiment Royal Artillery and the capability of 16 Regiment is being enhanced by the creation of a fourth battery. The possible configuration of 16 Regiment on mobilisation will then be four batteries each of two troops with four fire units per troop. In July 2004 the MoD announced the disbandment of the RAF Regiment Rapier squadrons.

Rapier in all of its versions has now been sold to the armed forces of at least 14 nations. We believe that sales have amounted to over 25,000 missiles, 600 launchers and about 350 radars.

ARTILLERY LOCATING DEVICES

MSTAR
Weight 30 kg; Wavelength J – Band; Range in excess of 20 kms.

MSTAR is a Lightweight Pulse Doppler J – Band All Weather Radar that has replaced the ZB 298 in the detection of helicopters, vehicles and infantry. Powered by a standard army field battery this radar will also assist the artillery observer in detecting the fall of shot. The electroluminescent display that shows dead ground relief and target track history, also has the ability to superimpose a map grid at the 1:50000 scale to ease transfer to military maps. MSTAR can be vehicle borne or broken down into three easily transportable loads for manpacking purposes.

MSTAR is used by Forward Observation Officers. There are believed to be around 100 MAOV (Warrior Mechanised Artillery Observation Vehicles) equipped with MSTAR. MSTAR is believed to cost about £50,000 pounds per unit at mid 1999 prices and in total about 200 MSTAR equipments are in service throughout the British Army.

COBRA
Cobra (Counter Battery Radar)is a 3-D Phased Array Radar that has been developed for West Germany, France and the UK. Cobra came into service with 5 Regt RA in mid 1999. The

dominant cost element of the Cobra Radar is the antenna, which probably accounts for about 70% of the unit price. There are believed to be about 20,000 Gallium Arsenide integrated circuits in each antenna. This enables the equipment to produce the locations of multiple enemy artillery at extremely long ranges, and the radar is able to cope with saturation type bombardments. In addition there is a high degree of automated software, with high speed circuitry and secure data transmission to escape detection from enemy electronic countermeasures.

Cobra therefore appears to be an ideal equipment for operation in conjunction with MLRS. 5 Regt is believed to field three Cobra Troops, each Troop consisting of three radars.

MAMBA – Mobile Artillery Monitoring Battlefield Radar (Ericsson ARTHUR)
(possibly eight available)

This is an artillery hunting radar which was deployed operationally for the first time in April 2002. MAMBA automatically detects, locates and classifies artillery, rockets and mortars and carries out threat assessment based on weapon or impact position. All acquired data is automatically transmitted to a combat control centre. The equipment also incorporates its own basic command, control and communications system for direct control of counter-battery fire. The contract value is believed to be in the region of £30 million.

Mamba's detection range is 20 km (howitzer) and 30 km (rockets) with a circular error probable (CEP) of around 30 m at extreme range.

The system, which is mounted on a Alvis Hagglunds BV206 tracked vehicle is easily transportable by aircraft or helicopters. Reports from operational areas suggest that this system has been extremely successful.

Phoenix UAV

Phoenix is an all-weather day or night, real time surveillance system which consists of a variety of elements. The twin boom UAV (unmanned air vehicle) provides surveillance through its surveillance pod, the imagery from which is datalinked via a ground data terminal (GDT) to a ground control station (GCS). This controls the overall Phoenix mission and is used to distribute the UAV provided intelligence direct to artillery forces, to command level, or to a Phoenix troop command post (TCP). The principle method of communication from the GCS to artillery on the ground is via the battlefield artillery engagement system (BATES).

Powered by a 19kW (25hp) Target Technology 342 two stroke flat twin engine, the Phoenix air vehicle (with a centrally mounted fuel tank) is almost entirely manufactured from composites such as Kevlar, glass fibre, carbon reinforced plastics and Nomex honeycomb. The principal subcontractor was Flight Refuelling of Christchurch in Dorset.

The modular design UAV can be launched within one hour of reaching a launch site and a second UAV can be dispatched within eight minutes from the same launcher. The wing span is 5.5 m and the maximum launch weight 175 kgs. The manufacture, GEC states that "Flight endurance is in excess of four hours, radius of action 50 kms and the maximum altitude 2,700 m (9,000 feet)."

A flight section consists of a launch and recovery detachment and a ground control detachment. The launch and recovery detachment consists of three vehicles; the launch support vehicle, with several UAVs and mission pods in separate battlefield containers, plus operational replacement spares and fuel; the launch vehicle, which features a pallet-mounted lifting crane, the hydraulic catapult and launch ramp, a pre-launch detonator device, built-in test equipment, and the Land Rover recovery vehicle which is fitted with cradles for the air vehicle and mission pod. The ground control detachment consists of two vehicles, the ground control station and the Land Rover towed ground data terminal.

The British Army has one regiment (32 Regiment) equipped with Phoenix. Each of the three Phoenix batteries in 32 Regiment are believed to be equipped with 27 x UAV, with associated ground support equipment and a battery has enough resources to launch 72 flights. The total cost of the programme was £227 million and each Phoenix aircraft is believed to cost approximately £300,000. The overall initial purchase was 198 Phoenix.

Watchkeeper UAV

In July 2005 a £700 million contract was awarded to Thales to provide the Royal Artillery with an unmanned air vehicle (UAV) named Watchkeeper designed for all weather, Intelligence, Surveillance, Target Acquisition and Reconnaissance (ISTAR) use.

Watchkeeper will probably enter service in 2010. There will be a payload capacity of 150 kg, an endurance of around 17 hours and an all up weight of 450 kg. Watchkeeper will be based on the Elbit Hermes 450 UAV design.

The Watchkeeper UAV capability is part of the UK's plans for a Network Enabled Capability that will provide UK commanders with accurate, timely and high quality information, including imagery. Watchkeeper will be fully integrated into the wider command and control digitised network, passing data quickly to those who need it. Watchkeeper will be operated and deployed by 32 Regt Royal Artillery to meet the information requirements of HQ Land Manoeuvre Commanders.

Watchkeeper will almost certainly replace the Phoenix UAV system (the current UAV in service with the UK's Armed Forces) although it remains a possibility that elements of Phoenix may continue in service as part of the overall capability transition.

Desert Hawk

Desert Hawk is a small and portable UAV surveillance system which provides aerial video reconnaissance. It has a flight time of approximately one hour, and can fly almost anywhere within a 10 km radius of its ground control station. Desert Hawk weighs 3.2 kg, has a length of 0.86 m and a wingspan of 1.32 m. The system can be used for a variety of tasks, such as force protection for convoys and patrols, route clearance, base security, reconnaissance or target tracking. It has both day and night time (thermal imaging) capability.

The acquisition costs of the Desert Hawk UAVs procured for 32 Regiment Royal Artillery were around £1.8 million.

Desert Hawk has an extremely good record over the last two years supporting UK forces in Afghanistan.

Predator (RAF)

In late 2006 the MoD announced the establishment of an RAF UAV operations squadron as the home for its two General Atomics MQ-9 Predator B aircraft. The Predator contract value is in the region of £37 million and an initial operating capability will probably exist from late 2007. Predator carries a range of cameras, heat sensors and missiles that provide 'a bird's eye view' of the battlefield, day and night. It also has extraordinary endurance, being able to stay aloft for 20 hours or more. The system usually flies at about 100 mph and can fly at 25,000 feet.

Project Taranis

In December 2006 the MoD announced the award of a £124 million contract to BAE Systems for Project Taranis, a project to develop unmanned aerial vehicle (UAV) technology. BAE Systems will lead an industry team including Rolls-Royce, Qinetiq, and Smiths Aerospace.

Taranis will be one of the world's largest UAV demonstrators, about the size of a Hawk jet (about 11 m in length), and will integrate stealth technology around an intelligent, autonomous system. It will also test the potential to carry ground attack weapons.

Sound Ranging

Sound Ranging (SR) locates the positions of enemy artillery from the sound of their guns firing. Microphones are positioned on a line extending over a couple of kilometres to approximately 12 kilometres. As each microphone detects the sound of enemy guns firing, the information is relayed to a Command Post which computes the location of the enemy battery. Enemy locations are then passed to Artillery Intelligence and counter battery tasks fired as necessary. Sound Ranging can identify an enemy position to within 50 m at 10 kms. The only Sound Ranging assets remaining in the Royal Artillery are those with 5 Regt RA at Catterick.

The UK has one battery equipped with Mark 2 HALO ASP (advanced sound ranging system), an acoustic weapons locating equipment specifically for use in out of area or sensitive operations where flying UAVs might be sensitive. The ASP system was deployed in March 2003 and is expected to be in service until 2017.

BMETS

The Battlefield Meteorological System BMETS came into service in 1999 and replaces AMETS which entered service in 1972 and provided met messages in NATO format. However, with AMETS there was only one system for each division resulting in a high radius of data application and the system was vulnerable because it used an active radar.

With the extreme range of modern artillery and battlefield missiles, very precise calculations regarding wind and air density are needed to ensure that the target is accurately engaged. BMETS units can provide this information by releasing hydrogen filled balloons at regular intervals recording important information on weather conditions at various levels of the atmosphere.

To benefit from current technology BMETS uses commercially available equipment manufactured by VAISALA linked to the Battlefield Artillery Target Engagement System

(BATES). It is a two vehicle system with a detachment of five in peace, six in war. It is deployed with all regular field artillery and MLRS regiments.

BMETS can operate in all possible theatres of conflict worldwide where the Meteorological Datum Plain (MDP) varies from 90 m below to 4000 m above sea level, and can be used with a variety of radiosonde types to sound the atmosphere to a height of up to 20 km. Measurements are made by an ascending radiosonde. This is tracked by a passive radiotheodolite which provides wind data, air temperature, atmospheric pressure and relative humidity from the datum plan for each sounding level, until flight termination. In addition virtual temperature, ballistic temperature and ballistic density are calculated to a high degree of accuracy. Cloud base is estimated by observation. The data is then processed by receiver equipment in the troop vehicles to provide formatted messages to user fire units via the existing military battlefield computer network.

Air Defence Alerting Device (ADAD)
An infra-red thermal imaging surveillance system that is used by close air defence units to detect hostile aircraft and helicopter targets and directs weapon systems into the target area. The air defence missile operators can be alerted to up to four targets in a priority order. This passive system which is built by Thorn EMI has an all weather, day and night capability.

CHAPTER 7 – ARMY AVIATION

AVIATION SUPPORT

Battlefield helicopters have played a major role in UK military operations since the 1960s. The Army Air Corps battlefield helicopter fleet has accumulated a vast amount of operational experience in recent years, and is arguably a more capable force than that possessed by any other European nation.

The flexibility of battlefield helicopters was demonstrated in 2003 during Operation TELIC in Iraq. Here 3 Regiment, Army Air Corps, with two Pumas from the Support Helicopter Force attached, was deployed forward as a combined-arms battle group, initially within 16 Air Assault Brigade and later in conjunction with 7 Armoured Brigade. The battle group had responsibility for an area that extended over 6,000 square kilometres, and provided a versatile combat arm during the warfighting phase. In the immediate aftermath of hostilities, helicopters proved to be the most efficient means of covering the vast operational area allocated to British forces, and also in distributing humanitarian aid to isolated villages.

FORCE STRUCTURE

The Army obtains its aviation support from Army Air Corps (AAC), which is an organisation with eight separate regiments and a number of independent squadrons and flights.

AAC manpower is believed to number some 2,000 personnel of all ranks, including about 500 officers. Unlike the all-officer Navy and Air Force helicopter pilot establishments, almost two-thirds of AAC aircrew are non-commissioned officers. The AAC is supported by REME and RLC personnel numbering some 2,600 all ranks. Total AAC-related manpower is believed to be some 4,600 personnel of all ranks.

With certain exceptions, during peace, all battlefield helicopters come under the authority of the Joint Helicopter Command (JHC).

The introduction into AAC service of the WAH-64D Apache Longbow attack helicopter is transforming AAC doctrine, organisation, and order of battle. The British Army designation of the type is Apache AH Mk1. As of early 2007, the AAC continues a process of organisational transformation with the UK Army having taken the decision to concentrate the Apache AH Mk 1 into three Attack Regiments.

The AAC is to equip these three Aviation Attack Regiments with a total of 48 x Apache AH Mk 1 attack helicopters. Pilot training on Apache is well under way, and AAC and RAF Support Helicopter Squadrons are being forged into a new Air Manoeuvre Arm within 16 Air Assault Brigade which includes two Battalions of the Parachute Regiment. The three newly equipped Attack Regiments will be 9 Regt at Dishforth in Yorkshire, and 3 and 4 Regts at Wattisham in Suffolk – with a full operating capability expected by late 2007.

Each attack regiment will have 2 x attack squadrons equipped with 8 x Apache AH Mk1 attack helicopters and 1 x support squadron equipped with 8 x Lynx. The Gazelle Helicopter has already started to be phased out by several units as the Apache AH Mk 1 is being introduced. The capability gap left will be filled by introducing the Battlefield Light Utility Helicopter (BLUH) in this capacity. Several Gazelle Helicopters will, however, continue to be retained for specialist tasks as required. The Lynx Helicopter will also be phased out as the Apache AH Mk 1 will replace it in its attack helicopter role. Ultimately, however, the Lynx will be replaced by the new Battlefield Reconnaissance Helicopter (Future Lynx).

The current (2007) AAC Regimental and Squadron locations are shown below.

Army Air Corps force structure and helicopters during early 2007

Regiment	Squadron	Location	Helicopter/ aircraft	Fleet (estimate)
1 Regiment	652, 661	Germany	Lynx	16
2 (Trg) Regiment	668, 670, 671, 673, 676	Middle Wallop	Apache, Lynx, Gazelle	36 (variable)
3 Attack Regiment	653, 662 & 663	Wattisham	Apache, Lynx	24
4 Attack Regiment	654, 659 & 669	Wattisham	Apache, Lynx	24
5 Regiment	665	Aldergrove	Gazelle	8
6 Regiment (V)	667	Bury St Edmunds	Support (1 more sqn forming)	n/a
7 Regiment (V)	658, 666	Netheravon	Gazelle	12
9 Attack Regiment	656, 664, 672	Dishforth	Apache, Lynx	24
Independent units				
Joint Special Forces Aviation Wing	657	Odiham	Lynx	12
Development & Trials	667	Middle Wallop	All types	Variable
Initial Training	660	Shawbury	Squirrel HT 1	12

Flights include 3 (TA) Flight (Leuchars), 6 (TA) Flight (Shawbury), 7 Flight (Brunei), 8 Flight (Hereford, 12 Flight (Germany), 25 Flight (Belize), 29 BATUS Flight – Canada

Note: AAC Attack Helicopter units will co-locate at Wattisham Airfield in Suffolk during late 2007/early 2008. The new hub will be formed by exchanging two Lynx squadrons from Wattisham (659 Squadron Army Air Corps and 669 Squadron Army Air Corps) with two Apache squadrons from Dishforth in Yorkshire (656 Squadron Army Air Corps and 664 Squadron Army Air Corps).

The AAC Centre at Middle Wallop in Hampshire acts as a focal point for all Army Aviation, and it is here that the majority of corps training is carried out. Although the AAC operates some fixed-wing aircraft for training and liaison flying, the main effort goes into providing helicopter support for the land forces. About 300 AAC helicopters are believed to be in operational service in early 2007.

Employment of aviation

Following significant development during World War II, Army Aviation formally joined the Army order of battle in the early 1950s. Since then its place on the battlefield has developed rapidly as an integral element of the Army's manoeuvre forces. The introduction of attack helicopters clearly identifies the shift of emphasis from combat support towards the combat role, particularly within air manoeuvre operations, and establishes the AAC as the sixth combat arm of the British Army. However, despite this changing emphasis, the Army also has a continuing essential requirement for army aviation to provide both combat support and combat service support roles.

THE AVIATION MISSION

Combat Aviation: To find, fix and strike, either independently, or as the lead element, or as a constituent of combined arms groupings, throughout the depth of the battlefield and the 24 hour battle, and throughout the full spectrum of operations.

Combat Support Aviation: To provide enabling capabilities for combined arms operations, throughout the depth of the battlefield and the 24 hour battle, and throughout the full spectrum of operations.

Roles of Army Aviation

In a Combat Role: To conduct air manoeuvre using direct fire and manoeuvre, as part of the land battle component.

In a Combat Support Role: To provide ISTAR (intelligence, surveillance, target acquisition and reconnaissance) as a collection asset in its own right or potentially as a platform for other sensors, including ECM (electronic countermeasures): NBC (nuclear, chemical and biological) reconnaissance: ESM (electronic support measures): radar and other electronic systems.

Other tasks may include:

To provide direction of fire support (ground/air/maritime/special forces).

To provide mobility for combat forces.

To assist in command and control, including acting as airborne command posts.

To provide a limited extraction capability.

In a Combat Service Support Role: To provide movement for personnel and materiel including casualty evacuation (CASEVAC).

Army Aviation doctrine

Army aviation operations rely for their effect on integration into combined arms groupings (e.g. brigades and battle groups) of which army aviation forms an element, the most pivotal of which is its place within air manoeuvre forces.

In the context of Land Operations, Air Manoeuvre seeks decisive advantage through the exploitation of the third dimension by combined-arms forces centred on rotary-wing aircraft, but within an overall joint operations framework.

Until 2004, the Army Lynx was the main AAC battlefield helicopter, and the only one with a combat role. Consequently, the AAC has had no previous experience of what some might describe as true Attack Helicopter operations. With the introduction of the Apache AH Mk 1 into service, doctrine has evolved to accommodate this new capability. The experience of other Apache operators (particularly the US Army) has proved to be invaluable.

JOINT HELICOPTER COMMAND (JHC)

The majority of AAC helicopters are assigned to the Joint Helicopter Command which reports to HQ Land Command. The primary role of the JHC is to deliver and sustain effective Battlefield Helicopter and Air Assault assets, operationally capable under all environmental conditions, in order to support the UK's defence missions and tasks. Major formations under JHC command are as follows:

- All Army Aviation Units
- RAF Support Helicopter Force
- Commando Helicopter Force
- Joint Helicopter Force (Northern Ireland)
- 16 Air Assault Brigade
- Combat Support Units
- Combat Service Support Units
- Joint Helicopter Command and Standards Wing

Our estimate for the JHC service personnel total is approximately 13,500 (includes RAF and Royal Navy personnel).

Our figures suggest that during early 2007 the JHC had about 268 aircraft (forward fleet) available.

Army
76 x Lynx AH7/AH/9
52 x Gazelle
38 x Apache Mk1
6 x Bell 212
3 x A109

Royal Air Force
25 x Chinook HC2/2a
24 x Puma HC1
15 x Merlin HC3

Royal Navy
25 x Sea King HC4
4 x Sea King HC6

In a normal non-operational environment (with the exception of Lynx), each individual aircraft is resourced to fly approximately 400 hours per year. The Lynx fleet is resourced for 23,900 hours, which averages 206 hours per aircraft.

AAC ORGANISATION
We would expect an AAC Regiment to be organised on the lines shown in the diagrams below.

Army Air Corps – Attack Regiment

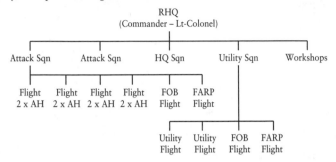

```
                        RHQ
             (Commander – Lt-Colonel)

Attack Sqn    Attack Sqn    HQ Sqn    Utility Sqn    Workshops

Flight  Flight  Flight  Flight  FOB    FARP
2 x AH  2 x AH  2 x AH  2 x AH  Flight Flight

                              Utility  Utility  FOB    FARP
                              Flight   Flight   Flight Flight
```

Totals: 8 x LUH (Light Utility Helicopters)
         16 x AH (Attack Helicopters)

Notes: FOB – Forward Operating Base: FARP- Forward Arming and Refuelling Point.

Army Air Corps – Divisional Aviation Regiment

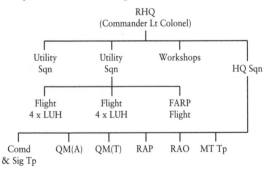

```
                        RHQ
             (Commander Lt Colonel)

Utility        Utility        Workshops
Sqn            Sqn                          HQ Sqn

Flight         Flight         FARP
4 x LUH        4 x LUH        Flight

Comd        QM(A)   QM(T)   RAP   RAO   MT Tp
& Sig Tp
```

Total: 16 x LUH (Light Utility Helicopters)

Future Helicopter Fleet Requirements

A recent MoD report identified the future helicopter fleet requirements for Army mission tasks under three contingency levels, as shown in the table.

Future helicopter force structure – Army component

	Small-scale contingency	*Medium-scale contingency*	*Large-scale contingency*
Attack helicopters	34	36	48
Support helicopters	44	65	110
Total	78	101	158

ARMY AVIATION TRAINING

The School of Army Aviation at Middle Wallop in Hampshire trains Army pilots using the Army's front line aircraft, the Islander, the Gazelle, the Lynx and the Apache AH Mk 1. It also trains soldiers to support these aircraft on the ground, to protect their operating bases, to provide communications between the ground and aircraft, and to arm and refuel them. The training activity conducted by SAAvn is divided into ground training and flying training. Ground training is conducted by 2 Regiment AAC and consists of:

Phase 2 training to provide special to arm training for recruits on completion of their basic training at Winchester Army Training Regiment, and,

Phase 3 training to provide career progress courses for trained soldiers.

Flying training is conducted by Flying Wing and consists of:

Army Flying Grading

Operational Training Phase of the Army Pilots Course

Conversion to the Army Air Corps operational aircraft

The AAC Centre at Middle Wallop is under the ownership of the Army Training and Recruitment Agency (ATRA). There is also a detachment of 132 Aviation Support Squadron, Royal Logistics Corps, which comes under the Joint Helicopter Command, based at the AAC Centre. The Headquarters of the Director of Army Aviation is also based at Middle Wallop. There are 12 Attack Helicopters allocated to the School of Army Aviation for training purposes.

HQ DAAvn (Director Army Aviation) is responsible for providing advice and support on Army Aviation and AAC training matters. In this regard HQ DAAvn is responsible for the training policy for both aircrew and ground crew. The School of Army Aviation (SAAvn) undertakes AAC Special-to-Arm training. AAC Soldier Basic Training takes place at ATR Winchester.

The AAC recruits pilots from three main sources:

Direct Entry (Officers only)

The ranks of the AAC (Corporals and above)

Officers and soldiers from other arms and branches of the Service (Corporal and above)

Officers join the Corps after completing the Commissioning course at the Royal Military Academy Sandhurst. Unlike the all-officer Navy and Air Force helicopter pilot establishments, almost two-thirds of AAC aircrew are non-commissioned officers. Within the Army, NCOs, of at least LCpl rank with a recommendation for promotion, from within the AAC and from the remainder of the Army may also apply for pilot training. NCO pilots spend the majority of their service flying and many go on to be commissioned as Officers, normally to fill specialist flying appointments such as flying instructors.

There are three phases to selection for Army pilot training:

Aircrew Selection tests are conducted at RAF College Cranwell. These tests are common to the three Services and last two days. Army candidates require a minimum aircrew aptitude score of 80/180 to progress onto the next phase. RAF/RN require higher scores, but the Army is able to accept a lower score at this point, as Army candidates also have to pass Army Flying Grading which the AAC considers a far more accurate indicator of potential to be an Army pilot.

Army Flying Grading (AFG) is conducted at Middle Wallop. This consists of 13 hours, over a three week period, in a Slingsby Firefly 160. The aim of this course is to test aptitude in a live flying environment and to identify whether students have the capability to become an Army pilot.

Students who have successfully demonstrated the necessary flying potential at AFG will progress onto the final phase at the Pilot Selection Centre. This is run by HQ SAAvn and selection includes aptitude tests, a medical, and finally a selection interview.

Flying training
There are several stages in AAC flying training.

Groundschool
The Army Flying Course starts with four weeks of groundschool instruction at RAF College Cranwell. Students learn the basic building blocks of aviation – such as Meteorology, Principles of Flight, Aircraft Operations, Navigation and Technical instruction.

Elementary Flying Training (EFT)
EFT is the first element of Army Flying Training at RAF Barkston Heath. This phase consists of 40 flying hours of elementary fixed- wing flying training over 14 weeks on the Slingsby Firefly (260).

Aeromedical and Survival Training
After EFT, students complete a week of aeromedical and survival training at RNAS Yeovilton, Lee-on-Solent and Plymouth.

Defence Helicopter Flying School
The Defence Helicopter Flying School (DHFS) at RAF Shawbury provides basic single-engine helicopter training for the three Services and some overseas countries. The DHFS also provides advanced twin-engine helicopter training for RAF aircrew and other special courses for the three Services.

At the DHFS, much of the training effort is contracted out to FBS Ltd – a consortium of Flight Refuelling Aviation, Bristow Helicopters Ltd and Serco Defence. All DHFS military and civilian instructors are trained by the Central Flying School (Helicopter) Squadron. The single-engine basic flying course incorporates some 36 flying hours over nine weeks on the Squirrel helicopter with the instructors of No 660 Squadron. Army students complete nine weeks training before they leave to start their Operational Training Phase at Middle Wallop.

Operational Training Phase (OTP)

The penultimate phase is conducted at the School of Army Aviation at Middle Wallop. Training is focused on converting helicopter pilots into Army pilots. It starts with a week of tactics training, preparing students for the military part of the course. The OTP phase involves 82 flying hours in 18 weeks, and is conducted on the Squirrel helicopter.

Conversion to Type (CTT)

The final phase is conducted at the School of Army Aviation at Middle Wallop. Before being posted to a regiment, students have to convert onto an operational helicopter type. The Conversion to Type (CTT) course takes around nine weeks. At Middle Wallop, Apache aircrew and ground crew training is conducted by Aviation Training International Limited (ATIL).

Conversion to Role (CTR)

Once a pilot has been converted onto type at Middle Wallop, he or she will proceed to a Regiment. At the Regiment a special CTR course will be held to bring the pilot up to combat ready status.

Helicopter crews

In mid 2006 the number of actual and required helicopter crew personnel for each regular regiment of the AAC was as follows:

Regiment	Helicopter Crew Established (Required)	Helicopter Crew Held (Actual)
1 Regt AAC	60	54
3 Regt AAC	85	57
4 Regt AAC	85	63
5 Regt AAC	93 (31 from 1 Apr 2007)	64
9 Regt AAC	85	69

These figures include qualified helicopter instructors and regimental headquarters personnel, whose primary role is not as helicopter crew. The figures do not include aviation crewmen, such as air door gunners and winch operators. The established figure for 5 Regiment AAC will reduce to 31 by 1 April 2007, as part of the planned reductions in Northern Ireland. The deficits shown in the table in 3, 4 and 9 AAC Regiments are mainly due to the re-roling of these regiments to Apache helicopters. As a consequence of re-roling, some aircrew are posted away for re-training.

AAC Aircraft

In 2007, the AAC aircraft fleet comprises four types: Apache AH Mk1, Lynx AH7/9, and Gazelle helicopters, and the fixed-wing BN-2 Islander/Defender aircraft. Contractor-owned Bell 212s are also used by the Army flight in Brunei as a utility and transport helicopter. Over the next ten years, the MoD plans to invest some £3bn in helicopter platforms to replace and enhance the existing capability. In light of the improved security situation in Northern Ireland, the MoD plans to make some reductions in overall helicopter numbers.

Apache (AH Mk1)

(67 ordered and delivered) Gross Mission Weight 7,746 kgs (17,077 lb); Cruise Speed at 500 m 272 kph; Maximum Range (Internal Fuel with 20 minute reserve) 462 kms; General Service Ceiling 3,505 metres (11,500 ft); Crew 2; Carries – 16 x Hellfire II missiles (range 6,000 metres approx); 76 x 2.75" CRV-7 rockets; 1,200 30mm cannon rounds; 4 x Air-to-Air Missiles; Engines 2 x Rolls Royce RTM-332.

The UK MoD ordered 67 Apache based on the US Army AH-64D manufactured by Boeing in 1995. Boeing built the first eight aircraft, and partially assembled the other 59. The UK Westland helicopter company undertook final assembly, flight testing and programme support at their Yeovil factory. Full operating capability for all three Apache Attack Regiments is expected by June 2007.

We believe that there will be 48 operational aircraft in three regiments (each of 16 aircraft). The remaining 19 aircraft will be used for trials, training and a war maintenance reserve (WMR).

The Apache can operate in all weathers, day or night, and can detect, classify and prioritise up to 256 potential targets at a time. Apart from the 'Longbow' mast-mounted fire control radar, the aircraft is equipped with a 127 x magnification TV system, 36 x magnification thermal imaging, and 18 x magnification direct view optics. The missile system incorporates Semi-Active Laser and Radio Frequency versions of the Hellfire missile, whose range is at least 6 kms. Apart from the Rolls-Royce engines, specific British Army requirements include a secure communications suite and a Helicopter Integrated Defensive Aids System (HIDAS). Programme cost is some £3 billion.

It is believed that an air-to-air weapon capability will continue to be investigated and trials of the Shorts Starstreak missile onboard an AH-64 have continued in the US. Any longer term decision to proceed will be based on the results of these US Army trials.

The night vision system of 67 Apache AH Mk1 attack helicopters is to be upgraded in the near future. The M-TADS/PNVS, which is designated Arrowhead, will replace the existing forward-looking infra-red (FLIR) and daylight television image intensifier with new sensors to provide improved target identification over longer ranges, better pilot performance and reduced life-cycle costs. Army Air Corps (AAC) aviators are said to have been keen to proceed with the upgrade, because the damp UK climate significantly degrades the effectiveness of the existing Target Acquisition and Designation Sight/Pilot Night Vision Sensor

The Apache AH Mk 1 presents a completely new capability for the AAC with significant implications for Air Manoeuvre doctrine in Land and Joint Operations. The Apache certainly gives the British Army the 'punch' necessary for operations during the next decade. First reports from operational areas suggest that the Apache AH Mk 1 has been a resounding success.

Lynx AH – Mark 7/9
(112 in service) Length Fuselage 12.06 m; Height 3.4 m; Rotor Diameter 12.8 m; Max Speed 330 kph; Cruising Speed 232 kph; Range 885 km; Engines 2 Rolls-Royce Gem 41; Power 2 x 850 bhp; Fuel Capacity 918 litres (internal); Weight (max take off) 4,763 kg; Crew one pilot, one air-gunner/observer; Armament 8 x TOW Anti-Tank Missiles; 2-4 7.62 mm machine guns; Passengers-able to carry 10 PAX; Combat radius approximately 100 kms with 2 hour loiter.

Until the introduction of Apache, Lynx was the helicopter used by the British Army to counter the threat posed by enemy armoured formations. Armed with 8 x TOW missiles the Lynx was the mainstay of the British armed helicopter fleet.

With the introduction into service of the Apache AH Mk 1 Lynx is now only used as a utility helicopter providing fire support using machine guns, troop lifts, casualty evacuation and many more vital support battlefield tasks.

Although the total Lynx inventory is 112 aircraft we believe that there are currently 99 available (77 Lynx Mark 7 and 22 Lynx Mark 9).

Gazelle
(Approx 107 available) Fuselage Length 9.53 m; Height 3.18 m; Rotor Diameter 10.5 m; Maximum Speed 265 kph; Cruising Speed 233 kph; Range 670 km; Engine Turbomeca/Rolls-Royce Astazou 111N; Power 592 shp; Fuel Capacity 445 litres; Weight 1,800 kg (max take off); Armament 2 x 7.62 mm machine guns (not a standard fitting).

Gazelle is the general purpose helicopter in use by the AAC, and it is capable of carrying out a variety of battlefield roles. Gazelle is a French design built under licence by Westland Aircraft. It is equipped with a Ferranti AF 532 stabilised, magnifying observation aid. The fleet is now some 30 years old and due to be withdrawn progressively by 2018 – being replaced by the Battlefield Reconnaissance Helicopter (BRH).

A-109

(4 in service) Fuselage Length 10.7 m; Rotor Diameter 11.0 m; Cruising Speed 272 kph; Range 550 kms; Service Ceiling 4570 m; Engines 2 x 420-shp Allison 250-C20B turboshafts; Fuel Capacity 560 litres; Weight 1,790 kg; Max Take Off Weight 2600 kg; Crew Pilot plus observer + 7 pax.

The AAC is believed to operate four of these light general purpose helicopters for liaison flying and special tasks. The aircraft are part of 8 Flight.

BN-2 Islander

(6 in Service) Crew 2; Length Overall 12.37 m; Max Take Off Weight 3,630 kg; Max Cruising Speed at 2,135 m (7,000 ft and 75% of power) 257 kph (154 mph); Ceiling 4,145 m (13,600 m); Range at 2,137 m (7,000 ft and 75% of power) 1,153 km (717 miles); Range with Optional Tanks 1,965 kms (1,221 miles).

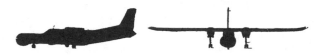

This type is the only fixed-wing aircraft that the AAC operates. The AAC BN-2 Islanders carry the Thorn EMI CASTOR (Corps Airborne Stand Off Radar) that is designed to provide intelligence information in the Forward Edge of the Battle Area (FEBA) and beyond while operating well within friendly territory. The radar, located in the nose cone of the aircraft has a 360 degree scan and offers wide coverage against moving and static targets.

The Islander has been routinely deployed with 1 Flight AAC in Northern Ireland, and also deployed with British Army SFOR contingents in the former Yugoslavia. More recently, the Army acquired three more of the type under an Urgent Operational Requirement (UOR) for service in Iraq. The first of these was delivered in October 2004. Defensive aids system dispensers are installed in pods under the aircraft wings to improve survivability when flying into high-threat airfields in Iraq, such as Baghdad International, Basra and Al Amara. The new aircraft have the designation BN2T-4S AL.1 Defender

Battlefield Reconnaissance Helicopter (BRH)
In time the Battlefield Reconnaissance Helicopter (formerly known as the Battlefield Light Utility Helicopter) will replace the capability currently provided by the Gazelle AH 1 and Lynx Mk 7 and Lynx Mk 9.

The UK MoD announced in 2006 that the UK's Armed Forces will receive 70 of the highly advanced BRH (sometimes known as Future Lynx) helicopters which will be used for everything from battlefield reconnaissance, casualty evacuation and troop transport, to detecting and destroying fast naval attack craft. The contract provides 40 aircraft for the AAC and 30 for the Royal Navy. The contract also provides an option for a further 10 aircraft, possibly five for the Army and five for the Navy.

The new aircraft are expected to enter service from 2014 and will incorporate a range of technological improvements including: configurable cockpit display, networked enabled capability, more powerful engines, better defensive aids and a new tail rotor system. Technology improvements mean that the aircraft will have greater reliability, resulting in significant reductions to support and maintenance costs over life of the aircraft which will stay in service for 30 years.

Aircraft will be built by Augusta Westland and the the contract is expected to cost in the region of £1 billion (about £14 million per aircraft).

RAF Support
The second agency that provides aviation support for the Army is the Royal Air Force. In general terms, the RAF provides helicopters that are capable of moving troops and equipment around the battlefield, and fixed-wing fighter ground attack (FGA) aircraft that provide close air support to the troops in the vicinity of the Forward Edge of the Battlefield Area (FEBA). The RAF also provides the heavy air transport aircraft that will move men and material from one theatre of operations to another. In general terms, the RAF support (other than helicopters) available is as follows:

RAF Support Helicopters

Squadron	Aircraft	Location
7 Squadron	5 x Chinook HC2	Odiham
18 Squadron	18 x Chinook HC2	Odiham
27 Squadron	10 x Chinook HC2	Odiham
28 Squadron	22 x Merlin	Benson
33 Squadron	15 x Puma HC1	Benson
78 Squadron	1 x Chinook HC2,	Mount Pleasant,
	2 x Sea King HAR 3	Falkland Islands
230 Squadron	12 x Puma HC1	Aldergrove

Puma

(27 in squadron service – probably 45 available) Crew 2 or 3; Fuselage Length 14.06 m; Width 3.50 m; Height 4.38 m; Weight (empty) 3,615 kg; Maximum Take Off Weight 7,400 kgs; Cruising Speed 258 km/ph (192 mph); Service Ceiling 4,800 m; Range 550 kms; 2 x Turbomeca Turmo 111C4 turbines.

Following the retirement of the last Wessex in 2003, the Puma is now the oldest helicopter in RAF service. The 'package deal' between the UK and France on helicopter collaboration dates back to February 1967. The programme covered the development of three helicopter types – the Puma, Gazelle and Lynx. Production of the aircraft was shared between the two countries, the UK making about 20% by value of the airframe, slightly less for the engine, as well as assembling the aircraft procured for the RAF. Deliveries of the RAF Pumas started in 1971. Capable of many operational roles, Puma can carry 16 fully equipped troops, or 20 at light scales. In the casualty evacuation role (CASEVAC), six stretchers and six sitting cases can be carried. Underslung loads of up to 3,200 kg can be transported over short distances and an infantry battalion can be moved using 34 Puma lifts. 41 x RAF Puma helicopters received an avionics upgrade between 1994 and1998.

RAF Pumas are due to be phased out of service in 2010.

Chinook

(34 available) Crew 3; Fuselage Length 15.54 m; Width 3.78 m; Height 5.68 m; Weight (empty) 10,814 kgs; Internal Payload 8,164 kgs; Rotor Diameter 18.29 m; Cruising Speed 270 km/ph (158 mph); Service Ceiling 4,270 m; Mission Radius (with internal and external load of 20,000 kgs including fuel and crew) 55 kms; Rear Loading Ramp Height 1.98 m; Rear Loading Ramp Width 2.31 m; Engines 2 x Avco Lycoming T55-L11E turboshafts.

The Chinook is a tandem-rotored, twin-engined medium-lift helicopter and the first aircraft entered service with the RAF in 1982. It has a crew of four (pilot, navigator and two crewmen) and is capable of carrying 54 fully equipped troops or a variety of heavy loads up to approximately 10 tons. The triple hook system allows greater flexibility in load carrying and enables some loads to be carried faster and with greater stability. In the ferry configuration with internally mounted fuel tanks, the Chinook's range is over 1,600 km (1,000 miles). In the medical evacuation role the aircraft can carry 24 stretchers.

RAF Chinook aircraft were upgraded to the HC2 standard between 1993 and 1996 for some £145million. The HC2 upgrade modified the RAF Chinooks to the US CH-47D standard. New equipment included infra-red jammers, missile approach warning indicators, chaff and flare dispensers, a long-range fuel system, and machine gun mountings. In 1995, the UK MoD purchased a further 14 x Chinooks (6 x HC2 and 8 x HC3) for £240 million.

During 2003 the Chinook Night Enhancement Package (NEP) was installed in the HC2 fleet. The NEP was based upon experience gained during operations in Afghanistan in 2001 and allows Chinook aircraft to operate at night and in very low-light conditions, often at the limit of their capabilities.

HC2 aircraft are due to be phased out during 2010 and HC2A aircraft in 2015.

The RAF awaits the delayed entry into service of eight Chinook Mk3 helicopters configured for special operations. Reports in late 2006 indicated that the Defence Aviation Repair Agency is likely to receive a contract to install the Thales 'Top Deck' avionics system on the Chinook HC3s. If and when the HC3s enter service they will join 7 Squadron at RAF Odiham. The programme is likely to cost between £50 to £60 million and the aircraft may be available during late 2008.

EH101 Merlin Mk 3
(22 available) Crew 2; Length 22.81 m; Rotor Diameter 18.59 m; Max Speed 309 k/ph (192mph); Engine 3 x Rolls Royce/Turbomeca RTM 322 three-shaft turbines of 2,312 shp each; Up to 35 fully equipped troops can be carried or 16 stretchers and a medical team.

The EH101 Merlin Mk 3 is the newest RAF helicopter, the RAF having ordered 22 EH101 (Merlin) support helicopters for £755m in March 1995. Merlin is a direct replacement for the Westland Wessex, and it operates alongside the Puma and Chinook in the medium-lift role. Its ability to carry troops, artillery pieces, light vehicles and bulk loads, means that the aircraft is ideal for use with the UK Army's 16 Air Assault Brigade. Deliveries took place between 2000-2002.

The aircraft can carry a load of 24-28 troops with support weapons. The maximum payload is 4,000 kg and Merlin has a maximum range of 1,000 km, which can be extended by external tanks or by air-to-air refuelling. The Merlin Mk 3 has sophisticated defensive aids, and the aircraft is designed to operate in extreme conditions with corrosion-proofing for maritime operations. All weather, day/night precision delivery is possible because of GPS navigation, a forward-looking infra-red sensor and night vision goggle compatibility. In the longer term, the aircraft could be fitted with a nose turret fitted mounting a .50 calibre machine gun.

RAF Merlin Mk 3 are due to be phased out of service in 2030.

Royal Navy Support Helicopters

Squadron	Aircraft	Location
845 Squadron	10 x Sea King HC4	Yeovilton
846 Squadron	10 x Sea King HC4	Yeovilton
848 Squadron	19 x Sea King HC4	Yeovilton
847 Squadron	6 x Lynx AH7	Yeovilton

RAF TRANSPORT AIRCRAFT

Hercules C3
Crew 5/6; Capacity 92 troops or 64 paratroops or 74 medical litters; Max freight capacity 43,399 lb/19,685 kg; Length C1 – 29.79 m C3 – 34.69 m; Span 40.41 m; Height 11.66 m; Weight Empty 34,287 kg; Max All-up Weight 45,093 kg; Max speed 374 mph/602 kph; Service Ceiling 13,075 m; Engines 4 x Allison T-56A-15 turboprops.

The C-130 Hercules is the workhorse of the RAF transport fleet. Over the years it has proved to be a versatile and rugged aircraft, primarily intended for tactical operations including troop carrying, paratrooping, supply dropping and aeromedical duties. The Hercules can operate from short unprepared airstrips, but also possesses the endurance to mount long-range strategic lifts if required. As a troop carrier, the Hercules can carry 92 fully armed men, while for airborne operations 62 paratroops can be dispatched in two simultaneous 'sticks' through the fuselage side doors. Alternatively, 40 paratroops can jump from the rear loading ramp. As an air ambulance the aircraft can accommodate 74 stretchers.

Freight loads that can be parachuted from the aircraft include: 16 x 1 ton containers or 4 x 8,000 pound platforms or 2 x 16,000 pound platforms or 1 x platform of 30,000 pounds plus. Amongst the many combinations of military loads that can be carried in an air-landed operation are: 3 x Ferret scout cars plus 30 passengers or 2 x Land Rovers and 30 passengers or 2 x Gazelle helicopters.

Of the original 66 C1 aircraft, some 31 have been given a fuselage stretch producing the Mark C3. The C3 'stretched version' provides an additional 37% more cargo space. Refuelling probes have been fitted above the cockpit of both variants and some have received radar warning pods under the wing tips.

The C-130 LTW (RAF Lyneham Transport Wing) appears to have a total of 43 aircraft (C3/C4/C5).

Hercules C4/C5 (C-130J)

The RAF has replaced some of its Hercules C1/C3 aircraft with second-generation C-130Js (C4/C5) on a one-for-one basis. Twenty-five Hercules C4 and C5 aircraft were ordered in December 1994, and the first entered service in 2000. Deliveries were completed by 2003 at a total cost of just over £1bn. The C4 is the same size as the older Hercules C3 which features a fuselage lengthened by 4.57 m (15ft 0 in) more than the original C1. The Hercules C5 is the new equivalent of the shorter model. With a flight deck crew of two plus one loadmaster, the aircraft can carry up to 128 infantry, 92 paratroops, eight pallets or 24 CDS bundles. The Hercules C4/C5s have new Allison turboprop engines, R391 six-bladed composite propellers and a Full Authority Digital Engine Control (FADEC). This propulsion system increases take off thrust by 29% and is 15% more efficient. Consequently, there is no longer a requirement for the external tanks to be fitted. An entirely revised 'glass' flight deck with head-up displays (HUD) and four multi-function displays (MFD) is fitted, replacing many of the dials of the original aircraft. These displays are compatible with night-vision goggles (NVG).

Tristar

(8 in service) Crew 3; Passengers 265 and 35,000 pounds of freight; Length 50.05 m; Height 16.87 m; Span 47.35 m; Max Speed 964 km/ph (600 mph); Range 6,000 miles (9,600 kms); Engines 3 x 22,680 kgs thrust Rolls Royce RB 211-524B4 turbofans.

The Tristar normally cruises at 525mph and with a payload of 50,000 pounds has a range in excess of 6,000 miles. The aircraft entered service in early 1986 with No 216 Sqn which reformed at RAF Brize Norton on 1 Nov 1984.

VC-10

(16 in service) Crew 4; Carries 150 passengers or 78 medical litters; Height 12.04 m; Span 44.55 m ; Length 48.36 m; Max Speed (425 mph); Range 7596 kms; All Up Operational Weight 146,513 kgs; Engines 4 x Rolls Royce Conway turbofans.

The VC-10 is a fast transport aircraft which is the backbone of Strike Command's long-range capability, providing flexibility and speed of deployment for British Forces. This multi-purpose aircraft can be operated in the troop transport, freight and aeromedical roles in addition to maintaining scheduled air services.

The VC10 is due to be replaced in RAF service by the Airbus A400M and the Future Strategic Tanker Aircraft.

C-17 Globemaster

(4 in service) Crew of 2 pilots and 1 loadmaster; Capacity Maximum of 154 troops; Normal load of 102 fully-equipped troops, up to 172,200 lb (78,108 kg) on up to 18 standard freight pallets or 48 litters in the medevac role: Wingspan 50.29 m; Length overall 53.04m; Height overall 16.8 m; Loadable width 5.5m; Cruising speed 648 kph (403 mph); Range (max payload) 4,444 km (2,400 miles); Engines 4 x Pratt and Whitney F117 turbofans.

The C-17 meets an RAF requirement for an interim strategic airlift capability pending the introduction of Future Transport Aircraft (A400). The decision to lease four C-17 aircraft for some £771 m from Boeing was taken in 2000, and the aircraft entered service in 2001. The lease is for a period of seven years, with the option of extending for up to a further two years. The C-17 fleet is capable of the deployment of 1,400 tonnes of freight over 3,200 miles in a seven day period. The aircraft is able to carry one Challenger 2 MBT, or a range of smaller armoured vehicles, or up to three WAH-64 Apache aircraft at one time. Over 150 troops can be carried. Inflight refuelling increases the aircraft range. No 99 Sqn has some 158 flight crew and ground staff.

A400M (Previously Future Large Aircraft – FLA)

The MoD committed to 25 x Airbus A400M in 2000 to meet the Future Transport Aircraft (FTA) requirement for an air lift capability to replace the remaining Hercules C-130K C1/C3 fleet. The A400 is a collaborative programme involving eight European nations (Germany, France, Turkey, Spain, Portugal, Belgium, Luxembourg and United Kingdom), procuring a total of 180 aircraft. The expected UK cost is some £2.4 billion for 25 aircraft. The projected in-service date has slipped from 2007 to 2010.

The A400M should provide tactical and strategic mobility to all three Services. The capabilities required of the A400M include the ability to operate from well established airfields and semi-prepared rough landing areas, in extreme climates and all weather by day and night; to carry a variety of vehicles and other equipment, freight, and troops over extended ranges; to be capable of air dropping paratroops and equipment; and to be capable of being unloaded with the minimum of ground handling equipment. The A400M should also meet a requirement for an airlift capability to move large single items such as attack helicopters and some Royal Engineers' equipment.

The most commonly quoted argument in favour of the A400M over the C-130J is that this aircraft could carry a 25 ton payload over a distance of 4,000 km. Thus, it is argued that a fleet of 40 x A400M could carry a UK Brigade to the Gulf within 11.5 days, as opposed to the 28.5 days required to make a similar deployment with 40 x C-130s. To operate a fleet of 40 x A400M would of course require aircraft from elsewhere in Europe. In any event, we believe that the RAF will probably retain its C-17s, and will operate a mixed transport fleet comprising the C-130J, A-400 and C-17.

Deliveries are expected between 2009 and 2025 with operational capability from 2011.

The Joint Force Harrier (JFH) was established on 1 April 2000 and brought together the Sea Harrier FA.2 squadrons, previously under Naval Air Command, with the RAF's Harrier GR 7/7A squadrons in a new command within RAF Strike Command. However, less than two years later, it was announced that the Sea Harrier FA.2 was to be retired early from the JFH under a development that will see the JFH standardise on the RAF's Harrier GR 9/9A. Announcing the move in 2002, UK MoD officials said the type rationalisation was in preparation for the introduction of the Future Joint Combat Aircraft and the Future Aircraft Carrier in 2012.

The MoD explained that the optimum development of the JFH is to support only one Harrier type to its end of service life, the 'more capable GR 9'. The Sea Harrier FA.2 was therefore withdrawn from service between 2004 and March 2006.

As from April 2007 the JFH will consists of 4 x squadrons as follows:

800 Naval Air Squadron	9 x Harrier GR 7/7A	Cottesmore
801 Naval Air Squadron	9 x Harrier GR 7/7A	Cottesmore
1 Squadron RAF	9 x Harrier GR 9/9A	Cottesmore
4 Squadron RAF	9 x Harrier GR 7/7A	Cottesmore

All four squadrons should have 12 pilots and eventually all will operate the Harrier GR 9/9A and T 12.

We would expect the AAC armed helicopter to deal with the localised armoured threats to a British force on operations, with RAF aircraft (such as the Harrier used on larger targets at a great distance from the forward edge of the battle area. However, high performance modern aircraft are very expensive and fast jet pilots take up to three years to train. It would only be sensible to risk such valuable systems when all other options had failed. In addition, the strength of enemy air defences would probably allow only one pass to be made over the target area. A second pass by fixed- wing aircraft after ground defences had been alerted would be problematical.

Helicopters in UK service
During January 2007 the UK MoD produced the following figures for helicopters in service with all three armed services, and the length of in-service life.

Helicopter type	Fleet size	In-service date	Planned out of service date
Attack Helicopter	67	2001	2030
Chinook Mk 2	34	1993	2015
Chinook Mk 2a	6	2000	2025
Lynx Mk 7 & Mk 9	112	1977	2012
Lynx Mk 3 & Mk 8	73	1976	2012/2014
Merlin Mk 1	42	1999	2029
Merlin Mk 3	22	2000	2030
Puma Mk 1	45	1971	2010

Gazelle Mk 1	115	1973	2018
Sea King Mk 3/3A	25	1978	2017
Sea King Mk 4	33	1979	2012
Sea King Mk 5	16	1981	2017
Sea King Mk 6	4	1988	2006
Sea King Mk 6c	5	2004	2008
Sea King Mk 7	11	2002	2017
Agusta A109	4	1984	2008

In addition to the aircraft above, the UK MoD contracts for a Commercially Owned Military Registered (COMR) fleet of helicopters. These helicopters are on the Military Register and flown by military aircrew, but are owned and maintained by commercial operators.

Helicopter type and location	Number	Contract let	Contract expires
Bell 412 / Shawbury	11	1997	2012
Bell 412 / Cyprus	4	2003	2008
Bell 212 / Belize	3	2003	2008
Bell 212 / Brunei	3	1993	2008
Bell 212 /Middle Wallop	1	2004	2007
Dauphin / Plymouth	2	1996	2007
Single Squirrel / Shawbury	27	1997	2012
Single Squirrel / Middle Wallop	10	1997	2012
Twin Squirrel (AS355N) / Northolt	4	2006	2011
Sikorski S61N / Falklands	2	1983	2011

Although planned out of service and contract expiry dates have been given, the UK MoD has emphasised that no decisions have yet been taken on the shape of the future helicopter programme, or the individual components within it.

CHAPTER 8 – ENGINEERS

OVERVIEW

The engineer support for the Army is provided by the Corps of Royal Engineers (RE). Known as Sappers, the Royal Engineers are one of the Army's six combat arms, and are trained as fighting soldiers as well as specialist combat engineers. The Corps of Royal Engineers performs highly specialised combat and non-combat tasks, and is active all over the world in conflict and during peace. The Corps has no battle honours, its motto *'ubique'* (everywhere), signifies that it has taken part in every battle fought by the British Army in all parts of the world.

Force structure

At the beginning of 2007, the RE had a regular Army establishment of some 9,460 personnel and a strength of 8,780 personnel. These figures are for UK trained regular army (including Full Time Reserve Service Personnel) and exclude Gurkhas, and mobilised reservists. This large corps comprises 16 regular regiments (including two training regiments) and five TA regiments – presently organised as follows:

Royal Engineers: Regular Army units and locations during 2007

Unit	Location	Country	Notes
21 Engineer Regiment	Osnabruck	Germany	1 (UK) Division
22 Engineer Regiment	Perham Down	UK	3 (UK) Division
23 Engineer Regiment	Woodbridge	UK	16 Air Assault Brigade
24 Commando Regiment	Barnstaple	UK	3 Commando Brigade (from late 2007)
25 Engineer Regiment	Antrim	UK	Air Support
26 Engineer Regiment	Ludgershall	UK	3 (UK) Division)
28 Engineer Regiment	Hameln	Germany	Amphibious Engineers, 1 Armoured Division
32 Engineer Regiment	Hohne	Germany	1 (UK) Division
33 Engineer Regiment	Wimbish	UK	EOD
35 Engineer Regiment	Paderborn	Germany	1 (UK) Division
36 Engineer Regiment	Maidstone	UK	3 (UK) Division
38 Engineer Regiment	Ripon	UK	3 (UK) Division
39 Engineer Regiment	Waterbeach	UK	RAF Support
42 Engineer Regiment	Hermitage	UK	Geographic survey

The former Gurkha Engineer Regiment QGE (Queen's Gurkha Engineers) now forms part of 36 Engineer Regiment, comprising 50 Headquarters Squadron, two wheeled field squadrons (20 Field Squadron and 69 Gurkha Field Squadron) and an engineer logistic squadron (70 Gurkha Field Support Squadron). The listing of Regiments by role is as follows:

	Germany	UK
Engineer Regiments	4	5
Air Assault Regiment		1

Commando Regiment	1
EOD Regiment	1
Geographic Regiment	1
Resident N Ireland Regiment	1
Training Regiments	2
TA Engineer Regiments	5

There are also a number of independent engineer squadrons in the UK, as shown in the next table:

Royal Engineers: Specialist units and locations during early 2007

Unit	Location	Country	Notes
12 (Air Support) Engineer Brigade	Waterbeach	UK	Air support (39, 71(V) and 73(V) Regts
29 (Corps Support) Engineer Brigade	Aldershot	UK	Corps support (75 (V) and 101 (V) Regts
62 Cyprus Support Squadron	Cyprus	Cyprus	Cyprus
Military Works Force	Nottingham	UK	Gurkhas
Works Group RE (Airfields)	Wallingford	UK	Airfields
Engineer Resources	Bicester	UK	Logistics
Engineer Training Advisory Team (ETAT)	Sennelager	Germany	Training
Joint Aeronautical and Geospatial Organisation	Hermitage	UK	Geographic survey
Band of the Corps of Royal Engineers	Chatham	UK	Band

Territorial Army Royal Engineer Regiments and independent units are shown below:

Royal Engineers: Territorial Army units and locations in 2007

Unit	Location
71 Engineer Regiment (V)	Leuchars
72 Engineer Regiment (V)	Gateshead
73 Engineer Regiment (V)	Nottingham
75 Engineer Regiment (V)	Warrington
Royal Monmouthshire RE (Militia)	Monmouth
101 Engineer Regiment (V) EOD	Ilford
131 Independent Commando Squadron (V)	London
135 Independent Geographic Squadron (V)	Ewell
591 Independent Field Squadron (Volunteers)	Bangor (N Ireland)
HQ RE Territorial Army	Aldershot
Central Volunteer HQ RE	Minley
Military Works Force	Minley
170 (Infrastructure Support) Engineer Group	Chilwell

Contingents of Royal Engineers (including Volunteer Reservists) are likely to be deployed in all combat zones, including most recently Afghanistan, Iraq, Balkans, Democratic Republic of Congo, Georgia, Liberia and Sierra Leone.

Future Army Structure (FAS)

Under the late 2004 FAS proposals the following enhancements to the Royal Engineers are being implemented:

a. A new Commando Engineer Regiment (24 Commando Engineer Regiment) is in the process of being formed.

b. An Air Support RHQ and associated HQ and Support Squadron is being established by the re-roling of 25 Engineer Regiment's RHQ and HQ and Support Squadron following Northern Ireland Normalisation.

c. An additional EOD squadron is being formed.

d. Two additional Close Support (CS) squadrons are being formed in order to provide support to all battlegroups within the armoured and mechanised brigades.

e. The resources cells in Field Support Squadrons are being decaderised.

f. The geographic capability is being enhanced.

g. Counter mobility support is being established within the specialist brigades.

h. Engineer reconnaissance will be embedded into formation reconnaissance regiments.

i. The Military Work Force will be enhanced and 535 Specialist Team Royal Engineers transferred from Northern Ireland on 'Normalisation'.

COMBAT ENGINEERING ROLES

Combat engineer support to military operations may be summarised under the following headings:

♦ Mobility
♦ Counter-mobility
♦ Protection

Mobility

The capability to deliver firepower, troops and supplies to any part of the battlefield is crucial to success. Combat engineers use their skills to overcome physical obstacles both natural and man-made, ensuring that armoured and mechanised troops can reach their targets and fight effectively.

Combat Engineers employ a wide variety of equipment, including tank-mounted, amphibious and girder bridges, to cross physical barriers. This equipment can be rapidly deployed to any part of the battlefield to ensure minimum interruption to progress.

Combat engineers are trained and equipped to clear enemy minefields which block or hinder movement. All combat engineers are trained to clear minefields by hand with the minimum risk. They also employ a number of explosive and mechanical devices to clear paths through minefields.

Combat engineers are also trained to detect and to destroy booby traps.

Improving the mobility of own and friendly forces may include the following tasks:

Route clearance and maintenance

Construction and maintenance of diversionary routes

Routes to and from hides

Bridging, rafting and assisting amphibious vehicles at water obstacles

Detection and clearance of mines and booby traps

Assisting the movement of heavy artillery and communications units

Preparation of landing sites for helicopters

Counter-mobility
Counter-mobility is the term used to describe efforts to hinder enemy movement. Combat engineers aim to ensure that hostile forces cannot have freedom of mobility. Combat engineers are trained in the use of explosive charges to create obstacles, crater roads and destroy bridges. In this role, the combat engineer may be required to delay detonation until the last possible moment to allow the withdrawal of friendly forces in the face of an advancing enemy.

Combat engineers are also responsible for laying anti-tank mines, either by hand or mechanically, to damage vehicles and disrupt enemy forces. Combat engineers are trained to handle these devices safely and deploy them to maximum effect. Combat engineers are also trained for setting booby traps.

Earthwork defences, ditches and obstacles – one of the earliest forms of battlefield engineering – are also used to prevent the advance of enemy vehicles. Hindering enemy movement may include the following tasks:

Construction of minefields

Improvement of natural obstacles by demolitions, cratering, and barricades

Nuisance mining and booby traps

Route denial

Construction of obstacles to armoured vehicle movement, such as tank ditches

Protection
Construction of field defences is a core task for combat engineers. The capability to protect troops, equipment and weapons is critical. Combat engineers provide advice and assistance to the other parts of the Land Forces and the other services on the best methods of concealment

and camouflage, and use mechanised plant to construct defensive positions and blast-proof screens.

Protection for troops in defensive positions may include field defences, minefields, wire, and other obstacles. Because of their commitment to other primary roles, there may be little engineer assistance available for the construction of defensive positions. What assistance can be given would normally be in the form of earth-moving plant to assist in digging, and advice on the design and methods of construction of field defences and obstacles.

Combat Engineers Military Works units have design and management teams that can provide military infrastructure support to all armed services and other government departments. Secondary protection roles include:

Water and power supply in forward areas

Technical advice on counter-surveillance with particular reference to camouflage and deception

Destruction of equipment

Intelligence

A major Engineer commitment in the forward area is the construction, maintenance and repair of dispersed airfields for aircraft and landing sites for helicopters.

Non-Combat Engineering
Combat engineers also perform non-combat tasks during national peacetime contingencies and multilateral peace support operations in foreign countries, including:

General support engineering, including airfield damage repair and repair of ancillary installations for fuel and power, construction of temporary buildings, power and water supplies, repair and construction of POL pipelines and storage facilities, and construction and routine maintenance of airstrips and helicopter landing sites

Survey – including maps and aeronautical charts

Explosive Ordnance Disposal – including terrorist and insurgent bombs

Traffic Movement Lights for mobilisation and exercises

Postal and courier services for all the Armed Forces

Recent coalition and peace support operations have highlighted the importance of combat engineers in all spheres of military activity. During the period 1993-2007, the multitude of tasks for which engineer support has been requested has stretched the resources of the Corps to its limit. Engineers are almost always among the first priorities in any call for support: tracks must be improved, roads built, accommodation constructed for soldiers and refugees, clean water provided and mined areas cleared. For example during 2003, 22 Engineer Regiment (operating in Iraq) was tasked to supply a quick fix to problem areas along the diesel pipeline for the Oil Security Force (OSF), and to ensure regular supplies of water for the Iraqi population in Basra and the surrounding urban areas.

Engineer Regiment

A possible organisation for an Engineer Regiment deployed on operations with 1 (UK) Division could be as follows:

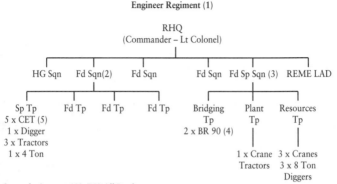

Engineer Regiment (1)

RHQ
(Commander – Lt Colonel)

HG Sqn   Fd Sqn(2)   Fd Sqn   Fd Sqn   Fd Sp Sqn (3)   REME LAD

Sp Tp   Fd Tp   Fd Tp   Fd Tp   Bridging   Plant   Resources
5 x CET (5)   Tp   Tp   Tp
1 x Digger   2 x BR 90 (4)
3 x Tractors
1 x 4 Ton   1 x Crane   3 x Cranes
                                             Tractors   3 x 8 Ton
                                                          Diggers

Strength: Approx 650–750 All Ranks

(1)This Regiment would send most of its soldiers to man the engineer detachments that provide support for a Division's battlegroups; (2) A Field Squadron will have approximately 68 vehicles and some 200 men; (3) Field Support Squadron; (4) or Medium Girder Bridge; (5) Combat Engineer Tractor.

This whole organisation is highly mobile and built around the AFV 432 and Spartan series of vehicles. In addition to the Regimental REME LAD, each squadron has its own REME section of some 12-15 men.

The smallest engineer unit is the Field Troop which is usually commanded by a Lieutenant and consists of approximately 44 men. In an Armoured Division, a Field Troop will have up to four sections, each mounted in an APC. Some Engineer Regiments in UK may have only three sections and may be mounted in wheeled vehicles such as Land Rovers and 4-Ton Trucks. An engineer troop will deploy with most of its equipment scale (known as G1098), stores and explosives to enable it to carry out its immediate battlefield tasks.

An Engineer Field Troop assigned to work in support of a battlegroup operating in the area of the FEBA would normally resemble the following:-

Field Troop Organisation

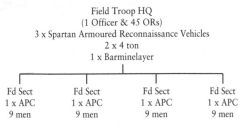

Field Troop HQ
(1 Officer & 45 ORs)
3 x Spartan Armoured Reconnaissance Vehicles
2 x 4 ton
1 x Barminelayer

Fd Sect	Fd Sect	Fd Sect	Fd Sect
1 x APC	1 x APC	1 x APC	1 x APC
9 men	9 men	9 men	9 men

Engineer amphibious capability and specialist support is provided by elements of 28 Engineer Regiment in Germany and 412 Amphibious Engineer Troop (V).

The UK Engineer Field Regiment (Regular and TA) is generally a wheeled organisation that would normally have 2 x Field Squadrons, a Support Squadron and possibly an Airfield Damage Repair (ADR) Squadron. Engineer regiments supporting 3 (UK) Division are likely to be structured along the lines of the Armoured Divisional Engineer Regiment.

33 Engineer Regiment (EOD) is currently configured as follows: 3 Field Squadrons (EOD) which each have a unique operational role and one Headquarters and Support Squadron (EOD) who hold specialist EOD support equipment. Additionally there is an Explosive Ordnance Clearance (EOC) Group who work as an independent team.

33 Engineer Regt (EOD)

22 HQ &Sp Sqn	21 Fd Sqn	49 Fd Sqn	58 Fd Sqn	EOC	REME
(EOD)	(EOD)	(EOD)	(EOD)	Group	LAD

23 Engineer Regiment (Air Assault) was established in September 2002 and officially formed on 7 January 2003 to provide engineer support to 16 Air Assault Brigade.

COMBAT ENGINEER TRAINING

All RE officers undergo officer training at RMA Sandhurst (44 weeks) before taking the Royal Engineers Troop Commanders Course (RETCC) with 1 and 3 RSME Regiments. The RETCC is 27 weeks long. All RE officers are expected to have or to obtain university degree-level engineering qualifications, and many qualify for higher degrees in the course of their career.

Recruit training for other ranks involves three phases:

♦ Soldier training (12 to 32 weeks)
♦ Combat engineer training (10 weeks)
♦ Trade training (10 – 49 weeks)

For both officers and other ranks, specialist engineer training is mainly conducted by 1 and 3 Royal School of Military Engineer (RSME) Regiments based at Chatham and Blackwater. 1 RSME Regiment is the support regiment for training. During a year, some 8000 students may pass through 1 RSME Regiment, many of whom have recently joined the army and who have arrived at Chatham for a long engineering course lasting, in some cases, up to 44 weeks. 1 RSME Regiment incorporates the Construction Engineer School at Chatham, where civil and mechanical engineering skills are taught.

3 RSME Regiment is responsible for combat engineer training. The Combat Engineer School is located at Minley. 55 and 57 Training Squadrons are responsible for Combat Engineer and Assault Pioneer training, and Driver Training Troop, 63 Training Support Squadron, is responsible for ABLE and RE Module Driver training.

Combat Engineering Vehicles

Combat Engineer Tractor
(73 available) Weight 17,010 kg; Length 7.54 m; Height 2.67 m; Road Speed 56 kph; Road Range 480 kms; Fuel Capacity 430 litres; Engine Rolls-Royce C6TCR; Engine Power 320 bhp; Crew 2; Armament 1 x 7.62 mm machine gun.

The FV180 Combat Engineer Tractor (CET), which entered service in 1977, is a versatile tracked AFV that can clear obstacles, dig pits, prepare barriers and recover other vehicles that become stuck or damaged. In short, it is an armoured vehicle that can assist in a variety of engineer battlefield tasks, and has an impressive amphibious capability. The 100 m winch cable can be fired from the CET by rocket and, using an anchor, can assist in dragging the vehicle up steep slopes and over river banks. CET is found mainly in the Divisional Engineer Regiments and the UK Engineer Regiments. India has 39 x CET in service and Singapore is believed to have another 18.

Terrier
Terrier is a lightly armoured highly mobile, general support engineer vehicle optimised for battlefield preparation in the indirect fire zone. It will replace the existing FV180 Combat Engineer Tractor from 2008, providing mobility support (obstacle and route clearance), counter-mobility (digging of anti-tank ditches and other obstacles) and survivability (digging of trenches and Armoured Fighting Vehicle slots). Terrier is claimed to be faster, more mobile and with more effective armour and mine protection than the FV-180 CET.

142

Terrier will be operated by a crew of two – or may be operated remotely in particularly hazardous environments. The vehicle must also be able to tow a trailer carrying fascines, trackway and the GIAT Viper minefield breaching system; clear scatterable mines; remove or enhance obstacles, and establish routes while keeping pace with other armoured vehicles such as the Challenger 2 MBT and the Warrior ICV. Terrier will be fitted with day and night vision systems and, although (at 30 tonnes) twice as heavy as CET, it will be air-portable in An-124, C17 or A400M transport aircraft. The Terrier manufacturer (OEM) is BAe Systems. Current indications are that 65 vehicles have been ordered in a contract that over the life of the Terrier programme is believed to be worth some £700 million.

Trojan and Titan

The Trojan and Titan are new armoured engineer vehicles based on a common tank chassis – the Challenger 2 MBT. The replacement of the Chieftain AVRE and AVLB systems by the ETS means that the British Army has a common heavy armour fleet based on the Challenger 2 MBT chassis. Both vehicles are manufactured by the Alvis subsidiary of BAe Systems. These vehicles represent the first armoured engineer vehicles specifically designed (rather than adapted from battle tank chassis) for their role and incorporate the very latest mobility and survivability features, many of which are also planned for Challenger 2. Improved visibility is achieved by incorporating direct and indirect vision devices with low light, image intensifying and thermal imaging capabilities. The interior, and to some extent the exterior, of the vehicles have been designed around the crew station positions.

A contract worth £250 million was awarded during early 2001 for the supply of 66 vehicles – 33 x Trojan and 33 x Titan. Deliveries to the RE commenced in late 2006.

Trojan Armoured Vehicle Royal Engineers (AVRE)

(33 on order with first vehicles in service from late 2006) Crew 3; Weight (est) 62,500 kg; Max Road Speed 59 kph; Road Range 450 km; Powerpack comprises Perkins CV12 diesel engine, David Brown TN54 enhanced low-loss gearbox and the OMANI cooling group; Auxiliary Power Unit (APU) is also fitted; Engine Power 1,200 bhp; Armament 7.62mm GPMG; Stowage for crew man-portable Light Anti-Tank Weapons; Fitted with NBC protection system.

Trojan is designed to open routes through complex battlefield obstacles and clear a path through minefields. Standard equipment includes a winch and a knuckle-arm excavator shovel. A Pearson Engineering Full-Width Mine Plough can be mounted at the front to clear mines and a Pearson Engineering Pathfinder clear lane-marking system can also be fitted. It can also carry fascines to drop into ditches and tow a trailer-mounted Python rocket-propelled mine-clearing system. Trojan has the flexibility to support a wide range of operations, including humanitarian missions.

Titan Armoured Vehicle Launcher Bridge (AVLB)

(33 on order with first vehicles in service from late 2006) Crew 3; Weight (est) 62,500 kg; Max Road Speed 59 kph; Road Range 450 km; Powerpack comprises Perkins CV12 diesel engine, David Brown TN54 enhanced low-loss gearbox and the OMANI cooling group; Auxiliary Power Unit(APU)is also fitted; Engine Power 1,200 bhp; Carries BR-90 Close

Support Bridges; No. 10 (length 26 m, span 21-24.5 m); No. 11 (length 16 m, span 14.5m); & No.12 (length 13.5 m, span 12 m); Armament 7.62 mm GPMG; Stowage for crew man-portable Light Anti-Tank Weapons; Fitted with NBC protection system.

Titan is designed to cross gaps of up to 60 m laying a selection of close support bridges. It can carry and lay the current range of In-Service No 10, 11 and 12 Close Support Bridges, providing ground manoeuvre formations with improved operation of the bridges enabling them to be laid in a greater range of terrain conditions.

BR90 Bridges

The RE BR-90 family of bridges are built from a range of seven modular panels of advanced aluminium alloy fabrication. These are interchangeable through the various bridge types, to form two interconnecting trackways with a 4 m overall bridge width and a 1 m girder depth. BR90 is deployed with Royal Engineer units in both Germany and the UK. The production order was valued at approximately £140 million in 1993. These bridges entered service from 1999, and comprise the following elements:

♦ General Support Bridge
♦ Close Support Bridge
♦ Two Span Bridge
♦ Long Span Bridge

Close Support Bridge – This consists of three tank-launched bridges capable of being carried on a tank bridgelayer and a Tank Bridge Transporter truck.

There are three basic Tank Launched Bridges (also known as Close Support or Assault Bridges): the No 10, No 11 and No 12.

General Support Bridge – This system utilises the Automated Bridge Launching Equipment (ABLE) that is capable of launching bridges up to 44 m in length. The ABLE vehicle is positioned with its rear pointing to the gap to be crossed and a lightweight launch rail extended across the gap. The bridge is then assembled and winched across the gap supported by the rail, with sections added until the gap is crossed. Once the bridge has crossed the gap the ABLE launch rail is recovered. A standard ABLE system set consists of an ABLE vehicle and 2 x TBT carrying a 32 m bridge set. A 32 m bridge can be built by 10 men in about 25 minutes

Spanning Systems – There are two basic spanning systems. The long span system allows for lengthening a 32 m span to 44 m using ABLE and the two span system allows 2 x 32 m bridge sets to be constructed by ABLE and secured in the middle by piers or floating pontoons, crossing a gap of up to 60 m.

BR-90 carrier – The Unipower 8x8 TBT is an improved mobility transporter for the BR 90 bridging system. It can carry one No 10 bridge or two No 12 bridges. The TBT can self load from, and off-load to, the ground. The TBT task is to re-supply the Chieftain and Titan AVLB with replacement bridges.

Medium Girder Bridge (MGB)

The MGB is a simple system of lightweight components that can be easily manhandled to construct a bridge capable of taking the heaviest AFVs. The MGB has been largely replaced by the BR90 system, although some MGB have been retained for certain operational requirements. Two types of MGBs are fielded: Single span bridge – 30 m long which can be built by about 25 men in 45 minutes; Multi span bridge – a combination of 26.5 m spans: a two span bridge will cross a 51 m gap and a three span bridge a 76 m gap. If necessary, MGB pontoons can be also be joined together to form a ferry.

Class 16 Airportable Bridge

In service since 1974 and a much lighter bridge than the MGB, the Class 16 can be carried assembled under a Chinook helicopter or in 3 x 3/4 ton vehicles with trailers. A 15 m bridge can be constructed by 15 men in 20 minutes. The Class 16 can also be made into a ferry which is capable of carrying the heaviest AFVs. In the near future, the British Army will replace the Class 16 bridge with the Future Light Bridge (FLB) systems. This bridge will also be capable of being used as a ferry.

M3 Ferry

(20 available for operations) Weight 24,500 kg; Length 12.74 m; Height 3.93 m; Width 3.35 m; Width (bridge deployed) 6.57 m; Max Road Speed 80 kph; Water Speed 14 kph; Road Range 725 kms; Crew 3.

The M3 can be driven into a river and used as a ferry or, when a number are joined together from bank to bank, as a bridge, capable of taking vehicles as heavy as the Challenger MBT. The M3 has a number of improvements over the M2 which it has replaced (the M2 was in service for over 25 years). The M3 can deploy pontoons on the move, in or out of water; it needs no on-site preparation to enter the water; it can be controlled from inside the cab when swimming and its control functions have been automated allowing the crew to be reduced from four to three.

A single two-bay M3 can carry a Class 70 tracked vehicle, where two M2s would have been required for this task with additional buoyancy bags. Eight M3 units and 24 soldiers can build a 100 m bridge in 30 minutes compared with 12 M2s, 48 soldiers and a construction time of 45 minutes. The M3 is only 1.4 m longer and 3,300 kg heavier than the M2. It is still faster and more manoeuvrable on land and in water. A four-wheel steering facility gives a turning diameter of 24 m.

By early 1999, 38 x M3 rigs had been delivered and 30 of these (including four of seven pre-production vehicles) went to 28 Engineer Regiment in Germany. The unit cost was believed to be in the region of £1.2 million.

Mine Clearance

Python

Trailer Weight 136 kg; Hose Length; 230 m; Cleared Zone; 180 m x 7.3 m wide.

Python is a minefield breaching system that replaces the Giant Viper in RE service. The Python has the ability to clear a much longer 'safe lane' than its predecessor. It is also faster into action and far more accurate. It can clear a path 230 m long and 7 m wide through which vehicles are safe to pass.

The system works by firing a single rocket from a newly designed launcher trailer which has been towed to the edge of a mined area. Attached to the rocket is a coiled 230 m long hose packed with one and a half tons of powerful explosive. After the hose lands on the ground it detonates and destroys or clears any mines along its entire length. It is claimed that in a cleared lane, over 90% of anti-tank mines will have been destroyed.

Mine Warfare

Anti-tank minefields laid by the Royal Engineers will usually contain Barmines (anti-tank) or Mk.7 (anti-tank) mines and anti-disturbance devices may be fitted to some Barmines. Minefields will always be recorded and marked; they should also be covered by artillery and mortar fire to delay enemy mine clearance operations and maximise the attrition of armour. ATGWs are often sited in positions covering the minefield that will give them flank shoots onto enemy armour; particularly the ploughs or rollers that might spearhead a minefield breaching operation.

Shielder

Shielder provides the facility to create anti-tank barriers quickly and effectively. The system consists of modular dispensers of anti-tank mines which can be fired to either side or to the rear, mounted on a flatbed version of the Stormer Armoured Personnel Carrier. The anti-tank mines have a programmable life, at the end of which they self-destruct.

Ordered in 1995, Shielder is derived from the US Alliant Techsystems M163 Volcano system. It is believed that the total value of the order was approximately £110 million for 29 x Volcano systems, anti-tank mines, training, spares and the Stormer flatbed carrier. The first vehicles entered service in 1999.

Barmine (Anti-Tank)

Weight 11 kg; Length 1.2 m; Width 0.1 m; Explosive Weight 8.4 kg.

The Barmine is usually mechanically laid by a plough-type trailer that can be towed behind an AFV 432 or Warrior. The Barmines are manually placed onto a conveyor belt on the layer from inside the APC. The minelayer automatically digs a furrow, lays the mines into it at the correct spacing and closes the ground over them. Up to 600 mines can be laid in one hour by one vehicle with a three man crew. A full width attack (FWAM) fuse and an anti-disturbance fuse are available for Barmine; these are secured on the ends of the mine, adjacent to the pressure plate.

Claymore Mine (Anti-Personnel)
Weight 1.58 kg; Length 210 mm; Width 30 mm; Charge Weight 0.68 kg.

The Claymore Mine has a curved oblong plastic casing mounted on a pair of bipod legs. The mine is positioned facing the enemy and fired electrically from distances up to 300 m away. On initiation, the mine scatters about 700 ball-bearings out to a range of 50 m across a 60 degree arc. First purchased from the US in 1963, the Claymore is an effective anti-infantry weapon that is likely to remain in service for many years to come.

Off-Route Mine (Anti-Tank)
Length 0.26 m; Weight 12 kg; Diameter 0.2 m; Range 75 m.

This French mine is designed for vehicle ambush. The mine is placed at the side of the road and a thin electric 'breakwire' laid out across the vehicle's path. The mine is initiated when the vehicle breaks the wire; a shaped charge known as a 'Misznay Schardin Plate' fires an explosively formed projectile into the side of the vehicle.

Mine Detection

L77A1 Mine Detectors
Weight Packed with all accessories 6.5 kg; Weight Deployed ready for use 2.2 kg; Approximate Battery Life 45 hrs; Detection Depth (metal AT mine) 0.6 – 0.7 m.

The 4C, formerly the standard mine detector of the British Army since until the late 1990s, has been replaced by the Ebinger EBEX-420PB. The Army have designated the detector L77A1 and assigned it the NATO Stock Number 6665-99-869-3649. The L77A1 is a lightweight modular design which uses pulse induction technology to locate the metallic content of mines. The battery compartment and electronics are built into the tubular structure, and an audible signal provided to the operator via a lightweight earpiece. The sensitivity is such that even modern plastic mines with a minimal metallic content can be detected to a depth of 15 cm.

CHAPTER 9 – COMMUNICATIONS

OVERVIEW

The Royal Corps of Signals (R Signals) is the combat arm that provides the communications throughout the command system of the Army. Individual battle groups are responsible for their own internal communications, but in general terms, all communications from Brigade level and above are the responsibility of the Royal Signals.

Information is the lifeblood of any military formation in battle and it is the responsibility of the Royal Signals to ensure the speedy and accurate passage of information that enables commanders to make informed and timely decisions, and to ensure that those decisions are passed to the fighting troops in contact with the enemy. The rapid, accurate and secure employment of command, control and communications systems maximises the effect of the military force available and consequently the Royal Signals act as an extremely significant 'Force Multiplier'. The Corps motto is 'First In Last Out'.

Force structure

The Royal Corps of Signals provides about 9% of the Army's manpower with nine Regular regiments (with a tenth forming), one training regiment, and 11 Territorial Army regiments, each generally consisting of between three and up to six Squadrons with between 600 and 1,000 personnel. As of the beginning of 2007 the corps was slightly over strength with 8,640 personnel against a liability of 8,440.

Royal Signals personnel are found wherever the Army is deployed including every UK and NATO headquarters in the world. The Headquarters of the Corps is at the Royal School of Signals (RSS) located at Blandford in Dorset.

Royal Signals units based in the United Kingdom provide command and control communications for forces that have operational roles both in the UK itself, including Northern Ireland, and overseas including mainland Western Europe and further afield wherever the Army finds itself. There are a number of Royal Signals units permanently based in Germany, Holland and Belgium from where they provide the necessary command and control communications and Electronic Warfare (EW) support for both the British Army and other NATO forces based in Europe. Royal Signals personnel are also based in Cyprus, the Falkland Islands, Belize and Gibraltar.

ROLES OF MILITARY COMMUNICATIONS

Communications have enabling capabilities that support all military operations in war and peace. These roles may be summarised under the following headings:

Command and Control: Communications enable commanders at all levels to exercise command and control over their own forces. Communications enable commanders to receive information, convey orders and move men and materiel, and select and position their attacking and defensive forces to maximum effect in order to take advantage of their own strengths and enemy weaknesses.

The capacity to deliver firepower, troops and supplies to any part of the battlefield is crucial to success. From the earliest days of messengers, flags, bugles and hand signals, this has been vital to successful command. Modern electronic communications systems have vastly added to this capacity, increasing the distances over which Command and Control can be exercised – from line of sight or hearing to any geographical area where forces are deployed.

Computerised Command Information: Communications enables commanders to receive information from the field and rear to build up a picture of the state and disposition of their own forces as well as enemy forces. Commanders have always sought to have the fullest possible information on the dispositions and states of both their own and enemy forces – but were typically limited by restraints of time, space and information carrying capacity.

Computer hardware and software – allied to the geographical spread, bandwidths and data-carrying capacity of modern military networks – have removed many of these constraints. Computer processing power enables information received from all sources to be sorted into meaningful patterns of use to commanders.

Such sources include:

> Voice and data reports from troops in the field
> Intelligence reports
> Mapping
> Battlefield sensors
> Multi-spectral imaging from ground reconnaissance units
> Reconnaissance and surveillance satellites, aircraft, helicopters and unmanned aerial vehicles
> Electronic Warfare systems on ground, air and sea platforms

In modern war, to capture the full scope of computer information systems, this communications effect is typically described as Command, Control, Communications, Computers, Intelligence, Surveillance and Reconnaissance (C4ISR)

Electronic Warfare: Secure communications deny the enemy knowledge of own and friendly force activities, capabilities and intelligence (Communications Security). Communications enable the penetration, compromise and destruction of enemy communication systems (Electronic Warfare).

ROYAL SIGNALS MISSIONS
Royal Signals units have three principal missions:

Communications Engineering: Communications units design, build and dismantle the tactical communications networks at division and brigade levels.

Communications Operations: Communications units operate the tactical communications networks at division and brigade levels, and also battalion and battalion group level in the case of a detached formation. In conventional divisional and brigade level operations, battalions will typically be responsible for their own communications.

Communications Management: Communications units are responsible for the management of the whole communications nexus at division and brigade level.

These missions will need to be performed in all phases of battle:

Offensive: In the offensive: setting up command posts, setting up area communications networks and setting up wire networks to connect battalions to brigades and elsewhere as far as possible. Can set up air portable communications systems shortly after a foothold is secured on air base.

Advance: In the advance: continuing to keep forward and area communications running and providing logistics and maintenance needs for company and brigade forces as appropriate. Running wire forwards as far as possible with the advance, Setting up alternate Brigade HQs. Relocating and maintaining relay and retransmission points and ensuring communications to rear and flanks remain open.

Defensive: In the defence: re-enforcing command posts and relay points. Increasing the complexity and robustness of wire networks. Providing alternate and redundant communications for all users.

Withdrawal: In the withdrawal: Preventing communications assets falling into enemy hands, setting up alternate command posts on the line of withdrawal, running wire networks backwards to rear. Keeping nodes open and supplying logistics and maintenance support as required.

Non-Combat missions: Communications perform non-combat roles during peacetime, including national peacetime contingencies and multilateral peace support operations in foreign countries.

Royal Signals Units

Royal Signals: Regular Army units during early 2007

Unit	Location	Notes
1 Sig Bde	Germany	Supports Allied Rapid Reaction Corps (ARRC)
2 (NC) Sig Bde	Corsham HQ	Mainly TA, national communications during contingencies
11 Sig Bde	Donnington HQ	1,000 Regular and 2,500 TA personnel, communications for JRRF
3 (UK) Div HQ	Bulford	Divisional command and control communications & Sig Regt
2 Sig Regt	York	With 11 Signal Bde, currently equipping with Cormorant system
10 Sig Regt	Corsham	Information Communications Services & Information Management
14 Sig Regt (EW)	Brawdy	Electronic Warfare
21 Sig Regt (Air Sp)	JHF	Communications for the RAF Support Helicopter Force and AAC Apache

22 Sig Regt	Stafford	Ptarmigan/Falcon (1)
30 Sig Regt	Bramcote	Strategic satellite communications to Land & Joint Task Forces
1(UK)AD and Sig Regt	Germany	Communications for 1st (UK) Armd Div HQ and Bdes
7 (ARRC) Sig Regt	Germany	Part of 1 Sig Bde, supports Allied Rapid Reaction Corps (ARRC)
16 Sig Regt	Germany	Part of 1 Sig Bde, supports Allied Rapid Reaction Corps (ARRC)
11 Signal Regt	Blandford	Training Regt, responsible for Phase 2 and 3 signals training
Queens Gurkha Signals	Various	Supports 2 x Gurkha Inf Bns, 2 and 30 Sig Regts, and others
209 Sig Sqn	Catterick	Independent Sqn, supporting 19 Light Brigade HQ
213 Sig Sqn	Lisburn	Independent Sqn, supporting Northern Ireland
215 Sig Sqn	Tidworth	Independent Sqn, supporting 1 Mechanised Bde within 3 Div
216 Sig Sqn	Colchester	Independent Sqn, supporting 16 Air Assault Bde HQ
228 Sig Sqn	Bulford	Independent Sqn, supporting 12 Mech Bde HQ
238 Sig Sqn	London	Independent Sqn, supports London Military District
242 Sig Sqn	Edinburgh	Independent Sqn, supports Army in Scotland & Northern England
261 Sig Sqn	Germany	Independent Sqn, supports 101 Logistics Bde HQ
262 Sig Sqn	Aldershot	Independent Sqn, supports 102 Logistics Bde HQ
264 Sig Sqn	Hereford	Independent Sqn, supports Special Forces
200 Sig Sqn	Germany	Independent Sqn, supporting 20 Armd Brigade HQ
204 Sig Sqn	Germany	Independent Sqn, supporting 4 Armd Brigade HQ
207 Sig Sqn	Germany	Independent Sqn, supporting 7 Armd Brigade HQ
628 Sig Tp	Netherlands	Independent Tp, supports AFNORTH HQ
CCU & JSSU	Cyprus	Cyprus Communications Unit and Joint Service Signal Unit
JCU (FI)	Falklands	Joint Communications Unit (Falkland Islands)

22 Signal Regiment (1)

In April 2007 22 Signal Regiment was formed under the terms of the Future Army Structure proposals. The regiment consists of a new regimental headquarters and three squadrons, involving the transfer of 248 Squadron from Colerne (Wiltshire) and 222 Squadron from

Bulford (Wiltshire), plus the creation of the new 217 Squadron formed largely from personnel of 219 Squadron (York).

22 Signal Regiment with approximately 570 personnel will be located at the former site of RAF Stafford and will be co-located with the Tactical Supply Wing of the Joint Helicopter Command.

TA Units

The Royal Signals TA is structured as follows:

a. Within 2 (NC) Signals Brigade there are a total of eight signals regiments (mainly TA) and four sub-units which provide NC (National Communications) in support of the Home Defence MACA (Military Aid to the Civil Authority). In addition, where necessary these units provide support to other government departments and agencies.

b. Within 11 Signal Brigade there are three Ptarmigan regiments providing a composite Ptarmigan Regiment to the Allied Rapid Reaction Corps.

Major Royal Signals Territorial Army (TA) units are shown in the next table.

Royal Signals : Territorial Army units during early 2007

Unit	Location
2 (NC) Sig Bde	Corsham HQ
11 Sig Bde	Donnington HQ
31 Sig Regt (V)	London
32 Sig Regt (V)	Scotland
33 Sig Regt (V)	Lancashire & Cheshire
34 Sig Regt (V)	Yorkshire, Durham & Northumberland
35 Sig Regt (V)	South and West Midlands
36 Sig Regt (V)	East Anglia and Essex
37 Sig Regt (V)	Wales, Midlands, Lancashire
38 Sig Regt (V)	Yorkshire, Notts, Derbyshire, Leicester, Lancashire
39 Sig Regt (V)	Somerset, Gloucester, Home Counties,
40 Sig Regt (V)	Ireland
71 Sig Regt (V)	London, Essex
Central Volunteer Headquarters (CVHQ) Royal Signals	London
1 (RBY) Sig Sqn (V)	Milton Keynes (Special Communications)
2 Sig Sqn (V)	Dundee
63 Sig Sqn (V)	Independent Sqn, supports TA SAS units
81 Sig Sqn (V)	Corsham

FUNCTIONS OF MILITARY COMMUNICATIONS

Military communications roles undertaken by the Royal Signals may be divided into three separate functions:

Strategic communications: Communications between the political leadership, military high command, and military administrative and field commands at the divisional level. In terms of capability as opposed to function, modern communications systems increasingly blur the distinction between strategic and tactical systems as a consequence of technological advance.

Tactical communications: Communications between field formations from corps to division through brigade down to battalion level.

Electronic Warfare: The security of own forces and friendly forces communications, and the penetration, compromise and degradation of hostile communications.

TRAINING

All Royal Signals officers undergo officer training at RMA Sandhurst (44 weeks) before taking the Royal Signals Troop Commanders Course at the Royal School of Signals at Blandford Camp. Royal Signals officers are expected to have, or to obtain university degree-level engineering qualifications.

Recruit training for other ranks involves two phases:

♦ Phase 1 – Soldier training (11 to 21 weeks: apprentices 6 months)

♦ Phase 2 – Trade training (7 – 50 weeks)

Every Royal Signals soldier, whether from the Army Training Regiment Lichfield, or the Army Apprentices College Arborfield, carries out trade training at the Royal School of Signals at Blandford Camp. The length of the course depends on the trade chosen, varying from seven weeks up to 50. All trades will carry out a common module of Basic Signalling Skills and a computer literacy module before specialising. Special Operators attend an introductory course of two weeks at the Royal School of Signals before completing their training at the Defence Special Signal School in Chicksands.

11 Signal Regiment is responsible for the special to arm training for both officers and other ranks. The Royal School of Signals at Blandford Camp conducts approximately 144 different types of courses and numbering over 714 courses run per year. There are in excess of 5,250 students completing courses throughout the year with about 1,000 students on courses at any one time. These figures equate to approximately some 470,000 Man Training Days a year.

Organisation

We would expect the organisation of a Signal Regiment supporting an armoured division to be as follows:

Armoured Divisional Signal Regiment Organisation

```
                        Regimental HQ
      ┌──────────────┬──────────────┬──────────────┐
   1 Sqn          2 Sqn          3 Sqn       3 x Brigade
   Trunk         Main HQ       Alt HQ Trunk   Sig Sqns
  Equipment      SAN (1)        SAN (2)         (3)
```

Notes: (1) SAN – Secondary Access Node (2) A Divisional HQ will have two HQs to allow for movement and possible destruction. The main HQ will be set up for approx 24 hrs with the alternate HQ (Alt HQ) set up 20-30 kms away on the proposed line of march of the division. When the Main HQ closes to move to a new location the Alt HQ becomes the Main HQ for another 24 hour period. (3) Expect a Brigade Sig Sqn to have a Radio Troop and a SAN Troop.

Equipment

Royal Signals units are currently operating the following types of major equipment:

Static strategic communications
Mobile strategic satellite communications
Fixed and mobile electronic warfare (EW) systems
Tactical Area Communications – corps to brigade down to battalion HQ
VHF Combat Net Radios – battalion and sub-units
Tactical HF and UHF radios – battalion and sub-units
Radio Relay (carrying telephone & teleprinter links)
Teleprinters, Fax, CCTV and ADP Equipment
Computer Information Systems
Local area networks (LAN) and wide area networks (WAN) for computers
Line

Tactical Area Communications

The principal tactical role of the Royal Signals is to provide corps to brigade level communications that link higher commands to battalion HQs. The area communications systems used by the Royal Signals include:

Ptarmigan

Ptarmigan is a mobile, secure battlefield system that incorporates the latest technology and has been designed to improve communications reliability, capacity and interoperability. Ptarmigan remains the core equipment for the British Army Tactical Trunk Communications System, and has undergone a number of upgrades to be better prepared to meet the challenges of changing deployments and new operational requirements. This has included the introduction of an Air Portable Secondary Access Node (SAN) for 16 Air Assault Brigade. The General Purpose Trunk Access Port (GPTAP) software enhancement will allow improved interconnectivity to other nation's tactical systems.

Bowman is shortly to replace the HQ infrastructure element of Ptarmigan. In time, Ptarmigan is due to be replaced by Falcon, which will not be in service for several years. Falcon is expected to build on the lessons learned from the current introduction of Cormorant.

Built by Siemens-Plessey Christchurch (now part of BAe Systems) in the mid 1980s, Ptarmigan is a user-friendly, computer controlled communications system which was initially designed to meet the needs of the British Army in Germany. The system consists of a network of electronic exchanges or Trunk Switches that are connected by satellite and multi-channel radio relay (Triffid) links that provide voice, data, telegraph and fax communications.

The Trunk Switch, radio and satellite relays together with their support vehicles, comprise a 'Trunk Node' and all field headquarters include a group of communications vehicles that contain an Access Switch which can be connected to any Trunk Switch giving access to the system. This ensures that headquarters have flexibility in both siting and facilities, and that trunk communications then present no constraints on operations. Additionally Ptarmigan has a mobile telephone or Single Channel Radio Access (SCRA) which gives isolated or mobile users an entry point into the entire system.

Falcon

In March 2006 the UK MoD signed a contract with BAe Systems Insyte for the first increment of the Falcon Secure Trunk Communication System. Falcon will provide a modem, secure communications infrastructure for deployed formations and operating bases. As such it will help to deliver an information infrastructure that will provide the UK Armed Forces with the network enabled capability required in the 21st century. The contract is valued at over £200 million and the equipment will enter into service at the turn of the decade (possibly 2011).

Euromux

EUROMUX is a trunk system manufactured by Racal (now part of the French Thales group), which is similar in principle to the Ptarmigan system, and is interoperable with the trunk systems of other NATO armies. Triffid is used to provide the relay links within the system.

Cormorant

In service with 2 Signal Regiment, Cormorant will deliver new area communications capabilities to British Forces and the prime contractor for the Cormorant programme is the European EADS company. Cormorant will comprise two primary equipments: a local access component, based on an ATM switch, which will provide digital voice subscriber facilities and a high speed data LAN for over 20 Headquarters; and a wide area component will allow the interconnection of these Headquarters, on a 'backbone' communications network across a large geographical area as well as the means to interconnect with single service and multinational systems.

Designed to link all components of a Joint Force, the system will enable the force to deploy and operate its Wide Area Network (WAN) communications system in either peacekeeping roles or in a fully operational military deployment. The system is fully containerised and can be operated in either vehicle mounted or dismounted mode. Each small HQ is designed to scale up in line with the requirements of a particular operation.

A Cormorant network can consist of the following vehicle-mounted (or dismounted) installations:

- Local Area Support module
- Core Element
- Bearer Module
- Long-Range Bearer Module (Tropo)
- Management Information Systems
- Interoperable Gateways
- Tactical Fibre Optic cabling
- Short-Range Radio

Triffid

Radio relay links within Ptarmigan are provided by Triffid, which is radio equipment that has three interchangeable radio frequency modules known as 'heads'. Each Triffid link carries the equivalent of up to 32 voice circuits at a data rate of 512 kb/s plus an engineering circuit.

Promina

Promina networks deliver pulse code modulation (PCM) and compressed digital analogue voice, video conferencing, Internet Protocol (IP) frame relay, Asynchronous transfer mode (ATM) and legacy Synchronous and Asynchronous data services over satellite, microwave, radio and leased line services.

It is extensively used to multiplex Ptarmigan, ATacCS, and JOCS systems alongside traditional voice, video and fax services over a common bearer. Promina networks form the core of NATO and Joint Force HQs, and are deployable for rapid reaction corps.

Combat Net Radio

VHF Combat Net Radios (CNR) provide the main tactical communications for battalions and battlegroups with their sub-units down to section level. CNR communications are the responsibility of the units themselves, and the Royal Signals have no direct role in supporting these networks. Like other combat arms, Royal Signals units are equipped with CNR for their own tactical communications.

Bowman

The Bowman family of digital radios, and the associated Combat Infrastructure Platform (CIP), are key to the plans of the Ministry of Defence (the Department), to transform military communications and enable the Armed Forces to operate more effectively and at a quicker pace. The pressing need to replace the ageing Clansman radios used since the 1970s with reliable, secure voice communications has made Bowman one of the UK Army's top priorities.

By enabling transmission of large quantities of electronic data Bowman is intended to provide information on the position of UK forces, and forms the underlying network to carry the CIP (Combat Infrastructure Programme). CIP is intended to replace and automate many existing manual processes for command and control on the battlefield. It is also key to plans for 'Network Enabled Capability'; joining up military communications and electronic systems in a 'network of networks'. The ability to see the position of UK forces, on screens in vehicles and headquarters, should amongst other benefits, help to reduce the frequency of 'friendly fire' incidents.

The secure radio capability provided by Bowman has only recently begun to enter service, later than originally intended, Though Bowman was declared in service in March 2004 and many useful new capabilities have since been delivered, conversion of vehicles and units has been slower than envisaged. The Bowman project covers all the VHF and HF radio configurations used as manpacks or installed in land, sea and air platforms.

The Royal Signals is playing a major role in the introduction into service of Bowman. The outline Bowman conversion programme is as follows:

2004 – 2006: 12 Mechanised Brigade; 4 Armoured and 7 Armoured Brigades; 1 Mechanised Brigade; 16 Air Assault Brigade and 3 Commando Brigade.

2007 – 2008: 19 Light Brigade and 20 Armoured Brigade

The programme involves conversion of up to 15,700 land vehicles, 141 naval vessels, and 60 helicopters (mainly Chinook and Merlin), with training for some 75,000 service personnel. Contracts worth £2.4 billion were placed with General Dynamics UK, in 2001 for Bowman and in 2002 for the Combat Infrastructure Programme (CIP). Around 45,000 Personal Role Radios, 47,000 manpack and vehicle radios, and 26,000 computer terminals are being acquired.

The system is being designed to provide, in conjunction with Ptarmigan, Cormorant, and in time (probably from about 2011 onward) Falcon, integrated digital communications network across the whole battlefield.

Reports in early 2007 suggested that work is proceeding on how best to improve the portability of the Bowman VHF manpack radio, aiming to deliver an improved solution for specific roles which will be based on a re-engineered and lighter radio. This should be introduced over the next two years.

Satellite Communications (SATCOM)
30 Signal Regiment deploys transportable and manpack satellite ground stations – VSC501, Talon, and in the future Reacher – to provide communications links for headquarters or small groups located in remote parts of the world via its SKYNET 4B satellite system and the new Skynet 5 satellites.

Skynet 5 satellite series
A new series of SKYNET 5 satellites is expected to enhance SATCOM facilities in the future. In 2003, the Skynet 5 contract was awarded to Paradigm. The company is tasked with delivering secure military satellite communications to UK armed forces around the world. The contract is worth around £2 billion over 20 years. This is one of the largest private finance initiatives (PFI) of its kind. Skynet 5 became operational in 2007.

The capacity of Skynet 5 is expected to be about 2.5 times greater than the existing system. Users will be able to send and receive information much more quickly. The Skynet 5 series (A, B and C) will deliver military satellite communication services to the Armed Forces until 2018.

Skynet 5A: During April 2007 Skynet 5A was launched. Skynet 5A, is the first of three satellites to be launched under a £3 billion Private Finance Initiative (PFI) programme which has seen the UK MoD working in partnership with Paradigm Secure Communications, who are the service providers, and EADS-Astrium, who built the satellite itself.

The satellite, with its antenna technology and high power and data rates, provides a significant enhancement to operational capability for the UK Armed Forces – whether deployed in Iraq, Afghanistan or at sea. It is also being used in the field of welfare services, to provide 'free' messages between service personnel on operations and their families and friends.

The Skynet 5A communications satellite, in orbit 40,000 km above the earth's surface, beams communications signals between headquarters in the UK and British forces deployed across the globe.

The next satellite, Skynet 5B, is due to be launched towards the end of 2007 and Skynet 5C in 2008.

VSC501 satellite ground terminal
The VSC501 Enhanced is a Land Rover based mobile satellite ground terminal, which has recently been upgraded to automatically track satellites in their figure of eight orbit. Its first major deployment was to Iraq during the first Gulf War and it is currently in service in Iraq on Operation Telic.

Talon satellite ground terminal
Talon is a lightweight deployable terminal to fulfil both tactical and strategic roles. Talon is easily transported and set up, by a crew of two trained operators within 30 minutes. Talon has been successfully used by the ARRC (Allied Rapid Reaction Corps) in Germany for one year, and used extensively in the harsh conditions experienced during Operation Telic in Iraq.

Reacher satellite ground terminal
Reacher is designated as the replacement for the VSC 501, and will be provided in three types:
Reacher Medium – a land terminal specifically designed for X-Band Military Satellite Communications. Designed to operate with a Forward Operating Headquarters Unit, it is mounted on a Bucher Duro 6 x 6 vehicle and has a detachable Intermediate Group cabin and associated trailer.

Reacher Large – mounted on the same vehicle as the Reacher Medium, this unit has a larger antenna.

Reacher All Terrain – mounted on two BV206 vehicles and associated trailers.

All Reacher terminals are transportable using Chinook helicopters, C130 Aircraft, sea and rail.

NCRS

The NCRS HF communications system was accepted into service in 1995, and is known to be operated by 32 Signal Regiment (V) in Scotland. A total of 104 NCRS stations were made, consisting of 89 trailer-mounted mobile stations and 15 static, transportable stations. All the stations are identical with the exception of five mobile stations which have high power radios.

NCRS can provide a powerful national network capable of operating in the most extreme circumstances. The network can be deployed at short notice to support a wide range of national operations. NCRS stations include a variety of mobile, static, high and low powered types. Each detachment has a crew of six.

MOULD

Mould is an insecure VHF radio system that uses hilltop sites to provide national radio coverage. The radios are normally grouped together to form regional radio nets.

Army Fixed Telecommunications Systems

The peacetime management of the Army depends heavily on effective communications. The Royal Signals Army Fixed Telecommunication System (AFTS) provides all the telephone, telegraph, facsimile, data systems and radio and line links for the Army in the United Kingdom. AFTS is operated and maintained by 2 (National Communications) Brigade and the system serves over 40,000 subscribers. The staff required to operate the AFTS is approximately 1,100 of whom 40% are military personnel who are located all over the UK in six (Fixed Service) Signal Squadrons supported by operational, engineering, planning and co-ordination staff at Headquarters 2 (NC) Brigade at Corsham in Wiltshire.

One of the ADP systems in the UK is MAPPER, which stands for Maintenance, Preparation and Presentation of Executive Reports. This system is used both as a peacetime management aid to staffs in major headquarters but also for command and control of Military Home Defence and was expanded for use in the Gulf War when MAPPER stations were deployed to Saudi Arabia and linked back to the United Kingdom. Its success in the Gulf has led to the system being used in post-Gulf War operations including the Balkans.

In Germany the Telecommunications Group Headquarters based at Rheindahlen provides a sophisticated fixed communications system based on the Integrated Services Digital Network (ISDN). Project Rodin which is intended to modernise the fixed communications system for both the Army and the RAF in Germany will, when introduced, use state of the art digital technology and will be able to interact with other German and British military and civilian networks.

The Communications Projects Division (CPD) provides engineering support for military fixed communications systems worldwide. CPD is part of the Royal School of Signals at Blandford in Dorset.

BRAHMS

This is a voice encryption terminal equipment that provides secure speech over a civil or military phone system.

DUST

An encrypted telegraph system providing secure telegraph over a civil or military bearer system.

Computer Information Systems (CIS)

ATacCS

The Army Tactical Computer System (ATacCS) provides the British Army with a LAN (Local Area Network) and WAN (Wide Area Network) based command and control system for in and out of barracks use across the whole battlespace. The majority of system managers and maintainers for this system are Royal Signals personnel.

JOCS

The formation of the Joint Rapid Reaction Force led to a requirement for a joint computer system. The Joint Operational Command System (JOCS) was brought into service during 1999. This system provides a sophisticated operational picture, along with staff tools for controlling joint operations.

DCM

Deployable CIS Modules (DCM) are a combination of Local Area Network and Wide Area Network (LAN/WAN), Integrated Digital Exchanges, fibre optic connections and a satellite interface capability.

Wavell

Wavell is a battlefield automatic data processing computer system, designed to accept information from all the battlefield intelligence agencies, and produce this information on request in hard copy or on a VDU. Information is then used to assist commanders and their staff with the analysis of intelligence and subsequent conduct of operations. Each headquarters from Corps down to Brigade level is equipped with its own Wavell computers that are linked to the Ptarmigan system. Wavell was continually upgraded during the 1990s.

Slim

Slim has been developed to complement Wavell.

Vixen

Vixen has been designed to provide an automated system for processing of electronic intelligence. It is probably mounted in soft-skinned vehicles and deployed with the 14 Signal Regiment (EW) which amongst its many tasks listens to enemy signal traffic and passes vital intelligence to the operational staff. Vixen became operational in late 1992 and it is probable that the system is linked to the existing electronic direction finding equipment subsequently feeding results into the battlefield artillery target engagement system (BATES) and Wavell ADP systems. The cost of the Vixen system was believed to be in the region of £36.5 million.

CHAPTER 10 – COMBAT SERVICE SUPPORT

LOGISTIC OVERVIEW

In the British Army logistic support is based upon the twin pillars of service support (the supply chain) and equipment support (the maintenance of equipment).

Combat Service Support within the British Army is provided by the Royal Logistic Corps (RLC), the Royal Electrical and Mechanical Engineers (REME) and the Royal Army Medical Corps (RAMC).

Within any fighting formation logistic units from these Corps typically represent about 30% of the manpower total of a division, and with the exception of certain members of the RAMC all are fully trained fighting soldiers.

The task of the logistic units on operations is to maintain the combat units in the field which entails:

- ♦ Supply and Distribution – of ammunition, fuel, lubricants, rations and spare parts
- ♦ Recovery and Repair – of battle damaged and unserviceable equipment.
- ♦ Treatment and Evacuation – of casualties.

In an operational division the commanders of the logistic units all operate from a separate, self contained headquarters under the command of a Colonel who holds the appointment of the Division's Deputy Chief of Staff (DCOS). This headquarters, usually known as the Divisional Headquarters (Rear), co-ordinates the whole of the logistic support of the Division in battle.

Supplies, reinforcements and returning casualties pass through an area located to the rear of the division where some of the less mobile logistic units are located. This area is known as the Divisional Admin Area (DAA) and its staff are responsible for co-ordinating the flow of all materiel and personnel into and out of the Divisional Area.

THE ROYAL LOGISTIC CORPS (RLC)

The RLC is the youngest Corps in the Army and was formed in April 1993 as a result of the recommendations of the Logistic Support Review. The RLC results from the amalgamation of the Royal Corps of Transport (RCT), the Royal Army Ordnance Corps (RAOC), the Army Catering Corps (ACC), the Royal Pioneer Corps (RPC) and some elements of the Royal Engineers (RE). During January 2007 the RLC comprised 15,700 personnel and was at almost 100% of its established strength.

There are 20 Regular RLC Regiments (18 operational and two training regiments) and under the terms of the Future Army Structure the RLC TA is structured around 15 regiments plus the Catering Support Regiment RLC (V).

The RLC has very broad responsibilities throughout the Army including the movement of personnel throughout the world, the Army's air dispatch service, maritime and rail transport, operational re-supply, explosive ordnance disposal, which includes hazardous bomb disposal duties. Other areas of responsibility include the operation of numerous very large vehicle and stores depots both in the UK and overseas, the training and provision of cooks to virtually all units in the Army, the provision of pioneer labour and the Army's postal and courier service.

The principal field elements of the RLC are the Logistic Support and Transport Regiments whose primary role is to supply the fighting units with ammunition, fuel and rations (Combat Supplies).

A division usually has an integral Logistic Support Regiment which is responsible for manning and operating the supply chain to Brigades and Divisional units.

Logistic Support Regiment RLC

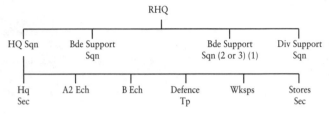

Note:
(1) A regiment could have two or three brigade support squadrons depending upon the size of the division/formation being supported.
(2) Depending on the composition of the formation being supported, some of these regiments may have an Artillery Support Squadron and/or a Postal and Courier Squadron. In addition for some operations a Tank Transporter Squadron may be required. The Artillery Support Squadron delivers artillery ammunition using DROPS vehicles. Tank Transporter Squadrons provide tank transporters that move armoured vehicles more rapidly and economically than moving them on their own tracks.

Brigade Support Squadron

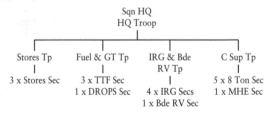

Divisional Support Squadron

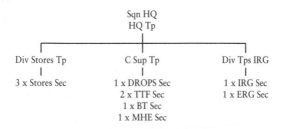

RLC Regiments have large sections holding stores both on wheels and on the ground. A division on operations will typically require about 1,000 tons of Combat Supplies a day but demand can easily exceed that amount in high intensity operations.

Battle groups in contact with the enemy can carry a limited amount of C Sups, particularly ammunition. As ammunition is expended, it is replenished from RLC vehicles located immediately to the rear of battle groups in an Immediate Replenishment Group (IRG) area. As the IRG vehicles are emptied they return to the RLC Squadron location and fully loaded replacements are automatically sent forward. This system ensures that a constant supply is always available to the battle group.

Ammunition and spares are generally carried on NATO standard pallets. These pallets are loaded to meet the anticipated requirements of particular units and if required, bulk consignments are broken down at the IRG location. Fuel is usually carried in bulk fuel tankers (TTFs) which top-up battle group vehicles direct. However there is still a requirement for a large number of the traditional jerricans. Within the NATO area large amounts of fuel can be delivered to the forward areas through the NATO Central European Pipeline System (CEPS).

During high intensity operations artillery ammunition constitutes by far the largest single element in the logistic pipeline. The bulk of this ammunition is delivered directly to the Royal Artillery guns, rocket and missile launchers by RLC Demountable Rack Off Loading and Pickup System (DROPS) vehicles from the Artillery Support Squadrons. DROPS vehicles are capable of meeting the requirement of even the highest intensity consumption.

RLC miscellaneous units

Apart from the RLC units that provide direct support to the operational formations, the RLC is either directly responsible for or co-located with other agencies at the following:

Ordnance Depots
Ammunition Depots
Army School of Ammunition
Army Petroleum Centre
Defence School of Mechanical Transport

Army School of Catering (Aldershot)
Royal Logistic Corps Training Centre (Deepcut)

Vehicles

Although many of the vehicles operated by the RLC are common to all arms, RLC units are in the main the majority users. During April 2005 a £1 billion contract awarded to MAN ERF, will see the delivery from late 2007 onwards of over 5,000 modern, versatile and robust support vehicles, with an option to buy up to 2,000 more.

The vehicles will be capable of transporting large quantities of bulk equipment to front-line troops wherever they are operating. The new fleet will consist of a mix of cargo and recovery vehicles. They will replace the MoD's tri-service fleet of four, eight and 14 tonne cargo vehicles and recovery trucks.

During 2005 the British Army vehicle fleet was based around the following vehicles:

Vehicle type	Army
Bedford 4 Tonne	5,002
Bedford 8 Tonne	1,460
Bedford 14 Tonne	900
Leyland-Daf Trucks	3,796
Ambulances operational	780
Ambulances non-operational	11
Land Rover operational	12,191
Land Rover non-operational	148

Daily Messing Rates

The allowances per day for catering purposes are based on a ration scale costed at current prices and known as the daily messing rate (DMR). The ration scale is the same for all three services and contrary to popular army belief the RAF are not supplied with wine etc at public expense. The rate per day is the amount that the catering organisation has to feed each individual serviceman or servicewoman.

The scale is costed to the supply source of the food items. When the source of supply is more expensive due to local conditions the DMR is set higher to take account of local costs. A general overseas ration scale exists for overseas bases and attachments. This scale has a higher calorific value to take into account the conditions of heat, cold or humidity that can be encountered.

RLC Catering Units feed the Army generally using detachments of cooks attached to units.

During early 2007 the daily messing rate (DMR) was approximately £1.51 per day per soldier in the UK. With this amount, RLC cooks in barracks have to provide three meals per day. The DMR for personnel serving in both Iraq and Afghanistan is £3.11 per day. These figures are adjusted on a monthly basis.

Ration scales vary according to location. The home ration scale in the UK is designed to provide 2,900 kilo-calories nett – that is, after loss through preparation and cooking. The general overseas ration scale used in overseas bases, includes an arduous duty allowance, to allow for climate and provides 3,400 kilo-calories nett. In field conditions, where personnel are fed from operational ration packs, 3,800 kilo-calories are provided.

Army cooks are trained at the The Defence Food Services School – Army (DFSS (A)) which was established in April 2004 as part of an organisation to serve the Army, Royal Navy and Royal Air Force. Before this, it was known as The Army School of Catering, founded in 1943, as part of the Army Catering Corps. DFSS (A) is located at Aldershot.

Postal

The Central Army Post Office (APO) is located in London and there are individual British Forces Post Offices (BFPO) wherever British Forces are stationed, plus Postal and Courier Squadrons with 29 Regiment (UK) and 24 Regiment (Germany). During the period 17 November-15 December 2004 approximately 112,000 kg of packets of mail (approximately 110 tons) were successfully processed by the British Forces Post Office Depot at Mill Hill so that they would reach service personnel deployed worldwide in time for Christmas.

THE ROYAL ELECTRICAL & MECHANICAL ENGINEERS – REME

Equipment Support remains separate from the other logistic pillar of Service Support and consequently the REME has retained not only its own identity but expanded its responsibilities. Equipment Support encompasses equipment management, engineering support, supply management, provisioning for vehicle and technical spares and financial management responsibilities for in-service equipment.

The aim of the REME is "To keep operationally fit equipment in the hands of the troops" and in the current financial environment it is important that this is carried out at the minimum possible cost. The equipment that REME is responsible for ranges from small arms and trucks to helicopters and main battle tanks. All field force units have some integral REME support (first line support) which will vary, depending on the size of the unit and the equipment held, from a few attached tradesmen up to a large Regimental Workshop of over 200 men. In war, REME is responsible for the recovery and repair of battle damaged and unserviceable equipment.

The development of highly technical weapon systems and other equipment has meant that REME has had to balance engineering and tactical considerations. On the one hand the increased scope for forward repair of equipment reduces the time out of action, but on the other hand engineering stability is required for the repair of complex systems.

Seven REME Equipment Support Battalions have been established. Six of these battalions provide second line support for the British contribution to the ACE Rapid Reaction Corps (ARRC) and formations in the UK. Three battalions are based in the UK and three battalions are based in Germany to support 1(UK) Armoured Division. An Equipment Support Aviation Battalion in the UK supports the Army Air Corps units assigned to the Joint Helicopter Command.

In January 2007 the REME had a total of 9,730 personnel against a requirement of 9,680.

There are currently four TA REME Equipment Support Battalions (1,557 personnel) but under the Future Army Structure proposals, each armoured and mechanised brigade will be supported by a REME Battalion.

REME Equipment Support Battalion (Outline)

The Close Support Company will normally deploy a number of FRG's (Forward Repair Groups) and MRGs (Medium Repair Groups) in support of brigades. The company is mobile with armoured repair and recovery vehicles able to operate in the forward areas, carrying out forward repair of key nominated equipment often by the exchange of major assemblies. It is also capable of carrying out field repairs on priority equipment including telecommunications equipment, and the repair of damage sustained by critical battle winning equipments.

The role of the General Support Company is to support the Close Support Companies and Divisional Troops. Tasks include the regeneration of fit power packs for use in forward repair and the repair of equipment back loaded from Close Support Companies. The General Support Company will normally be located to the rear of the divisional area in order to maximise productivity and minimise vulnerability.

Expect an Equipment Support Battalion to have approximately 450 personnel.

REME LAD (Light Aid Detachment)
Major divisional units have their own REME support organisation generally called the LAD which can vary in size from about 60 to 120 personnel. Usually commanded by a Captain, LADs are capable of quick repairs at the point of failure.

In manpower terms the REME LAD support available to the units of a division might resemble the following:

Armoured Regiment	120
Formation Reconnaissance Regiment	90
Armoured Infantry Battalion	90
Close Support Engineer Regiment	85
General Support Engineer Regiment	110
Field Regiment Royal Artillery	115
Air Defence Regiment Royal Artillery	160
Army Air Corps Regiment	130
Signals Regiment	60
RLC Logistic Support Regiment	75

Defence Medical Services Department (DMSD)

DMSD is the headquarters for the Defence Medical Services. The clinical director of the DMSD is the Surgeon General (SG). DMSD is a Joint Service organisation with personnel from all three services and MoD Civil Servants working together to ensure "Provision of strategic direction to the Defence Medical Services to ensure coherent delivery of all medical outputs".

Single Service Medical Care

The three armed forces maintain their own medical services that provide medical support worldwide in both peace and war.

Royal Naval Medical Service (RNMS)
Army Medical Services (AMS)
Royal Air Forces Medical Services (RAF MS)

Hospital Care

In the UK, hospital care is provided at Ministry of Defence Hospital Units (MDHU).

The Defence Medical Services Department (DMSD) has contracts with the NHS for provision of care in MDHUs, which are run as military units embedded within selected NHS hospitals. There are MDHUs at Derriford (Plymouth), Frimley Park (Aldershot), Northallerton (near Catterick), Peterborough and Portsmouth.

In addition, the Defence Medical Services runs a number of other units which include the Royal Centre for Defence Medicine (Birmingham) and the Defence Services Medical Rehabilitation Centre (Headley Court). There are also two military hospitals, one in Cyprus and the other in Gibraltar.

In Iraq the 'Role 3' Field Hospital at Shaibah provides medical support that includes primary surgery, an intensive care unit, medium and low dependency nursing care beds and diagnostic support, as well as emergency medical care.
Service personnel serving in Germany who require hospital care are treated in one of the five German Provider Hospitals.

Royal Centre for Defence Medicine (RCDM)

The RCDM in Birmingham provides a centre for military personnel requiring specialised care, and incorporates a facility for the treatment of service personnel who have been evacuated from an overseas deployment area after becoming ill or wounded/injured. RCDM also acts as a centre for the training of Defence Medical Service personnel.

In operation since 2001 the RCDM operates on a contract between the DMSD and the University Hospitals Birmingham (UHB) NHS Trust.

The RCDM is a Joint Service establishment with medical personnel from all three of the armed services wearing their respective Naval, Army, or Air Force uniforms.

Medical support to members of the British Army is provided by the Army Medical Services which consists of the following Corps:

Royal Army Medical Corps
Queen Alexandra's Royal Army Nursing Corps
Royal Army Dental Corps
Royal Army Veterinary Corps

The Royal Army Medical Corps (RAMC)

In peace, the personnel of the RAMC are based at the various medical installations throughout the world or in field force units and they are responsible for the health of the Army.

On operations, the RAMC is responsible for the care of the sick and wounded, with the subsequent evacuation of the wounded to hospitals in the rear areas. This is achieved by the provision of Close Support Medical Regiments (to treat front line casualties) and General Support Medical Regiments where more major procedures can be carried out some distance behind the front line, before evacuation to a Field Hospital where a full range of medical facilities is available.

Each Brigade has a medical squadron (from a Close Support Medical Regiment) allocated which is generally a regular unit (in some cases this may be a TA unit) that operates in direct support of the battle groups. These units are either armoured, airmobile or parachute trained. There are generally extra medical squadrons that provide support at the divisional level; once again these squadrons can be either regular or TA. These divisional squadrons provide medical support for the divisional troops and can act as manoeuvre units for the forward brigades when required.

All medical squadrons have medical sections that consist of a Medical Officer and eight Combat Medical Technicians. These sub-units are located with the battle group or units being supported and they provide the necessary first line medical support. In addition, the field provides a dressing station where casualties are treated and may be resuscitated or stabilised before transfer to a field hospital. These units have the necessary integral ambulance support both armoured and wheeled, to transfer casualties from the first to second line medical units.

Field hospitals may be Regular or TA and all are 200 bed facilities with a maximum of eight surgical teams capable of carrying out life saving operations on some of the most difficult surgical cases. Since 1990 regular medical units have been deployed on operations either in the Persian Gulf, the Former Yugoslavia, Sierra Leone, Afghanistan and Iraq.

Casualty Evacuation (CASEVAC) is by ambulance, either armoured or wheeled and driven by RLC personnel, or by helicopter when such aircraft are available. A Chinook helicopter is capable of carrying 24 stretcher cases and a Puma can carry six stretcher cases and six sitting cases.

In early 2007 there were 5 x regular medical regiments and three field hospitals. The TA provides 12 x independent field hospitals, 2 x General Support Medical Regiments and 1 x

Casualty Evacuation Regiment. The early 2007 personnel figure for the RAMC was 2,810 against a liability of 3,270.

The Queen Alexandra's Royal Army Nursing Corps (QARANC)
The QARANC is an all-nursing and totally professionally qualified Corps. Its male and female, officer and other rank personnel, provide the necessary qualified nursing support at all levels and cover a wide variety of nursing specialities. QARANC personnel can be found anywhere in the world where Army Medical Services are required.

During early 2007 the QARANC personnel total was approximately 840.

Royal Army Dental Corps (RADC)
The RADC is a professional corps that in mid 2004 consisted of 395 officers and soldiers. The Corps fulfils the essential role of maintaining the dental health of the Army in peace and war, both at home and overseas. Qualified dentists and oral surgeons, hygienists, technicians and support ancillaries work in a wide variety of military units – from static and mobile dental clinics to field medical units, military hospitals and dental laboratories.

During early 2007 the RADC personnel total was approximately 370.

The Royal Army Veterinary Corps (RAVC)
The RAVC look after the many animals that the Army has on strength. Veterinary tasks in today's army are mainly directed towards guard or search dogs, and horses for ceremonial duties. Personnel total in early 2007 was 190.

Service Health Professions
In mid 2006 totals for health professionals in the Defence Medical Services were as follows:

Post	Number in post
Biomedical Scientist	60
Clinical Physiologist	7
Combat Medical Technician (Army)	1,620
Dental Hygienists	69
Dental Surgery Support	390
Dental Technicians	42
Environmental Health Officer	29
Environmental Health Technicians	100
Health Inspector	2
Medical Admin (RAF)	330
Medical Assistant (Royal Marine and Commando)	66
Medical Assistant (General Duties)	470
Medical Assistant (RAF)	370
Medical Assistant (Submarine)	86
Operating Department Practitioners	120
Pharmacist	10
Pharmacy Technician	43

Physiotherapist	83
Radiographer	33
Tri-Service Totals	3,930

THE ADJUTANT GENERAL'S CORPS (AGC)

The Adjutant General's Corps formed on 1 April 1992 and its sole task is the management of the Army's most precious resource, its soldiers. The Corps absorbed the functions of six existing smaller corps; the Royal Military Police, the Royal Army Pay Corps, the Royal Army Educational Corps, the Royal Army Chaplains Department, the Army Legal Corps and the Military Provost Staff Corps.

The Corps is organised into four branches with early 2007 personnel figures as follows:

Staff and Personnel Support (SPS)	4,440
Provost	2,010
Educational and Training Services	340
Army Legal Services	100

The Role of SPS Branch

The role of SPS Branch is to ensure the efficient and smooth delivery of Personnel Administration to the Army. This includes support to individual officers and soldiers in units by processing pay and Service documentation, first line provision of financial, welfare, education and resettlement guidance to individuals and the provision of clerical skills and information management to ensure the smooth day to day running of the unit or department.

AGC (SPS) officers are employed throughout the Army, in direct support of units as Regimental Administrative Officers or AGC Detachment Commanders. They hold Commander AGC (SPS) and SO2 AGC (SPS) posts in district/Divisional and Brigade HQs and fill posts at the Adjutant General's Information Centre (AGIC) and general staff appointment throughout the Army headquarters locations.

AGC (SPS) soldiers are employed as Military Clerks in direct support of units within the AGC Field Detachments, in fixed centre pay offices, in headquarters to provide staff support and in miscellaneous posts such as embassy clerks, as management accountants or in AGIC as programmer analysts.

The principal functional tasks of AGC (SPS) personnel on operations are:

a. The maintenance of Field Records, including the soldiers 'Record of Service', casualty reporting and disciplinary documentation.

b. Clerical and staff support to Battle Group HQs and independent Sub Units such as Engineer and Logistic Squadrons.

c. The issue of pay and allowances to personnel.

d. The maintenance of Imprest Accounts (the MoD Public Accounts) which involve paying local suppliers for services, receiving cash from non-Army agencies such as NAAFI and Forces Post Office receipts.

e. The deployment of a Field Records Cell which co-ordinates all personnel administration in the field.

f. AGC (SPS) personnel play a full part in operational duties by undertaking such tasks as local defence, guard and command post duties. In addition, Command Officers can employ any soldier in their unit as they see fit and may require AGC (SPS) personnel to undertake appropriate additional training to allow them to be used in some specialist roles specific to the unit, or as radio operators or drivers.

Currently, about 70% of AGC (SPS) soldiers are based in UK, 20% in Germany and 10% elsewhere. The majority, currently 70% are serving with field force units, with the remaining 30% in base and training units or HQs, such as MoD.

Members of AGC (SPS) are first trained as soldiers and then specialise as Military Clerks. AGC (SPS) officers complete the same military training as their counterparts in other Arms and Services, starting as the Royal Military Academy, Sandhurst. They are required to attend all promotion courses such as the Junior Command and Staff Course, and to pass the standard career exams prior to promotion to the rank of Major.

The Role of the Provost Branch

Provost comprises the Royal Military Police (RMP), the Military Provost Staff (MPS) and the Military Provost Guard Service (MPGS). The main role of the RMP is to 'Police the Force', and 'provide Police Support to the Force'. The MPS provide advice and support to Commanders on all custody and detention issues. The MPGS is the Army's professional armed guarding service, established to release general service personnel from armed guarding duties.

Provost Mission: To provide the necessary military police, custodial and guarding service to the Army in order to ensure military effectiveness.

The Royal Military Police (RMP)

The RMP is regulatory body with unique investigative and policing skills and competencies which also undertakes military tasks complementary to its specialist role.

The RMP has three specialist areas:

Investigations: Supporting the Military Criminal Justice System is the highest priority for the RMP, who alone have the unique capability to deliver the full range of policing functions throughout the spectrum of conflict at home, in overseas garrisons and on operations. This police support is both proactive and visible, contributing to success on operations by enforcing the law, deterring crime and thus underpinning the Military Criminal Justice System.

Special Investigations: The Special Investigations Branch (SIB) of the RMP is responsible for all special and sensitive investigations. In high intensity conflict they continue to police, investigating a range of offences ranging from murder to fratricide; the investigative procedure is the same, only the operational context changes.

Close Protection (CP): RMP provide CP personnel and training for others on CP duties, both for at risk military personnel and those of other government departments. The RMP provides a core of trained manpower at high readiness to cover contingencies and can also generate Short Term Training Teams.

In addition, the RMP also provide:

- The provision of a specialist Crime Reduction service to reduce the opportunities for crime, to shape attitudes and to maintain morale.

- The regulation of movement and manoeuvre, such as route reconnaissance, route selection, signing and manning of routes, and the establishment of Military Police Stations and Posts.

- The training and mentoring of Indigenous Civilian and Police Forces through the provision of basic police training in the form of an investigative capability with crime scene management, interviewing skills, file preparation and possibly forensics.

- Special to arm advice directly to the operational commanders on: arrest and detention, searches of people, property or vehicles, incident control, and crime scene management. They will also provide surety to correct handling of evidence in support of pre-planned operations.

The Military Provost Staff (MPS)
The principal function of the Military Corrective Training Centre (MCTC) at Colchester, Essex, is to detain personnel, both male and female, of the three Services and civilians subject to the Services Disciplinary Acts, in accordance with the provisions of the Imprisonment and Detention (Army) Rules 1979. The MCTC is an establishment that provides corrective training for those servicemen and women sentenced to periods of detention; it is not a prison. The MCTC takes servicemen and women who have been sentenced to periods of detention from 14 days to two years. Up to 316 detainees can be held at the MCTC. The MCTC has extensive Military Training facilities and an Education Wing that includes trade training. The MPS has approximately 90 personnel.

The Military Provost Guard Services (MPGS)
The Military Provost Guard Service (MPGS) was established in 1997 as the Army's professional armed guarding service to relieve the Ministry of Defence Police and general service personnel from armed guarding duties at nominated Tri-Service locations.

The MPGS comprises regular soldiers employed on a Military Local Service Engagement that is restricted to the United Kingdom. All MPGS soldiers have had previous service experience and service may be up to the age of 55. The MPGS has approximately 1745 personnel.

The Role of the ETS Branch
The AGC (ETS) Branch has the responsibility of improving the efficiency, effectiveness and morale of the Army by providing support to operations and the developmental education, training, support and resettlement services that the Army requires to carry out its task. ETS personnel provide assistance at almost all levels of command but their most visible task is the manning of Army Education Centres wherever the Army is stationed. At these centres officers and soldiers receive the educational support necessary for them to achieve both civilian and military qualifications.

The Role of the ALS Branch

The AGC (ALS) Branch advises on all aspects of service and civilian law that may affect every level of the Army from General to Private soldiers. Members of the branch are usually qualified as solicitors or barristers.

Smaller Corps

THE INTELLIGENCE CORPS (Int Corps) – The Int Corps deals with operational intelligence, counter intelligence and security. Early 2007 the personnel strength of the Intelligence Corps was 1,440.

THE ARMY PHYSICAL TRAINING CORPS (APTC) – Consists mainly of SNCOs who are responsible for unit fitness. The majority of major units have a representative from this corps on their strength. Early 2007 personnel total was in the region of 440.

ROYAL ARMY CHAPLAIN'S DEPARTMENT (RAChD) – Provides officers and soldiers with religious and welfare support/advice. The RAChD has approximately 140 chaplains who represent all of the mainstream religions.

THE GENERAL SERVICE CORPS (GSC) – A holding unit for specialists. Personnel from this corps are generally members of the reserve army.

SMALL ARMS SCHOOL CORPS (SASC) – A small corps with the responsibility of training instructors in all aspects of weapon handling. Early 2007 personnel total was in the region of 150.

CHAPTER 11 – UNITS OF THE REGULAR ARMY (during late 2007)

The Cavalry
The cavalry consists of 11 armoured regiments and one mounted ceremonial regiment as follows:

The Household Cavalry
The Household Cavalry Regiment	HCR
The Household Cavalry Mounted Regiment	HCMRD

The Royal Armoured Corps
1st The Queen's Dragoon Guards	QDG
The Royal Scots Dragoon Guards	SCOTS DG
The Royal Dragoon Guards	RDG
The Queen's Royal Hussars	QRH
9th/12th Royal Lancers	9/12L
The King's Royal Hussars	KRH
The Light Dragoons	LD
The Queen's Royal Lancers	QRL
1st Royal Tank Regiment	1 RTR
2nd Royal Tank Regiment	2 RTR

The Infantry
Comprised of 36 battalions.

The Guards Division
1st Bn Grenadier Guards	1 GREN GDS
1st Bn Coldstream Guards	1 COLM GDS
1st Bn Scots Guards	1 SG
1st Bn Irish Guards	1 IG
1st Bn Welsh Guards	1 WG

There are generally three battalions from the Guards Division on public duties in London at any one time. When a Regiment is stationed in London on public duties it is given an extra company to ensure the additional manpower required for ceremonial events is available.

The Scottish Division
The Royal Scots Borderers, 1st Bn The Royal Regiment of Scotland	1 SCOTS
The Royal Highland Fusiliers, 2nd Bn The Royal Regiment of Scotland	2 SCOTS
The Black Watch, 3rd Bn The Royal Regiment of Scotland	3 SCOTS
The Highlanders, 4th Bn The Royal Regiment of Scotland	4 SCOTS
The Argyll and Sutherland Highlanders, 5th Bn The Royal Regiment of Scotland	5 SCOTS

The Queen's Division
1st Bn The Princess of Wales's Royal Regiment (Queen's and Royal Hampshire)	1 PWRR
2nd Bn The Princess of Wales's Royal Regiment (Queen's and Royal Hampshire)	2 PWRR
1st Bn The Royal Regiment of Fusiliers	1 RRF
2nd Bn The Royal Regiment of Fusiliers	2 RRF
1st Bn The Royal Anglian Regiment	1 R ANGLIAN
2nd Bn The Royal Anglian Regiment	2 R ANGLIAN

The King's Division
1st Bn The Duke of Lancaster's Regiment (King's, Lancashire and Border)	1 LANCS
2nd Bn The Duke of Lancaster's Regiment (King's, Lancashire and Border)	2 LANCS
4th Bn The Duke of Lancaster's Regiment (King's, Lancashire and Border)	3 LANCS
1st Bn The Yorkshire Regiment (Prince Of Wales's Own)	1 YORKS
2nd Bn The Yorkshire Regiment (Green Howards)	2 YORKS
3rd Bn The Yorkshire Regiment (Duke of Wellington's)	3 YORKS

The Prince of Wales's Division
1st Bn The Mercian Regiment (Cheshire)	1 MERCIAN
2nd Bn The Mercian Regiment (Worcesters and Foresters)	2 MERCIAN
3rd Bn The Mercian Regiment (Staffords)	3 MERCIAN
1st Bn The Royal Welsh (The Royal Welsh Fusiliers)	1 R WELSH
2nd Bn The Royal Welsh (The Royal Regiment of Wales)	2 R WELSH

The Rifles
1st Bn The Rifles	1 RIFLES
2nd Bn The Rifles	2 RIFLES
3rd Bn The Rifles	3 RIFLES
4th Bn The Rifles	4 RIFLES
5th Bn The Rifles	5 RIFLES

The Brigade of Gurkhas
1st Bn The Royal Gurkha Rifles	1 RGR
2nd Bn The Royal Gurkha Rifles	2 RGR

The Parachute Regiment
1st Bn The Parachute Regiment	1 PARA
2nd Bn The Parachute Regiment	2 PARA
3rd Bn The Parachute Regiment	3 PARA

The Royal Irish Regiment
1st Bn The Royal Irish Regiment	1 R IRISH

Since April 2002 there have been four infantry training battalions at the Infantry Training Centre located at Catterick in North Yorkshire.

Under Director Special Forces

The 22nd Special Air Service Regiment	22 SAS
Special Reconnaissance Regiment	SRR

The SAS can be classed as an infantry unit but the members of the regiment are found from all arms and services in the Army after exhaustive selection tests.

The Royal Regiment of Artillery (RA)

1st Regiment Royal Horse Artillery	1 RHA
3rd Regiment Royal Horse Artillery	3 RHA
4th Regiment	4 REGT
5th Regiment	5 REGT
7th Regiment Royal Horse Artillery	7 RHA
12th Regiment	12 REGT
14th Regiment	14 REGT
16th Regiment	16 REGT
19th Regiment	19 REGT
26th Regiment	26 REGT
29th Commando Regiment	29 REGT
32nd Regiment	32 REGT
39th Regiment	39 REGT
40th Regiment	40 REGT
47th Regiment	47 REGT

The Corps of Royal Engineers (RE)

21st Engineer Regiment	21 ENGR REGT
22nd Engineer Regiment	22 ENGR REGT
23rd Engineer Regiment	23 ENGR REGT
24th Commando Regiment	24 CDO REGT
25th Engineer Regiment	25 ENGR REGT
26th Engineer Regiment	26 ENGR REGT
28th Engineer Regiment	28 ENGR REGT
32nd Engineer Regiment	32 ENGR REGT
33rd Engineer Regiment (EOD)	33 ENGR REGT
35th Engineer Regiment	35 ENGR REGT
36th Engineer Regiment	36 ENGR REGT
38th Engineer Regiment	38 ENGR REGT
39th Engineer Regiment	39 ENGR REGT
42nd Engineer Regiment	42 ENGR REGT

There are two training regiments:

1st RSME Regiment	1 RSME REGT
3rd RSME Regiment	3 RSME REGT

The Royal Corps of Signals (R SIGNALS)

1st (UK) Armd Div HQ and Signal Regiment	1 SIG REGT
2nd Signal Regiment	2 SIG REGT
3rd (UK) Div HQ & Signal Regiment	3 SIG REGT
7th (ARRC) Signal Regiment	7 SIG REGT
10th Signal Regiment	10 SIG REGT
11th Signal Regiment (Trg Regt)	11 SIG REGT
14th Signal Regiment (Electronic Warfare)	14 SIG REGT
16th Signal Regiment	16 SIG REGT
21st Signal Regiment (Air Support)	21 SIG REGT
22nd Signal Regiment	22 SIG REGT
30th Signal Regiment	30 SIG REGT
Queen's Gurkha Signals	QGS

The Army Air Corps (AAC)

1st Regiment	1 REGT AAC
2nd Regiment (Training)	2 REGT AAC
3rd Regiment	3 REGT AAC
4th Regiment	4 REGT AAC
5th Regiment	5 REGT AAC
9th Regiment	9 REGT AAC

6th and 7th Regiments AAC are TA units.

THE SERVICES

The Royal Logistic Corps (RLC)

1st Logistic Support Regiment	1 LOG REGT
2nd Logistic Support Regiment	2 LOG REGT
3rd Logistic Support Regiment	3 LOG REGT
4th Logistic Support Regiment	4 LOG REGT
5th Territorial Army Training Regiment	5 (TRG) REGT
6th Supply Regiment	6 (SUP) REGT
7th Transport Regiment	7 (TPT) REGT
8th Transport Regiment	8 (TPT) REGT
9th Supply Regiment	9 (SUP) REGT
10th Transport Regiment	10 (TPT) REGT
11th Explosive Ordnance Disposal Regiment	11 (EOD) REGT
12th Logistic Support Regiment	12 LOG REGT
13th Air Assault Regiment	13 REGT
17 th Port and Maritime Regiment	17 (PORT) REGT

23rd Pioneer Regiment	23 (PNR) REGT
24th Postal, Courier & Movements Regiments	24 (PC&MOV) REGT
27th Transport Regiment	27 (TPT) REGT
29th Postal, Courier & Movements Regiment	29 (PC&MOV) REGT

The Queens's Own Gurkha Logistic Regiment (QOGLR) consists of a Regimental Headquarters and 2 x operational squadrons. 28 Transport Squadron serves with 10 Transport Regiment and 94 Stores Squadron with 9 Supply Regiment.

There are 2 x Combat Service Support (CSS) Battalions. One is with the Royal Marines 3rd Commando Brigade and another with 19 Light Brigade.

Royal Electrical and Mechanical Engineers (REME)

1st Bn REME	1 BN REME
2nd Bn REME	2 BN REME
3rd Bn REME	3 BN REME
4th Bn REME	4 BN REME
5th Bn REME	5 BN REME
6th Bn REME	6 BN REME
7th Bn REME	7 BN REME

Royal Army Medical Corps (RAMC)

1st Close Support Medical Regiment	1 CS MED REGT
3rd Close Support Medical Regiment	3 CD MED REGT
4th General Support Medical Regiment	4 GS MED REGT
5th General Support Medical Regiment	5 GS MED REGT
16th Close Support Medical Regiment	16 CS MED REGT
22nd Field Hospital	22 FD HOSP
33rd Field Hospital	33 FD HOSP
34th Field Hospital	34 FD HOSP

Military Bands

Following the latest (2007) re-organisation of military bands in late 2007 the Regular Army has 24 bands as follows:

Household Cavalry	70 musicians	2 bands
Grenadier Guards	49 musicians	1 band
Coldstream Guards	49 musicians	1 band
Scots Guards	49 musicians	1 band
Welsh Guards	49 musicians	1 band
Irish Guards	49 musicians	1 band
Royal Artillery	49 musicians	1 band
Royal Engineers	35 musicians	1 band
Royal Signals	35 musicians	1 band
Royal Logistic Corps	35 musicians	1 band
REME	35 musicians	1 band

Adjutant General's Corps	35 musicians	1 band
Army Air Corps	35 musicians	1 band
Royal Armoured Corps	70 musicians	2 bands
Scottish Division	35 musicians	1 band
Queens Division	35 musicians	1 band
Kings Division	35 musicians	1 band
Prince of Wales's Division	35 musicians	1 band
The Rifles	35 musicians	1 band
Parachute Regiment	35 musicians	1 band
Royal Irish Regiment	35 musicians	1 band
Royal Gurkha Rifles	35 musicians	1 band

CHAPTER 12 – RECRUITING, SELECTION AND TRAINING

OVERVIEW

Recruiting can best be described as the steps taken to attract sufficient men and women of the right quality to meet the Army's personnel requirements. Selection is the process that is carried out to ensure that those who are accepted into the Army have the potential to be good soldiers and are capable of being trained to carry out their chosen trade. Training is the process of preparing those men and women for their careers in the Army. Training is progressive and continues all the way through a soldier and an officers' career.

Since the end of the Cold War and due to changing operational commitments, there have been significant changes in the organisation and structure of army training – and the process of reform continues. The Adjutant General (Personnel and Training Command) has overall responsibility for army training, and had a budget of over £1.9bn in FY 2005/2006. Since 1997, the Army Training and Recruiting Agency (ATRA) have been responsible within the Adjutant General (Personnel and Training Command) HQ for the delivery of army recruiting and training.

In 2001, the Defence Training Review (DTR) conducted by the MoD identified possibilities for the rationalisation of defence training on a joint service basis. As one consequence of the review, the Directorate General Training and Education organisation (DG T&E) was launched in September 2002 to provide a much needed central strategy and policy focus to continue the drive for more effective and better value training. Another result was the Defence Training Review Rationalisation Programme. This programme has led to the creation of joint service Federated Defence Training Establishments (DTE), which has already impacted ATRA provision of Phase 2 and Phase 3 army training, and further changes are expected.

ARMY TRAINING AND RECRUITING AGENCY

The Army Training and Recruiting Agency (ATRA) is responsible for each stage of a potential recruit's progress from the recruiting office, through a Recruit Selection Centre, into recruit training, through specialist courses before they are finally posted to their regiment in the Field Army. The ATRA is headed by the Director General Army Training and Recruiting (DGATR), a Major General who is responsible for ensuring that sufficient men and women of the right quality are recruited to meet the needs of the service.

The ATRA Headquarters is based at Upavon in Wiltshire, close to many of the training units. Recruiting is carried out from about 123 sites in towns and cities throughout the country, and individual training is conducted at some 40 schools. With a permanent staff of about 12,000, the Agency is responsible for Ministry of Defence land, buildings and field assets valued at more than one and a quarter billion pounds.

The annual ATRA budget is approximately £700m from which ATRA is required to enlist about 13,000 recruits and to train a total of about 100,000 officers and soldiers. ATRA conducts almost 1,500 different types of courses, with over 6,000 actual courses run each year. There are an average of 12,000 officers and soldiers under training at any time. Across all training phases, the average annual unit cost of training a soldier or officer is around £19,000.

ATRA operations are divided into four inter-related functions: Recruiting, Recruit training (Phase 1), Specialist training (Phase 2), and Career training (Phase 3).

RECRUITING

An MoD committee called the Standing Committee Army Manpower Forecasts (SCAMF) calculates the numbers that need to be enlisted to maintain the Army's personnel at the correct level. The Committee needs to take account of changing unit establishments, wastage caused by servicemen and women leaving the service at the end of their engagements, and those who might choose to leave before their engagements come to an end (PVR – Premature Voluntary Release). The number required in each trade in the Army is assessed and figures are published at six monthly intervals so that adjustments may be made during the year.

Within ATRA, the Recruiting Group runs all Army Recruiting from the headquarters in Upavon. Recruiting activities take place all over the country, using the network of 125 Careers Offices, 61 Schools Advisers, 26 Army Youth Teams and 93 Regimental Recruiting Teams. The Commander Recruiting Group (CRG), a Brigadier serving in ATRA and his staff, located throughout the United Kingdom are responsible for the recruiting and selection to meet the personnel targets.

Potential recruits are attracted into the Army in a number of ways including advertisements on the television, on the internet and in the press. Permanently established recruiting teams from many Regiments and Corps tour the country and staff from the Armed Forces Careers Offices (AFCO) and Army Career Information Offices (ACIO) visit schools, youth clubs and job centres. There is a network of AFCOs and ACIOs located throughout the UK. There are also Army Careers Advisers who access schools and universities throughout the country. Young, recently trained soldiers are also sent back to their home towns and schools to talk to their friends about life in the Army and are regularly interviewed by the local press.

The overall national marketing (advertising) spend for FY2006-2007 was £25.8 million (for both Regular and TA). These activities included television and press advertising, the production of DVDs, leaflets, pamphlets and brochures as well as the overarching production and design costs.

Annual Army recruiting figures (intake to untrained strength) during the recent past are as follows:

	2004/2005	2005/2006	2006/2007
Officers	680	730	720
Soldiers	10,620	11,620	12,400

Outflow figures (untrained personnel leaving the army) in the recent past are:

	2004/2005	2005/2006	2006/2007
Officers	200	90	210
Soldiers	4,230	3,660	4,480

Outflow figures (trained personnel leaving the army) in the recent past are:

	2004/2005	2005/2006	2006/2007
Officers	900	980	1060
Soldiers	10,670	10,420	10430

SOLDIER SELECTION

Potential recruits are normally aged between 16 years and nine months and 27 years, except when they are applying for a vacancy as a junior soldier when the age limits are from 16 years to 18 years and six months. As a trained soldier the minimum length of service will be four years from the age of 18, or from the start of training, if over 18.

Under the selection system, a potential recruit will have a preliminary assessment at the ACIO. Here he or she will take the computer based Army Entrance Test (AET) which is designed to assess ability to assimilate the training required for the candidate's chosen trade. The staff at the ACIO will then conduct a number of interviews to decide on overall suitability for the Army. The ACIO staff will look at references from school or any employers and offer advice on which trade may be available and might suit the candidate. A preliminary medical examination will also be carried out that checks on weight, eyesight and hearing.

If these tests and interviews are successfully passed the candidate will be booked for further tests at the Recruit Selection Centre which is closest to his or her home. Recruit selection centres are at Lichfield, Pirbright, and Ballymena in Northern Ireland.

The candidates will remain at the RSC for an overnight stay and undergo another medical examination, a physical assessment test and an interview with a Personnel Selection Officer. The potential recruit will also see at first hand the type of training that they will undergo, and the sort of life that they will lead in barracks if successful in getting into the Army. Physical fitness is assessed based on a 'best effort' 1.5 mile timed run and some gymnasium exercises. After further interviews the candidate is informed if he or she is successful and if so is offered a vacancy in a particular trade and Regiment or Corps.

PHASE 1 BASIC TRAINING FOR RECRUITS

Basic Recruit or Phase 1 training comprises the Combat Infantryman's Course (CIC) for infantry and the Common Military Syllabus Recruit (CMSR) for all other British Army regiments and corps.

Recruit Physical Training Assessments – During Recruit Training personnel are assessed at different stages of training as follows:

Test	Introduction	Interim	Final
Heaves	2	4	6
Sit Up Test	1 Min (20 reps)	2 min (42 reps)	3 min (65 reps)
1.5 Mile Run	11 min 30 sec	11 mins	10 min 30 sec

As part of ATRA, the Initial Training Group (ITG) is responsible for Phase 1 (Basic) Training of the majority of soldier recruits, which is undertaken primarily at the four Army Training Regiments; Bassingbourn in Cambridgeshire, Winchester in Hampshire, Lichfield in

Staffordshire and Pirbright in Surrey. Exceptions to this are the adult Infantry recruits who go direct to the School of Infantry at Catterick.

ITG is also responsible for the Army Foundation College at Harrogate. The group is also responsible for the Recruit Selection Centres where potential soldier recruits undergo initial selection.

Until mid 2002 the Army training organisation carried out centralised Phase 1 Training at four Army Training Regiments (ATRs). Since then, infantry recruits do all of their training at the Infantry Training Centre (Catterick).

School of Infantry, Catterick
Catterick is the home of all Infantry Training at Phase 1 and Phase 2, except Junior soldiers destined for the Infantry who continue to receive Phase 1 training at Bassingbourn and at the Army Foundation College. Catterick comprises the Headquarters School of Infantry and the Infantry Training Centre, Catterick. Also under its Command are the Infantry Battle School at Brecon and the Infantry Training Centre at Warminster, which both provide Phase 3 training for Infantry officers and soldiers.

Combat Infantryman's Course
The Combat Infantryman's Course (CIC) is the framework upon which all regular infantry recruit training is based. The course equips recruits with infantry special to arms skills needed for a rifle platoon ready to deploy on an operational tour after minimal further appropriate pre-operational training in the Field Army. Successful completion of the CIC marks the end of initial army training.

The majority of recruits joining the infantry choose line infantry regiments; they undertake the standard CIC which lasts for 24 weeks. Recruits joining the Foot Guards, Parachute Regiment and the Gurkhas, carry out additional training to meet the particular needs of these regiments. Similarly, recruits from the Army Foundation College at Harrogate undertake a specially adapted, but shorter CIC.

The Combat Infantryman's Course (Single) is structured around three phases as follows:

<u>Weeks 1-6</u> Individual skills, drill, weapons training, fitness and fieldcraft.

<u>Weeks 7-21</u> Team skills, endurance training including long runs, patrolling skills.

<u>Weeks 22 – 24</u> Live firing and battle camp at Sennybridge in Wales.

The unit costs of recruiting and training infantry are substantial, as shown in the next table.

Costs of infantry recruiting and training (Phase 1 and Phase 2)

Infantry Group	Length of course (weeks)	Cost per trainee for financial year 2003–04 (£)
Line	24	£22,000
Guards	26	£26,000
Para	28	£37,000

Royal Irish Regiment recruits also undertake the CIC at Catterick.

Gurkhas

Recruits from Nepal joining the Royal Gurkha Rifles, Queen's Gurkha Engineers, Queen's Gurkha Signals and the Queen's Own Gurkha Transport Regiment are trained at the ITC on a 38 week CIC (G). This combines the normal Common Military Syllabus Recruits (CMS(R)) course taught at the Army Training Regiments with the CIC course and it includes a special English language and British culture package.

As many as 30,000 potential Gurkha recruits apply to join the British Army each year and between 150 and 200 are selected.

Army Training Regiments

Phase 1 training for all regiments and corps except infantry comprises Common Military Syllabus Recruit (CMSR). This includes training in the basic military skills required of all soldiers and incorporates weapon handling and shooting, drill, physical fitness, field tactics, map reading, survival in nuclear chemical and biological warfare and general military knowledge. It is an intensive course and requires the recruit to show considerable determination and courage to succeed.

Since 2002, Phase 1 training for regiments and corps excluding infantry is undertaken by four Army Training Regiments as shown below:

ATR Pirbright – The Household Cavalry, The Royal Logistic Corps, the Royal Electrical and Mechanical Engineers and the Royal Artillery.

ATR Winchester – The Royal Armoured Corps, The Army Air Corps, The Adjutant General's Corps (including the Royal Military Police), The Intelligence Corps, Army Medical services and Musicians.

ATR Lichfield – The Royal Engineers and The Royal Signals.

In 2005 ATRA conducted a study to evaluate the capacity requirements for Phase 1 soldier training, and to determine the most long term economical use of the existing Phase 1 training real estate. The study identified and developed a range of options including the feasibility of closing one of the ATRs.

Junior Entry recruits

ATR Bassingbourn is the centre for training of Junior Entry recruits, most of whom will be 16 years old. The new courses are called:

a. Army Development Course (ADC)   20 weeks.

b. Army Development Course (Advanced) or (ADC(A))   29 weeks.

Both courses will train the recruits in basic soldiering, but the ADC(A) course has an additional education element – Key Skills in literacy, numbers and communication.

Army Foundation College

The Army Foundation College (AFC) at Harrogate delivers Phase 1 (initial military) training to Junior Entry recruits destined for the Royal Armoured Corps, Royal Artillery and Infantry.

Recruits make their final capbadge selection after week 21. The aim of the course is to develop the qualities of leadership, character, and team spirit required of a soldier to achieve a full career in the Army. The 42-week course is a progressive and integrated package divided into three 14-week terms. It combines the Common Military Syllabus (Recruits) with Vocational Education and Leadership and Initiative Training. Recruits achieve a Foundation Modern Apprenticeship and up to Key Skills Level 3.

Entrants to the college are aged between 16 and 17 years. They are offered the opportunity to pursue a one year Army Foundation Course. This course provides a supportive environment and the Foundation Course allows students to develop a broad range of skills and qualifications that are equally valuable in both Army and civilian life. There are three main elements to the course:

There are 23 weeks of military training, which include basic or advanced soldiering, progressive physical training, infantry weapons, grenades, military leadership, marksmanship, parade ground drill. There is also a two week final exercise in the field.

There are five weeks of leadership and initiative training which takes in hill walking, hiking, caving, rock climbing, abseiling, and all kind of leadership and command tasks.

Lastly, there are 14 weeks of vocational education which can result in an NVQ or SVQ in Information Technology.

In April 2005 the decision was taken to close the Army Technical Foundation College (ATFC) at Arborfield, and transfer students to, principally, the Army Foundation College (AFC) at Harrogate, where a technical training stream was introduced.

The former Army Technical Foundation College (ATFC) at Arborfield delivered Phase 1 (initial military) training to Junior Entry recruits in the Technical Corps: the Royal Engineers, Royal Signals, Royal Logistic Corps and Royal Electrical and Mechanical Engineers.

Phase 2 Special to Arm Recruit Training

Phase 2 training is the 'Special to Arm' training that is required to prepare soldiers who have recently completed their basic Phase 1 training, to enable them to take their place in field force units of their Regiment or Corps. This phase of training has no fixed period and courses vary considerably in length.

The 2001 Defence Training Review triggered a rationalisation of Phase 2 training facilities towards a joint service provision, where appropriate.

From 2005 Phase 2 training for the major Arms and Services of the British Army has been carried out as follows:

Infantry – Infantry recruits do all of their recruit training (Phase 1 and Phase 2) at the Infantry Training Centre at Catterick.

The Royal Armoured Corps – Training takes place at the Armour Centre at Bovington Camp and Lulworth. Recruits into the Household Cavalry Regiment also undergo equitation training.

The Royal Artillery – Training takes place at the Royal School of Artillery at Larkhill in Wiltshire.

The Royal Engineers – Training takes place at the Combat Engineering School at Minley, the Construction Engineer School in Chatham and Blackwater and the Defence Explosive Ordnance Disposal School.

Royal Signals – Training takes place at the Royal School of Signals at Blandford in Dorset. Since April 2004, the Defence College of CIS (DCCIS), based at Blandford, subsumed the responsibilities of the Royal School of Signals (RSS), and the provision of Royal Navy and Royal Air Force Signals training.

Army Air Corps – Training takes place at the School of Army Aviation in Middle Wallop

The Royal Logistic Corps – Training takes place at the RLC Training Regiment and Depot at Deepcut and the School of Logistics at Marchwood – previously under the joint Defence Logistic Support Training Group (DLSTG) and since April 2004 under Defence College of Logistics (DCL), also based at Deepcut. Under these new arrangements, ATRA is also responsible for Royal Navy and Royal Air Force Logistics training. The Army School of Catering, Aldershot, the Army School of Ammunition at Kineton and the School of Petroleum, West Moors are also ATRA logistics training facilities, as is the Defence School of Transport at Leconfield.

Royal Electrical and Mechanical Engineers – Vehicle Mechanics are trained at Bordon and other trades at Arborfield. Since April 2004, the Electro Mechanical elements of the ATRA REME Training Group transferred to the new Defence College of Electro Mechanical Engineering under the command of the Naval Recruiting and Training Agency (NRTA). The Aeronautical elements of the REME Training Group transferred to the Defence College of Aeronautical Engineering under the command of the RAF Training Group Defence Agency (TGDA). The ATRA REME Training Group ceased to exist in name at the end of 2003.

The Adjutant General's Corps – Pay and Clerks are trained at the AGC Depot at Worthy Down near Winchester. The Army School of Training Support is at Upavon, the Defence School of Languages at Beaconsfield and the Defence Animal Centre at Melton Mowbray. From April 2002, the School of Finance and Management, previously part of the Group and located at Worthy Down, became part of the Defence Academy, although it will remain at Worthy Down for the present. From April 2004, the Royal Military Police (RMP) training school transferred to the Defence College of Policing and Guarding (DCPG) at Southwick Park, Portsmouth.

Intelligence Corps – Have trained since 1997 at the Defence Intelligence and Security Centre (DISC) in Chicksands in Bedfordshire. The DISC is responsible for training all personnel in intelligence, security and information support. In June 2003, command of the Defence School of Languages transferred to DISC, although the school remained at Beaconsfield.

Army Medical Services (AMS) – Made up of the Royal Army Medical Corps (RAMC), Royal Army Dental Corps (RADC), Queen Alexandra's Royal Army Nursing Corps (QARANC), and the Royal Army Veterinary Corps (RAVC). Training is conducted by the joint service

Defence Medical Training Organisation at Aldershot and Birmingham, the Defence Dental Agency at Aldershot, and the RAVC training centre at Melton Mowbray respectively.

CONDITIONS OF SERVICE – SOLDIERS AND OFFICERS

Length of Service

As a general rule, all recruits enlist on an Open Engagement. This allows a recruit to serve for 22 years from their 18th birthday or date of attestation, whichever is the later, and so qualify for a pension.

A soldier enlisted on this engagement has a statutory right to leave after four years reckoned from the 18th birthday or from three months after attestation, whichever is the later, subject to giving 12 months notice of intention to leave and providing the soldier is not restricted from leaving in any way. Certain employments, particularly those involving a lengthy training, carry a time bar which requires a longer period before soldiers have the statutory right to leave.

For the initial period after joining the Army individuals are able to be "Discharged As Of Right" (DAOR). There is no obligation to stay during this time. The length of the period of DAOR is six months for under 18s and three months for over 18s after turning up at the Army Training Regiment. Individuals after this time are committed to serve for a minimum engagement of four years. There are of course allowances made for medical and exceptional compassionate circumstances.

Officer Commissions

There are five main types of commission in the Army. These are:

The Short Service Commission (SSC) – the SSC is the normal first commission for those who become an officer in the Army. It is a commission for those who do not wish to commit to a long career but would like to benefit from the high quality training and exceptional experience available to young officers. The SSC is also a first step to a mid-length or full career in the Army. SSCs are awarded for a minimum of three years (six years for the Army Air Corps on account of the length of pilot training) but can be extended to eight.

Candidates for commissions should be over 17 years and nine months and under 29 years old when they begin officer training.

The Intermediate Regular Commission (IRC) – The IRC offers a mid length career for a maximum of 18 years and can be applied for after two years SSC, subject to being recommended. On completion of 18 years after the age of 40 the officer will be entitled to a lump sum and regular monthly payments, which will convert at 65 to a further lump sum and pension.

The Regular Commission (Reg C) – The Reg C offers a full career of 35 years or to age 60 whichever is first. It can be applied for after two years IRC, subject to recommendation. Those completing a full career will receive an immediate lump sum and pension from age 55.

Undergraduate Army Placement (UGAP) – UGAP is a Commission for highly motivated undergraduates studying at UK universities requiring a placement as part of their degree. Up to 10 places are available each year. In all other respects the commission is identical to the GYC.

Late Entry Commissions – A number of vacancies exist for senior Non Commissioned Officers and Warrant Officers to be granted commissions known as Late Entry Commissions. They attend the Late Officer Entry Course (LEOC) at Sandhurst before commencing their officer careers. Because of their age they generally do not rise above the rank of Lieutenant Colonel.

Educational Requirements

All except LE officers require an indicative level of 35 ALIS points (34 for Scottish Standards) gained from the best seven subjects at GCSE, or equivalent, which must include English language, mathematics and either a science subject or a foreign language.

In addition a score of 180 UCAS Tariff points must be acquired in separate subjects at AS and A level, or equivalent. These must include a minimum of two passes at A level, or equivalent, at grades A-E. Note that the General Studies paper does not qualify for UCAS Tariff points.

The attainment of a degree will normally override the requirement for UCAS Tariff points.

Officer Selection and Sandhurst (RMAS)

Officer candidates are normally advised by an Army Careers Adviser of the options open to them and they will also arrange for interviews and familiarisation visits to an appropriate Regiment or Corps. If the Regiment or Corps is prepared to sponsor a candidate they then guide him or her through the rest of the selection procedure. All candidates, except those seeking an Army Sixth Form Scholarship or entry to Welbeck – The Defence Sixth Form College, are required to attend a briefing at the Army Officer Selection Board (AOSB) at Westbury, Wiltshire for psychometric tests and a 24 hour briefing. So long as they meet the minimum standards they will be invited back for a three and a half day assessment also at AOSB. Here they will also undergo a medical examination.

RCB consists of a series of interviews and tests that assess the personality and the leadership potential in applicants. Candidates need to be themselves, be prepared to discuss the issues of the day and be physically fit. In 2003/04, RCB filtered over 3800 candidates down to 1673, of whom 1010 received passes, while Territorial Commissions Board (TCB) passed 221 out of 320 candidates.

All potential officers accepted for training attend the RMAS Commissioning Course which lasts for 44 weeks with three entries a year in January, May and September. After successfully completing the Sandhurst course a young officer then completes a further specialist course with his or her chosen Regiment or Corps. Females cannot be accepted in the Household Cavalry, The Royal Armoured Corps or the Infantry.

In 2003-2004, the RMAS commissioned 622 Direct Entry Officers into the British Army and trained 68 Foreign and Commonwealth Officers to the same standards. In addition, a further 175 Late Entry Officers and 92 Professionally Qualified Officers (PQOs) successfully completed Regular Army courses at the RMAS and 197 Territorial Army (TA) Officers and 82 TA PQOs were commissioned.

Welbeck – The Defence Sixth Form College/Army Sixth Form Scholarship

Welbeck DSFC offers a two year residential A level course to motivated young people who would like, in the future, a commission in one of the more technical branches of the three Services, as well as the MoD Civil Service. Of those destined for the Army, most Welbexians will be commissioned into the Royal Engineers, the Royal Signals, the Royal Logistic Corps or the Royal Electrical and Mechanical Engineers. Both potential Welbexians and those seeking an Army Sixth Form Scholarship attend a similar 24 hour selection board at AOSB.

PHASE 3 IN-SERVICE TRAINING

An officer or soldier will spend as much as one third of their career attending training courses. Following basic Phase 1 and Phase 2 training soldiers are posted to their units and progressive training is carried out on a continual basis. Training is geared to individual, sub-unit or formation level and units regularly train outside of the UK and Germany. As would be expected there are specialist unit training packages for specific operational commitments such as Northern Ireland, Former Yugoslavia, Afghanistan, and Iraq. For example the training package for personnel warned off for deployment to either Iraq or Afghanistan special-to-mission package. The training is carried out by specialist training advisory teams at the Army's Combined Arms Training Centre at Warminster and for Germany based units at the Sennelager Training Centre.

Phase 3 training facilities are the same as those listed under Phase 2, and also include the Defence Academy located mainly at Shrivenham. Defence Academy training and education facilities incorporate the Joint Services Command and Staff College at Shrivenham; The Defence Academy College of Management and Technology (previously known as the Royal Military College of Science, Shrivenham); The Royal College of Defence Studies;The Defence Leadership Centre, and The Defence School of Finance and Management. The Joint Doctrine and Concepts Centre is collocated at Shrivenham. A Joint Services Warrant Officer's School is part of the Joint Services Command and Staff College at Shrivenham.

Army Recruiting and Training Division – Staff Leadership School

In June 2007 the Army Recruiting and Training Division Staff Leadership School opened at Pirbright in Surrey. This purpose built school provides teacher training skills, mentoring and counselling to Army trainers including those who work with new recruits. The school will train all Army Training and Supervisory Staff at Initial Training establishments a process which will ensure consistent quality and standards of training across the Army.

Overseas Students

During any one year, about 4,000 students from over 90 different countries take part in training in the United Kingdom. The charges for training depend on the length of the course, its syllabus and the number taking part. Receipts from overseas governments for this training are believed to be in the region of £40 million annually.

Training areas outside the UK and Europe

The British Army's main training areas outside of the Europe are:

Canada – Suffield

British Army Training Unit Suffield (BATUS) has the responsibility to train battlegroups in the planning and execution of armoured operations through the medium of live firing and tactical test exercise. There are 6 x 'Medicine Man' battlegroup exercises each year in a training season that lasts from March to November.

Canada – Wainright

The British Army Training Support Unit at Wainwright (BATSU(W)) provides the logistic and administrative support for Infantry units at the Canadian Forces training base in Western Canada.

Kenya

British Army Training and Liaison Staff Kenya (BATLSK) is responsible for supporting Infantry battalion group exercises and approximately 3,000 British troops train in Kenya each year in a harsh unforgiving terrain ranging in altitude from 8,000 feet down to 2,300 feet. BATLSK has been based at its present site in Kahawa Barracks since Kenya's independence in 1963.

Belize

The British Army Training Support unit Belize (BATSUB) was formed on 1 October 1994. Its role is to give training and logistic support to Land Command units training in a tropical jungle environment. In general terms BATSUB costs about £3 million per year.

Jungle Warfare School

The Jungle Warfare Wing (JWW) is located at Brunei on the island of Borneo close to the border with Sarawak (Malaysia) and is supported by the British Army's Brunei Garrison. JWW exists to provide a jungle training facility to meet the requirement to train jungle warfare instructors for the Field Army of the United Kingdom's Land Forces.

Fitness Requirements

All recruits and soldiers of all ranks and ages are required to take a basic fitness test. At the Recruiting Selection Centres, potential recruits undergo a series of tests known as Physical Standards Selection for Recruits (PSSR). These are 'best effort' tests that take place in the gymnasium. Recruits are required to complete the 1.5 mile (2.4 km) run.

Adult Entry candidates have to complete the run within 14 minutes or less. All Junior Entrants – Army Foundation College, Army Technical Foundation College or the School Leavers Scheme – are required to complete the run in 14 minutes 30 seconds or less. Officer candidates at the AOSB have to undertake a multi stage fitness test (known as the Beep Test) and aim to achieve a personal standard of 10.2 for males and 8.1 for females, as well as a number of sit-ups and press-ups.

In-service fitness requirements seek to maintain these standards. Tests typically require a 2.4 km run on level ground and in training shoes, in 10.5 minutes for those under 30. There are gradually rising time limits for older personnel. For women the requirement for the 2.4 km run is 13 minutes.

Standard fitness tests currently applied for infantry personnel include:

- BPFA Basic Personal Fitness Assessment. Sit-ups, press-ups, and a 1.5 mile (2.4km) run, all carried out against the clock. This tests individual fitness generally. The minimum fitness goals are: 54 continuous sit ups (with feet supported) and a 2.4 km (1.5 mile) run in 11 minutes 45 seconds.

- ICFT Infantry Combat Fitness Test. A distance of three miles as a squad carrying 56 pounds of kit each, including personal weapon. Timed to be completed in one hour, individuals must stay with the squad, or be failed.

CHAPTER 13 – RESERVE FORCES

There have been reserve land forces in Britain since medieval times. Over time, the titles and structures of these reserve forces have changed, but until World War Two essentially comprised four separate elements: Volunteers, Militia, and Yeomanry provided the part-time, voluntary territorial forces; while retired Regular Army personnel made up the Army Regular Reserve on a compulsory basis, subject to diminishing obligations with age. Today the Army Reserve is formed from the same components – with the difference that the erstwhile Volunteers, Militia, and Yeomanry are now incorporated into a single volunteer force as the Territorial Army (TA). Some 40% of regular Army recruits are said to come from the TA and Army Cadet Force. Currently the TA costs an estimated £400 million a year – around 1.2% of the defence budget.

Army Reserve personnel strength

As of April 2006, the total army reserve strength amounted to some 166,000 personnel of all ranks. The Ready Reserve, comprising the Army Reserve and Territorial Army, numbered some 64,000 personnel.

Army Reserve manpower, as of April 2006

Component	Category	Officers	Other ranks	Total
Regular Reserve				
	Army Reserve	9,190	22,870	32,060
	Individuals liable to recall		110,720	95,520
Volunteer Reserve				
	Territorial Army	5,840	26,590	32,150
	Non-Regular Permanent Staff	270	840	1,070
	Officer Training Corps		4,780	4.780
Total Reserve Strength	Regular Reserve + Volunteer Reserve	15,060	159,310	166,040
Ready Reserve (= Army Reserve + TA)	Army Reserve + TA	15,060	48,590	64,210

Note: OTC (Officer Training Corps) personnel numbers assume typical substantive rank of LCpl

During late October 2006 the TA strength was reported at 35,300 and the Ready Reserve at 68,690.

More than 9,000 TA personnel were called up for service in Iraq and Afghanistan in 2003 and 2004. TA officers and soldiers continue to be an important element of the overall UK force commitment to operations in both Iraq and Afghanistan.

TYPES OF RESERVIST

Members of the Army Reserve fall into two main components:

- Retired regular reserve
- Volunteer reserve

Retired regular reserve

The Regular reserve is comprised of people who have a mobilisation obligation by virtue of their former service in the Regular Army. For the most part, these reservists constitute a standby rather than ready reserve, and are rarely mobilised except in times of national emergency or incipient war. Some 420 retired regular reservists were called-up for Iraq operations in 2003.

The Regular Reserve consists of Individual Reservists (IR), who have varying obligations in respect of training and mobilisation, depending on factors such as length of regular service, age and sex. Categories of Individual Reservists are as follows:

Officer Reserve – with a compulsory training obligation of four to six years after leaving regular or reserve service

Regular Reserve – non-commissioned officers and other ranks who have a compulsory training obligation of up to six years after leaving regular service

Long-term Reserve – men (but not women) who have completed their Regular Reserve obligation, who serve in this capacity until the age of 45 and who have no training obligation

Military pensioners – ex-regular personnel who have completed pensionable service, who have a legal liability for recall up to the age of 60 (55 is the maximum age in general practice), and who have no training obligation

Many ex-regulars join the Volunteer Reserve Forces after leaving regular service – giving them a dual Reserve status.

Volunteer Reserve

The Volunteer reserve consists mainly of people who have joined the Territorial Army directly from the civilian community. These personnel form the main part of the active, ready reserve for the British Army, train regularly, and are paid at the same rates as the regular forces on a pro-rata basis.

Most TA volunteers commit to a minimum of some 40 days training a year, comprising one drill night in a week, one week end in a month and 14 days annual training. Some reservists exceed these minima.

The Reserve Forces Act 1996 provided for other categories of reservists, such as:

Full Time Reserve Service (FTRS) – reservists who wish to serve full time with regulars for a predetermined period in a specific posting

Additional Duties Commitment – part-time service for a specified period in a particular post.

The Act also provided two new categories of service, including:

Sponsored Reserves, being contractor staff who have agreed to join the Reserves and have a liability to be called up when required to continue their civilian work on operations alongside the Service personnel who depend upon them. Some 1,500 sponsored reservists have served in Iraq.

Territorial Army units are widely dispersed across the country – much more so than the Regular Forces and in many areas they are the visible face of the Armed Forces. They help to keep society informed about the Armed Forces, and of the importance of defence to the nation, and have an active role supporting the Cadet organisations. They provide a means by which the community as a whole can contribute to Britain's security.

TA Personnel strength by rank	Strength
Total	36,260
Officers	5,350
Senior officers (Majors and above)	2,070
Junior officers (ranks up to Captain)	3,280
Soldiers	30,910
Warrant officers and sergeants	4,960
Other ranks (ranks up to Corporal)	25,950

Note: TA establishment total (liability) is 42,000. Figures for late 2006 and exclude Officer Training Corps (OTC).

THE TERRITORIAL ARMY IN THE FUTURE ARMY STRUCTURE (FAS)

FAS plans for the TA announced in 2005 are intended to make the TA even more useable and deployable. The British Army is working through the force generation issues highlighted by recent experience on operations. FAS plans for the TA and Regular Reserves include the following elements:

♦ The Army Board has agreed the new indicative structure, which sees the TA remain at its current size of about 42,000 (including Officer Training Corps). Some adjustment and re-roling will be required.

♦ The future TA structure will ensure a more relevant, capable and usable TA.

♦ The Infantry TA has reduced from 15 to 14 battalions and has integrated into the new infantry structure, restoring a true sense of identity at TA battalion level.

♦ In future, a unit will deploy with its Deployable Component (for the more likely routine operations) drawing on its Contingent Component (normally from the TA) for the most demanding operations. A unit will also have an Enabling Component (consisting of an established Rear Party and an Infrastructure Element for security and support).

Under the FAS plan, the TA order of battle is being revised to reflect the requirement to augment the regular deployable units (adjusted under FAS) for the most demanding Deliberate Intervention operations, as outlined below.

Infantry

The Infantry will be organised to support and complement the regular regimental structure, thereby restoring a true sense of identity at TA battalion level. There are now 14 x TA infantry battalions. These battalions provide reinforcement of the regular infantry, and resilience to the infantry structure in meeting enduring commitments when Defence Planning Assumptions are exceeded. Manpower has also been included to force-generate the capability of seven Defence Troops for Armoured and Formation Reconnaissance Regiments.

The affiliation of TA battalions will be driven by the revised Future Infantry Structure (FIS), assigning one TA battalion to each new two or three battalion regular regiments, and two TA battalions to a large regular regiment. To ensure viability, restructuring will be conducted on the basis of a minimum of 400 soldiers per battalion.

Royal Armoured Corps

The Yeomanry retain a broadly similar structure, with four regiments covering the national area. As a platform-centric Arm, the RAC has a requirement for the provision of AFV crewmen Individual Reinforcements (IRs), which will be a force driver above the Contingent Component (CC) requirement. In outline:

♦ One Yeomanry Regiment of up to five squadrons will be earmarked to provide IRs and formed troops to the Joint NBC Regiment and NBC IRs to formation reconnaissance regiments; the detailed requirement is subject to the Jt NBC Regt Study.

♦ One Yeomanry Regiment will provide the RHQ and one squadron of the Armoured Replacement Regiment. In addition, this Yeomanry Regiment will provide the CC and IRs to armoured regiments.

♦ One Yeomanry Regiment will provide the balance of the CC and IRs to armoured regiments.

♦ One Yeomanry Regiment will provide the CC and IRs to formation reconnaissance regiments.

Royal Artillery

The RA will continue to provide seven regiments, although the requirement for formed TA Ground-Based Air Defence (GBAD) regiments will be removed. The RA TA will adjust to provide the following:

♦ One Regiment will provide a RHQ, a long range communications capability and up to four patrols batteries; three from the TA, the fourth from the Regular Battery (4/73 Bty, 5 Regt RA).

♦ Three Close Support Regiments will support the three Regular AS 90 SPA Regiments and two Regular Light Gun Regiments. This represents an addition of one Gun Regiment.

♦ Two General Support Regiments, one providing support to the Regular regiments and the other support to HQ 1 Arty Bde and the Regular UAV Regiment.

- One GBAD Regiment, providing support to the Regular RAPIER SAM Regiment and IRs and support to the Regular HVM SAM Regiment.

Royal Engineers

The RE TA will include the current five regiment structure, potentially supplemented by one new regiment with additional sub-units. RE TA will be structured to provide sub units for discrete tasks. Where possible this will be achieved through capability pairing mechanisms. In addition, the RE TA will be designed to provide the following:

- A formed Air Support Squadron capable of independent operation.

- A formed Squadron to 33 Engr Regt (EOD).

- A formed Topographic Squadron to 42 Engr Regt (Geo).

- A formed Amphibious Troop to 28 Engr Regt.

- Military Works Force (V), providing specialist infrastructure support to the Force.

Royal Signals

The Royal Signals TA will be structured as follows:

- Three Ptarmigan regiments based within 11 Sigs Bde, providing a composite Ptarmigan Regiment to the ARRC.

- Within 2(NC) Sigs Bde, a total of eight signals regiments (including 36 and 40 Sigs Regts) and four sub-units that will provide National Communications units in support of the Home Defence role, plus other bespoke support.

- 63 Sigs Sqn (SAS) will continue to support the SAS.

- An Air Support Signal Troop will be provided for Joint Helicopter Command.

- In addition, Royal Signals TA will provide individual augmentees to Regular regiments.

Army Aviation

The AAC TA will be structured as follows:

- 7 Regt AAC (V) will continue to provide aviation support to HQ LAND for UK Mainland tasking only.

- 6 Regiment AAC (V) will form in East Anglia to support the Attack Helicopter Regiments.

- The remainder of the AAC TA will operate from two TA squadrons, to be embedded in the Regular structure. These will provide Light Utility Helicopter (LUH) pilots, additional capability and LUH door gunners.

Royal Logistic Corps

The RLC structure will be based around the provision of TA to second line, third line and theatre enabling units. The new structure will include 15 regiments and the Catering Support Regiment RLC (V).

Army Medical Services (AMS)

The AMS will comprise of two Divisional General Support Medical Regiments and one Medical Evacuation Regiment, together with 11 Field Hospitals and six squadrons. TA AMS will provide:

- A Divisional General Support Medical Regiment (V) for the Divisional Rear Area.

- A composite Field Support Hospital of 400 beds and a Biological Warfare (BW) facility of 50 beds.

- A Field Hospital of 25 beds will be provided for enduring operations.

- TA medical sub-units embedded in the close support and general support medical regiments, to provide individual augmentees.

Royal Mechanical and Electrical Engineers

The REME TA will consist of four battalions, providing:

- A formed Battalion to support Theatre Troops and the Lines of Communications (LoC).

- Formed Role 1 support.

- Individual augmentees, attributed to Regular REME units and to Role 1 support to other Arms and Services (subject to further scrutiny during implementation).

Royal Military Police

The RMP manpower liability will increase structured on the current four companies, with additional Military Provost Staff (MPS). The RMP TA will be structured to provide:

- Formed platoons to augment the RMP companies deploying with the manoeuvre brigades, and the Theatre Troops Company.

- Formed sub-units to provide enhanced Line of Communication coverage.

- A dedicated Prisoner of War (PW) handling capability and augmentation to Divisional capability.

Intelligence Corps

The TA Intelligence Corps structure is now based on two TA battalions providing individual augmentees to tactical HQs and units, and to operational and strategic HQs. It also provides formed Field Interrogation Teams.

TERRITORIAL ARMY (TA) COMMAND STRUCTURE AND ORGANISATION

The basic command structure and organisation of TA units is the same as for Regular units, by way of Regimental or Battalion, Brigade, Divisional and District Headquarters. In addition, the Directors of the various Arms and Services have the same responsibilities for the TA as their Regular units. At the Headquarters of Regional Forces, the Commander is also Inspector General of the TA.

Types of TA Units

The most familiar type of unit is the 'Independent'. This will be found at the local Territorial Army Centre (formerly called Drill Hall). One or more Army units will be accommodated at the centre, varying in size from a platoon or troop (about 30 Volunteers) to a Battalion or Regiment (about 600 Volunteers). These units will have their place in the Order of Battle, and as with Regular Army units, are equipped for their role. Most of the personnel will be part-time. Volunteers parade one evening each week and perhaps one weekend each month in addition to the annual two-week unit training period.

Some staff at each TA Centre will be regular soldiers. Many units have regular Commanding Officers, Regimental Sergeant Majors, Training Majors, Adjutants and Instructors. The Permanent Staff Instructors (PSI) who are regular Senior Non-Commissioned Officers, are key personnel who help organise the training and administration of the Volunteers.

In the main, TA Infantry Units have a General Purpose structure which will give them flexibility of employment across the spectrum of military operations. All Infantry Battalions, including Parachute Battalions, have a common establishment of three Rifle Companies and a Headquarters Company. Each rifle company has a support platoon with mortar, anti-tank, reconnaissance, Medium Machine Gun (MMG) and assault pioneer sections under command.

The other type of unit is the 'Specialist'. These are located centrally, usually at the Headquarters or Training Centre of the Arm or Corps. Their members, spread across the country, are mainly civilians who already have the necessary skills or specialities, and require a minimum of military training.

An example of these can be found in the Army Medical Services Specialist Units whose doctors, surgeons, nurses and technicians from all over the country meet at regular intervals, often in York, or at a training area at home or abroad. They are on the lowest commitment for training, which is the equivalent of just two weekends and a two week camp each year, or it can be even less for some medical categories.

Territorial Army Order of Battle, as identified in Mid 2007

Arm or Corps	Number of regiments or battalions
Infantry	14
Armour	4
Royal Artillery	7
Royal Engineers	5
Special Air Service	2
Signals	11
Equipment Support	4
Logistics	15
Intelligence Corps	2
Aviation	2
Medical	15 (1)
Military Police	2
Total	83

(1) Total includes 12 x independent field hospitals, 2 x General Support Medical Regiments and 1 x Casualty Evacuation Regiment.

RECRUITING AND TRAINING

Recruits need to be at least 17 years old in order to join the TA. The upper age limit depends on what an individual has to offer, but it is normally 30 for those joining as an officer and 32 as a soldier. There are exceptions to the upper age limit for those with certain specialist skills or previous military experience.

Unless recruits have previous military experience, when they join the TA they will have to undergo basic recruit training. This consists of a number of training weekends, midweek drill nights and finally a two-week recruit's course at one of the Army recruit training centres.

During this stage, recruits will learn basic soldiering skills according to the TA Common Military Syllabus. This covers areas as diverse as how to wear uniform, physical fitness, weapon handling, first aid, fieldcraft, map reading and military terminology.

Officer recruiting and training may take one of two forms. Officers can be recruited from the ranks, and appointed officer cadets by their unit commander, before taking the TA Commissioning Course at the Royal Military Academy, Sandhurst. Alternatively, the new direct entry officer training scheme allows potential officers to enter officer training right from the very start of their time in the TA. Initial Officer Training is designed to produce officers with the generic qualities to lead soldiers both on and off operations and includes three weeks spent on the TA Commissioning Course at the Royal Military Academy, Sandhurst.

MOBILISATION AND CALL OUT ISSUES

Before reservists can be mobilised and sent on operations, a Call Out Order has to be signed by the Defence Secretary. He has the power to authorise the use of reserves in situations of war or on humanitarian and peacekeeping operations.

Before they are sent to their postings, reservists must undergo a period of induction where they are issued with equipment, given medical examinations and receive any specialist training relevant to their operations. For the TA and the RMR, this takes place at the new Reserves Training and Mobilisation Centre.

Under the Reserve Forces Act 1996, principal call out powers would be brought into effect in a crisis by the issue of a call out order. Members of the Reserve Forces are then liable for service anywhere in the world, unless the terms of service applicable in individual cases restrict liability to service within the UK.

Call out powers are vested in and authorised by Her Majesty the Queen who may make an order authorising call-out:

♦ If it appears to her that national danger is imminent

♦ Or that a great emergency has arisen

♦ Or in the event of an actual or apprehended attack on the United Kingdom.

The Secretary of State for Defence may make an order authorising call out:

♦ If it appears to him that warlike preparations are in preparation or progress.

♦ Or it appears to him that it is necessary or desirable to use armed forces on operations outside the UK for the protection of life or property.

♦ And for operations anywhere in the world for the alleviation of distress or the preservation of life or property in time of disaster or apprehended disaster.

Under normal circumstances, the maximum continuous periods of permanent service which individuals can serve under the above powers are respectively three years, 12 months and nine months. In exceptional circumstances the three years may be increased to five and the 12 months to two years but under the third power, no extensions can be ordered beyond the maximum of nine months. Under each power, provisions also limit the maximum aggregated time a reservist can spend in permanent service over given lengths of time.

Reservists and employers may apply for deferral of, or exemption from call out. It is recognised that those called out may not find the outcomes of their initial applications to their satisfaction. Therefore a system of arbitration has been set up.

The Reserve Forces Act 1996 (RFA96) introduced two new types of reserve categories: Higher Readiness Reserves and Sponsored Reserves.

Higher Readiness Reserve (HRR): these are individuals, serving either as members of the volunteer reserves or as individual reserves, who have taken additional liability for call out at any time. They have skills that are in short supply in both the regular and reserve forces. Typically these might be linguists, intelligence staff, media operations staff and specialist support staff.

To be a HRR, a reservist must sign an agreement to that affect and his civilian employer must agree in writing, to his doing so. An agreement that may be followed by successive agreements, will be for one year. Whilst the agreement is in force the reservist may be called up to serve for up to nine months continuous service. As for other call out powers, appeals against call-out by reservists or employers may be heard.

The HRR has largely fallen into abeyance as the terms and conditions of service proved to be unattractive. The MoD has largely been able to attract sufficient numbers of reservists to serve on mobilised service and Full Time Reserve Service (FTRS).

Sponsored Reserves. There are a number of support functions that are carried out by civilians but which in war are carried out by service personnel, because servicemen must carry out the function on operations. This new category of reserve will allow some of these tasks to be put out to contract, providing that the contractor employs in his workforce a sufficient number of employees willing to serve as members of a reserve force in the Sponsored Reserve category. If the task was required to be carried out operationally, these employees could be called out to continue providing the required support as servicemen. Sponsored Reserves will have their own call out power and be subject to no other. This and their conditions of service are tailored to the commercial aspects of the concept.

Reserve Forces Act (RFA) 1996: Enables reimbursement to be made to Employers and Reservists for some of the additional costs of employees being called out. Some reservists will have financial commitments commensurate with their civilian salary and so provisions are in place to minimise financial hardship.

The MoD is also able to offset the indirect costs of employees being called out incurred by an employer, for example, the need to recruit and train temporary replacements. If employers or reservists are dissatisfied with the financial assistance awarded they may appeal to tribunals set up for this.

Full and Part Time Service: One provision of the RFA 96 is that reservists can now undertake periods of full or part time employment with the Armed Forces. This is not a call out but a voluntary arrangement to make it possible for the Services to make more flexible use of their manpower assets. There are no fixed time limits. If a task needs doing, there is sufficient budget and a suitable volunteer is available for the job, then it can be done.

Call Out Procedure: TA soldiers are called out using the same procedures as for Individual Reservist (IR), they are sent a Call Out Notice specifying the time, date and place to which they are to report. If TA Units or Sub-Units are called out, they form up with their vehicles and equipment at their TA Centres or other designated locations. They would then be deployed by land, sea and air to their operational locations in the UK or overseas. However, if TA personnel are called out as individuals, they would report to a Temporary Mobilisation Centre where they would be processed before posting to reinforce a unit or HQ.

IR are required to keep at home an Instruction Booklet (AB 592A), their ID card and a personalised Booklet (AB 592B). The AB 592A provides IR with general instructions on what they have to do if mobilised. It contains a travel warrant and a special cash order. The AB 592A is computer produced and updated quarterly as required to take account of such changes as address, medical category and age. It explains where the reservist is to report on mobilisation and arrangements for pay and allotments, next-of-kin, clothing held etc.

Under present legislation IR may only be mobilised if called out by Queen's Order. Mobilisation may involve only a few individuals/units or any number up to general mobilisation when all are called out. If mobilisation is authorised Notices of Call Out are despatched to those IR concerned by Recorded Delivery as the legal notification. Announcements of call out are also made by the press, radio and television.

Under the Reserve Forces Act 1996, IR are liable to call out under the same new provisions as described above for the TA. In addition, the Act brings the conditions relating to all three Services in line and includes officers and pensioners who were previously covered by separate legislation/Royal Warrants.

Pay: TA personnel are paid for every hour of training. They also receive an annual bonus, known as a bounty, subject to achieving a minimum time commitment. Travel costs for training are refunded. As of 2007, daily rates of pay are the same for TA personnel and their Regular Army equivalents. The latest 2007 rates are £39.80 (starting rate) for a Private to £125.75 for a Major (mid rate). The exact rate also varies according to particular trade and type of commitment.

Hourly income is taxable, but the Annual Bounty is a tax-free lump sum. The value of the bounty depends on the specific unit and individual training requirement but, on a higher commitment, TA soldiers and officers start by receiving £395 in their first year. After five years satisfactory service, this rises to £1,556.

The annual training commitment to qualify for bounty is:

♦ Independent Units: 27 days including 15 days continuous at camp.

♦ Specialist Units: 19 days including 15 days continuous at camp.

In each case, individuals may attend one or more courses aggregated to at least eight days duration in lieu of camp, with the balance of seven days being carried out in extra out-of-camp training.

Pensions: Provision has been made in RFA 96 for the protection of Reservist pension rights in the event of call up. The MoD is permitted to pay the employers contributions to a civilian pension scheme.

MANAGEMENT

Two structures have been set up within the Territorial Army in order to improve management of reserves:

♦ Reserves Manning and Career Management Division

♦ Reserves Training and Mobilisation Centre (RTMC)

The role of the first is to centralise the coordination of all personnel management for the TA, bringing it more into line with the regular Army and also providing a single focus for identifying and notifying individuals for mobilisation, while the second is in charge of administrative preparation, individual training and provision of human resources requirements of individual reservists. The RTMC, which was inaugurated in April 1999, managed a first group of reservists in May 1999 for the British forces stationed in Bosnia and Kosovo.

Some 6,800 volunteers were recruited in 2006 (year to October). In spite of these efforts, there appears to have been a constant decline in the number of reservists. The drop-out rate among volunteers can be as high as 30% in the three first years of their engagement.

Territorial Army and Volunteer Reserve Associations

At local level, administration and support of the major elements of the Reserve Forces are carried out through the TAVRAs, working within the context described in the 1996 Reserve Forces Act. This is a tri-Service role which has been carried out by the TAVRAs and their predecessor organisations for many years. It is an unusual arrangement, but has been found to be a successful one. The TAVRA system ensures that people from the local communities in which the Reserve Forces and cadets are based are involved in the running of Reserve and cadet units. It also provides Reserve Forces and cadets representatives with the right of direct access to Ministers, so that they can make representation about Reserves issues. This provides an important balance and ensures that the case for the Reserves is clearly articulated at a high level.

TAVRAs have a second role as administrators and suppliers of services to the Reserve and cadet forces organisations. To reflect the increasing operational integration of Army Reserve and Regular forces, there have been certain changes in the way in which TAVRAs are organised since 1998. It is important that regional commanders take on full responsibility for the operational standards of Army Reserve units in their area; as a result, TAVRA boundaries were altered and brought more in line with the Army's Regular command structure. The new arrangement also took account of the needs of the other Services' Reserve Forces and all the cadet organisations.

SaBRE (Supporting Britain's Reservists and Employees)
Formerly the National Employers' Liaison Committee (NELC)

SaBRE has grown out of the the National Employers' Liaison Committee (NELC) which was formed in 1986 with a brief to provide independent advice to Ministers on the measures needed to win and maintain the support of employers, in both the public and private sectors, for those of their employees who are in the Volunteer Reserve Forces (VRF). The committee is made up of prominent businessmen and is supported by the secretariat. SaBRE provides advice on:

♦ The ways of educating employers on the role of the Reserve Forces in national defence, the vital role employers have to play in giving their support, and the benefits to employers and their employees of Reserve Forces training and experience.

♦ The current problems and attitudes of employers in relation to service by their employees in the Reserve Forces.

♦ Methods and inducements needed to encourage and retain the support of employers.

♦ Appropriate means of recognising and publicising support given by employers to the Reserve Forces.

ARMY CADETS
Consists of two separate organisations, The Combined Cadet Forces and the Army Cadet Force:

The Role of the CCF
The Combined Cadet Force (CCF) is a tri-Service military cadet organisation based in schools and colleges throughout the UK. Although it is administered and funded by the Services it is a part of the national youth movement.

The CCF receives assistance and support for its training programme from the Regular and Reserve Forces, but the bulk of adult support is provided by members of school staffs who are responsible to head teachers for the conduct of cadet activities. CCF officers wear uniform but they are not part of the Armed Forces and carry no liability for service or compulsory training.

There are some 240 CCF contingents with 40,000 cadets, of whom about 25,000 are Army Cadets. The role of the CCF is to help boys and girls to develop powers of leadership through training which promotes qualities of responsibility, self-reliance, resourcefulness, endurance, perseverance and a sense of service to the community. Military training is also designed to demonstrate why defence forces are needed, how they function and to stimulate an interest in a career as an officer in the Services.

The Role of the ACF

The role of the Army Cadet Force (ACF) is to inspire young people to achieve success with a spirit of service to the Queen, country and their local community, and to develop the qualities of good citizenship, responsibility and leadership.

Some reports suggest that Army cadets make up between 25%-30% of regular army recruits. There are about 1,674 ACF detachments based in communities around the UK with a strength of around 44,000 cadets. The ACF is run by over 8,000 adults drawn from the local community who manage a broad programme of military and adventurous training activities designed to develop character and leadership. The Army Cadets are administered by the MoD. The total budget provided to the Army Cadets in 2007 is £50 million, which comprises:

Salaries (all forms)	£32 million
Cadets estate programme	£14 million
Cadet activities	£3 million
Travel and subsistence	£1 million

TERRITORIAL ARMY UNITS
Territorial Army units, as identified in late 2007

Unit	HQ Location	Company/Squadron/Battery location
Infantry		
52nd Lowland, 6th Bn The Royal Regiment of Scotland	Glasgow	Edinburgh/Galashiels/Bathgate; Ayr/Dumfries; Glasgow/ Motherwell; Edinburgh (Band).
51st Highland, 7th Bn The Royal Regiment of Scotland	Perth	Dundee/Kirkcaldy/Stirling; Aberdeen/Peterhead/Keith/Lerwick; Inverness/Stornoway/Wick; Dumbarton/Dunoon; Perth (Band).
3rd Bn The Princess of Wales's Royal Regiment (Queen's and Royal Hampshires)	Canterbury	Farnham/Camberley; Brighton/ Worthing; Dover/Rochester; Portsmouth; Canterbury (Band).
5th Bn The Royal Regiment of Fusiliers	Durham	Washington/Bishop Auckland/ Doncaster; Newcastle/Tynemouth; Ashington/Alnwick; Newcastle (Band).

3rd Bn The Royal Anglian Regiment	Bury St Edmunds	Norwich/Lowestoft; Lincoln; Leicester/Northampton; Chelmsford/Hertford; Peterborough (Band).
4th Bn The Duke of Lancaster's Regiment (King's, Lancashire and Border)	Preston	Liverpool; Blackburn; Workington/Carlisle/Barrow; Manchester/Bury; Liverpool (Band).
4th Bn The Yorkshire Regiment	York	York/Scarborough; Hull/Leeds/Beverley; Middlesborough/Northallerton; Huddersfield/Keighley; Barnsley/Sheffield; York (Band).
4th Bn The Mercian Regiment	Wolverhampton	Warrington/Stockport; Crewe/Stoke; Mansfield; Wolverhampton/Kidderminster/Burton-on-Trent; Birmingham; Shrewsbury; Wolverhampton (Band).
3rd Bn The Royal Welsh	Cardiff	Wrexham/Queensferry; Swansea/Aberystwyth; Pontypridd/Cardiff; Colwyn Bay/Caernarfon; Newport (Band).
6th Bn The Rifles	Exeter	Gloucester/Bristol; Taunton/Exeter; Dorchester/Poole; Bodmin/Plymouth; Exeter (Band).
7th Bn The Rifles	Reading	Oxford; Reading; Milton Keynes; London; Oxford (Band).
4th Bn The Parachute Regiment	Pudsey	White City/Croydon; Pudsey/St Helens/Hebburn; Glasgow/Edinburgh.
The Royal Irish Rangers	Portadown	Newtonards; Newtonabbey/Ballymena; Armagh/Enniskillen; Lisburn (Band).
The London Regiment	Battersea	Westminster/Catford; Edgware/Hornsey; Balham; Camberwell.

Royal Armoured Corps

Royal Yeomanry	Croydon	Swindon; Leicester; Croydon; Nottingham; Fulham; Clifton St, City (Band).

Royal Wessex Yeomanry	Wareham	Wareham; Salisbury; Cirencester; Barnstable/Paignton.
Royal Mercian & Lancastrian Yeomanry	Telford	Dudley; Telford/Hereford; Chester; Wigan.
Queen's Own Yeomanry	Newcastle	York/Hull; Ayr/Motherwell; Belfast; Cupar/Forfar; Newcastle/Sunderland.

Royal Artillery

Honourable Artillery Company	London	3 x Sqns, Band; all in London.
100 Regiment RA (V)	Luton	Luton; Bristol; Nottingham.
101 Regiment RA (V)	Newcastle	Blyth; Newcastle; South Shields; Leeds.
103 Regiment RA (V)	St Helens	Liverpool; Manchester; Bolton; Bolton (Band).
104 Regiment RA (V)	Newport	Newport; Worcester.
105 Regiment RA (V)	Edinburgh	Newtownards; Edinburgh; Arbroath.
106 Regiment RA (V)	London	Wolverhampton; London; Southampton.

Army Air Corps

| 7 Regiment AAC (V) | Netheravon | 2 x Sqns Netheravon |
| 6 Regiment AAC (V) | Bury St Edmunds | Bury St Edmunds/Swaffham; Dishforth. |

Royal Engineers

Royal Monmouthshire RE (Militia)	Monmouth	Cwmbran/Bristol; Gorseinon/Cardiff/Swansea; Walsall/Oldbury; Jersey.
71 Regiment RE (V)	Leuchars	Paisley/Barnsford Bridge; Cumbernauld; Kinloss; Kirkwall.
72 Regiment RE (V)	Gateshead	Sheffield/Bradford; Newcastle; Wakefield/Hull/Pontefract
73 Regiment RE (V)	Nottingham	Chilwell/Mansfield; Derby/Chesterfield; Northampton/Leicester; Nottingham (Band).

75 Regiment RE (V)	Warrington	Birkenhead/Widnes; Stoke on Trent/Cannock; Failsworth/ Ashton Under Lyne.
101 Regiment (EOD) (V)	Ilford	Holloway/White City; Catford/ Rochester; Tunbridge Wells/ Brighton/ Reigate.
131 Independent Commando Squadron (V)	London	Birmingham; Bath: Plymouth.
135 Independent Squadron (V)	Ewell	Hermitage; Southampton.
412 Amphibious Engineer Hameln Troop (V)		
170 Infrastructure Support Engineer Group (V)	Chilwell	
65 Works Group (V)	Chilwell	10 x Specialist Work Groups all at Chilwell
591 Independent Field Squadron	Bangor/Antrim	

Royal Signals

21 Signal Regiment (Air Support)	Bath	
31 Signal Regiment (V)	London	Coulsdon/Kingston on Thames; Eastbourne/Brighton; Banbury/ Oxford.
32 Signal Regiment (V)	Glasgow	Aberdeen/Elgin; East Kilbride; Edinburgh.
33 Signal Regiment (V)	Liverpool	Manchester; Liverpool; Runcorn.
34 Signal Regiment (V)	Middlesbrough	Leeds/Hull; Darlington/Newcastle; Hartlepool/Middlesbrough.
35 Signal Regiment (V)	Coventry	Birmingham; Newcastle-Under-Lyme; Rugby; Shrewsbury.
36 Signal Regiment (V)	Grays	Cambridge; Colchester/Ipswich/ Southend; Cambridge/Norwich; Cambridge/Aylesbury/Bedford.
37 Signal Regiment (V)	Redditch	Cardiff/Brecon; Stratford-Upon-Avon/Stourbridge; Coventry/Tennal Grange.
38 Signal Regiment (V)	Sheffield	Derby; Sheffield/Nottingham; Blackburn/Manchester.

39 Signal Regiment (V)	Bristol	Bristol/Gloucester; Windsor/Reading/Chertsey.
40 Signal Regiment (V)	Belfast	Belfast; Limavady; Bangor.
71 Signal Regiment (V)	Bexleyheath	Uxbridge; London/Whipps Cross; Chelmsford/Harlow.
1 (Royal Buckinghamshire Yeomanry) Signal Squadron (Special Communications) (V)	Milton Keynes	
2 Signal Squadron (V)	Dundee	
63 Signal Squadron (SAS) (V)	Thorney Island	London; Birmingham; Southampton; Poole; Hereford.
81 Signal Squadron (V)	Corsham	

Royal Logistic Corps

150 (Yorkshire) Transport Regt (V)	Hull	Hull; Leeds; Doncaster.
151 Transport Regiment (V)	Croydon	Brentwood/Ilford; Sutton/Maidstone; Barnet/Ilford; Southall/Clapham.
152 Transport Regiment (V)	Belfast	Londonderry/Coleraine; Belfast.
155 Transport Regiment (V)	Plymouth	Plymouth; Truro; Poole/Dorchester.
156 Transport Regiment (V)	Liverpool	Liverpool; Birkenhead; Manchester; Bootle.
157 Transport Regiment (V)	Cardiff	Cardiff; Swansea; Carmarthen/Haverford West.
158 Transport Regiment (V)	Peterborough	Bedford/Peterborough; Ipswich; Loughborough/Melton Mowbray.
159 Support Regiment (V)	Stoke	Telford; Glasgow; Tynemouth; West Bromwich/Stoke.
160 Transport Regiment (V)	Grantham	4 x Sqn all at Grantham
162 Movement Control Regiment (V)	Grantham	Swindon; 4 x Sqn at Grantham.
165 Port Regiment (V)	Grantham	Southampton/Isle of Wight; Grantham.
166 Support Regiment (V)	Grantham	5 x Sqns all at Grantham.

168 Pioneer Regiment (V)	Grantham	Grantham; Cramlington/Berwick/ Hexham; Coulby Newham/ Washington/Hartlepool.
17 Port & Maritime Regiment	Bicester	
88 Postal & Courier Regiment (V)	Grantham	4 x Sqns all at Grantham.
Catering Support Regiment	Grantham	3 x Sqns all at Grantham.
Scottish Transport Regiment (V)	Dunfermline	Dunfermline; Glasgow; Edinburgh; Irvine.

Royal Electrical & Mechanical Engineers

101 Battalion REME (V)	Wrexham	Prestatyn; Coventry; Manchester; Grangemouth.
102 Battalion REME (V)	Newton Aycliffe	Newton Aycliffe; Rotherham; Scunthorpe; Newcastle upon Tyne.
103 Battalion REME (V)	Crawley	Northampton/Corby/Leicester; Portsmouth; Ashford; Redhill.
104 Battalion REME (V)	Bordon	Bordon

Army Medical Services

201 Field Hospital (V)	Newcastle	Newton Aycliffe; Stockton-on-Tees; Carlisle.
202 Field Hospital (V)	Birmingham	Stoke on Trent; Oxford; Shrewsbury.
203 Field Hospital (V)	Cardiff	Swansea; Aberystwyth/Crickhowell; Llandudno.
204 Field Hospital (V)	Belfast	Ballymena; Newtownards; Armagh.
205 Field Hospital (V)	Glasgow	Glasgow; Aberdeen; Dundee; Edinburgh.
207 Field Hospital (V)	Manchester	Stockport/Ashton Under Lyne; Blackburn; Bury.
208 Field Hospital (V)	Liverpool	Ellesmere Port; Blackpool/ Lancaster.
212 Field Hospital (V)	Sheffield	Leeds; Beeston/Lincoln; York/ Bradford.
243 Field Hospital (V)	Bath	Exeter; Plymouth; Portsmouth; Poole.

256 Field Hospital (V)	London	Walworth; Kensington; Kingston; Bow.
306 Field Hospital (V)	York	
225 Divisional General Support Medical Regiment (V)	Dundee	Sunderland; Glenrothes; Dundee.
253 Divisional General Support Medical Regiment (V)	Belfast	Londonderry; Belfast;
254 Divisional General Support Medical Regiment (V)	Cherry Hinton	Norwich; Hitchin; Colchester.
144 Parachute Medical Squadron	London/Hornsey	Glasgow; Nottingham; Cardiff.
335 Medical Evacuation Regiment (V)	York	
4 General Support Medical Regiment	Maidstone	Maidstone; Leicester/Derby
5 General Support Medical Regiment	Hull	Hull/Grimsby/Castleford; Chorley

Adjutant General's Corps

4 Regiment, Royal Military Police	Aldershot	West Bromwich/Manchester; Brixton/Southampton.
5 Regiment, Royal Military Police	Edinburgh	Livingston/Lisburn; Stockton-on-Tees/Newcastle Upon Tyne.
Military Provost Staff (V)	Colchester	

Intelligence Corps

3 Military Intelligence Bn	London	London; Portsmouth.
5 Military Intelligence Bn (V)		London; Edinburgh/Newton Abbey; York/Gateshead; Bristol/Cardiff/Exeter; Birmingham/Chorley/Nottingham.

Special Air Service

21 Regiment SAS

23 Regiment SAS

Note: an / between locations denotes detachments of the same unit.

Territorial Army: Officer Training Corps Units
Aberdeen University Officer Training Corps
Birmingham University Officer Training Corps
Bristol University Officer Training Corps
Cambridge University Officer Training Corps
East Midlands University Officer Training Corps
City of Edinburgh University Officer Training Corps
Exeter University Officer Training Corps
Glasgow and Strathclyde Universities Officer Training Corps
Leeds University Officer Training Corps
Liverpool University Officer Training Corps
London University Officer Training Corps
Manchester and Salford University Officer Training Corps
Northumbrian University Officer Training Corps
Oxford University Officer Training Corps
Queens University Officer Training Corps
Sheffield University Officer Training Corps
Southampton University Officer Training Corps
Tayforth University Officer Training Corps
University of Wales Officer Training Corps

CHAPTER 14 – MISCELLANEOUS

The Military Hierarchy

Rank	Badge	Appointment Example
General (Gen)	Crown, Star & Crossed Sword with Baton	Chief of the General Staff
Lieutenant General (Lt Gen)	Crown & Sword & Baton	Commander ARRC
Major General (Maj Gen)	Star & Sword & Baton	Divisional Commander
Brigadier (Brig)	Crown & 3 Stars	Brigade Commander
Colonel (Col)	Crown & 2 Stars	Staff or School
Lieutenant Colonel (Lt Col)	Crown & 1 Star	Battle Group/Armoured Regiment/Infantry Bn
Major (Maj)	Crown	Sqn/Coy/Bty
Captain (Capt)	3 Stars	Squadron/Company 2ic
Lieutenant (Lt)	2 Stars	Troop/Pl Commander
2nd Lieutenant	1 Star (2/Lt)	Troop/Pl Commander
Warrant Officer First Class	Royal Coat of Arms on Forearm	Regimental Sergeant Major (WO 1) (RSM)
Warrant Officer Second Class	Crown on forearm	Company Sergeant Major (WO 2) (CSM)
Staff Sergeant (Ssgt)	Crown over 3 stripes	Coy/Sqn Stores (or Colour Sergeant)
Sergeant (Sgt)	3 stripes	Platoon Sergeant
Corporal (Cpl)	2 stripes	Section Commander
Lance Corporal	1 Stripe	Section 2ic (LCpl)

Modes of Address

Where appropriate soldiers are addressed by their generic rank without any qualifications, therefore Generals, Lieutenant Generals and Major Generals are all addressed as 'General'. Colonels and Lieutenant Colonels as 'Colonel', Corporals and Lance Corporals as ' Corporal'. Staff Sergeants and Colour Sergeants are usually addressed as 'Staff' or 'Colour' and CSMs as Sergeant Major. It would almost certainly be prudent to address the RSM as 'Sir'.

Private Soldiers should always be addressed by their title and then their surname. For example: Rifleman Harris, Private Jones, Bugler Bygrave, Gunner Smith, Guardsman Thelwell, Sapper Williams, Trooper White, Kingsman Boddington, Signalman Robinson, Ranger Murphy, Fusilier Ramsbotham , Driver Wheel, Craftsman Grease or Air Trooper Rotor. However, it should be remembered that regiments and corps have different customs and although the above is a reasonable guide it may not always be correct.

Regimental Head-Dress

The normal everyday head-dress of NCOs and Soldiers (and in some regiments of all ranks) is the beret or national equivalent. The norm is the dark blue beret. Exceptions are as follows:

a.	Grey Beret	The Royal Scots Dragoon Guards
		Queen Alexandra's Royal Army Nursing Corps
b.	Brown Beret	The King's Royal Hussars
		The Royal Wessex Yeomanry
c.	Khaki Beret	All Regiments of Foot Guards
		The Honourable Artillery Company
		The Royal Anglian Regiment
		The Duke of Lancaster's Regiment
		The Yorkshire Regiment
d.	Black Beret	The Royal Tank Regiment
e.	Rifle Green Beret	The Rifles~
		The Brigade of Gurkhas
		Adjutant General's Corps
f.	Maroon Beret	The Parachute Regiment
g.	Beige Beret	The Special Air Service Regiment
h.	Light Blue Beret	The Army Air Corps
i.	Scarlet Beret	Royal Military Police
j.	Cypress Green Beret	The Intelligence Corps

The Royal Regiment of Scotland wear the Tam-O-Shanter (TOS) and the Royal Irish Regiment wear the Corbeen.

Regular Army Rates of Pay as at 1st April 2007
(all figures are £ per annum)

Officers	Level 1	Highest Level
University Cadet	–	11,718
Second Lieutenant	–	22,679
Lieutenant	27,260	30,161 (Level 10)

Captain	34,934	41,544 (Level 9)
Major	44,004	52,071 (Level 9)
Lieutenant Colonel	61,760	68,272 (Level 9)
Colonel	71,521	79,048 (Level 9)
Brigadier	85,787	89,443 (Level 5)

Notes:
Rates of pay apply to both male and female officers.
QARANC Officers are commissioned as Lieutenants.

Adult soldiers are paid in two bands (spines). There is a Lower Spine (LS) and a Higher Spine (HS).

| | (LS) | (LS) | (HS) | (HS) |
Adult Soldiers	**Level 1**	**Level 7**	**Level 1**	**Level 7**
Private & LCpl	15,677	22,325	15,677	26,664
Corporal	24,328	25,422	25,422	30,574
Sergeant	27,652	31,429	30,180	34,025
SSgt & WO	30,610	36,511	34,047	39,850
Warrant Officer 1	35,564	40,650	38,771	43,076

Notes:
Pay scales apply to both males and females.
(2)   Young entrants aged 17 or over are paid £12,571 per annum.

Additional Pay	**£ per day**
Parachutists All ranks	5.07
Army Compressed Air Diver	7.89
Army NCO Pilot	14.64 (middle rate)
Army Helicopter Crewman	4.50
UWA*	2.32 (initial rate rising to 16.88)

Note: *UWA – Unpleasant Work Allowance

The Royal Marines

The Royal Marines (RM) are specialists in Amphibious Warfare and are a Royal Naval organisation. The Royal Marines number approximately 7,400 personnel and, since the end of the Cold War, and especially in recent years, the Corps appears to have reverted to its traditional role of being ready for operations anywhere in the world.

All Royal Marines, except those in the Royal Marines Band Service, are first and foremost, commando soldiers. They are required to undergo what is recognised as one of the longest and most demanding infantry training courses in the world. This is undertaken at the Commando Training Centre Royal Marines at Lympstone in UK's West Country, not far from Dartmoor. The titular head of the Royal Marines is always a Major General – Commandant General Royal Marines (CGRM).

The Royal Marines have small detachments in ships at sea and other units worldwide with widely differing tasks. However, the bulk of the manpower of the Royal Marines is grouped in battalion-sized organisations known as Commandos (Cdo). There are 3 Commando Groups and they are part of a larger formation known as 3 Commando Brigade (3 Cdo Bde).

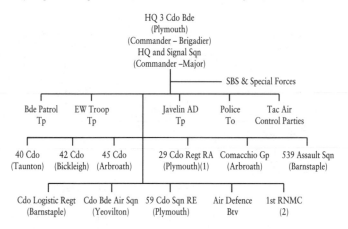

Note:
(1) 29 Cdo Regt RA has one battery stationed at Arbroath with 45 Cdo.
(2) 1st Bn The Royal Netherlands Marine Corps is part of 3 Cdo Bde for NATO assigned tasks. The Air Defence troop is equipped with Rapier. There are three regular Tactical Air Control Parties and one reserve. 539 Assault Squadron has hovercraft, landing craft and raiding craft.

1st Battalion The Rifles – 3 Commando Brigade's Fourth Manoeuvre Unit
From 1 April 2008 1 RIFLES will be attached to 3 Commando Brigade as a 4th Manoeuvre Unit. 3 Commando Brigade will then be able to provide both a brigade at high readiness for operations anywhere in the world and also support programmed operations.

1 RIFLES will remain on the Army list under the Full Command of the Chief of the General Staff but serve under the operational command of the Commander in Chief Fleet and the Commander of 3 Commando Brigade Royal Marines. The battalion will be structured as a Light Role Battalion and personnel will continue to wear the 1 RIFLES cap-badge.

Each Commando has the following organisation:

Commando Organisation

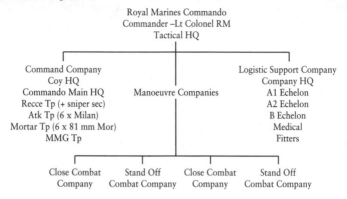

Note: There are 4 x Manoeuvre Companies:

♦ 2 x Close Combat Companies each with 3 x Fighting Troops (5 x officers and 98 other ranks).

♦ 2 x Stand Off Combat Companies one of which is tracked (Viking armoured vehicle) and the other wheeled. Each Stand Off Combat Company has 1 x Heavy Machine Gun Troop with 6 x 0.5 HMG, 1 x Anti-Tank Troop with 6 x Milan and 1 x Close Combat Fighting Troop (5 x officers and 78 other ranks).

♦ Total personnel strength is 692 all ranks.

♦ A troop (Tp) roughly equates to an army platoon and consists of about 30 men.

Locations.

Headquarters Royal Marines	(Portsmouth)
HQ 3 Commando Brigade Plymouth	(Stonehouse)
3 Commando Bde HQ & Signal Squadron	(Stonehouse)
3 Commando Bde Air Sqn	(RNAS Yeovilton)
40 Commando	(Taunton)
42 Commando	(Bickleigh)
45 Commando	(Arbroath)
Commando Logistic Regiment	(Barnstaple))
539 Assault Sqn Plymouth	(Barnstaple)
Fleet Protection Group	(Clyde)
Commando Training Centre	(Lympstone)
Royal Marines Stonehouse	(Plymouth)
Royal Marines Poole	(Poole)

| Amphibious Training & Trials Unit | (Bideford) |
| 1 Assault Group | (Poole) |

Royal Marines Reserve (RMR)

The RMR consists of about 600 personnel based around the following locations:

RMR London: The detachment is in London and is located alongside the HQ. The three remaining detachments are based in Chatham, Henley and Portsmouth.

RMR Merseyside: The Headquarters is in Liverpool where there is a detachment. The other two detachments are based in Birmingham and Manchester.

RMR Scotland: HQ is in Glasgow with the five remaining detachments based in Greenock, Edinburgh, Dundee, Aberdeen and Inverness.

RMR Tyne: A single location at Newcastle-on-Tyne

RMR Bristol: The main detachment is in Bristol which is located alongside the HQ. The four remaining detachments are based in Poole, Plymouth, Cardiff and Lympstone.

Special Boat Service

This organisation is the Naval equivalent of the Army's SAS (Special Air Service). Personnel are all volunteers from the mainstream Royal Marines and vacancies are few with competition for entry fierce.

Generally speaking only about 30% of volunteers manage to complete the entry course and qualify. The SBS specialises in mounting clandestine operations against targets at sea, in rivers or harbours and against occupied coastlines.

Comacchio Group/Fleet Protection Group Royal Marines (FPGRM)

This specialist company was formed in 1980, and has the task of guarding the UK's oil rigs and other associated installations from a variety of threats – in particular terrorist attacks.

During 2001 Comacchio Group was renamed as the Fleet Protection Group Royal Marines (FPGRM) and the unit moved from RM Condor to HMNB Clyde.

FPGRM is structured around 3 x rifle companies and 1 x headquarters company. Personnel strength is in the region of 533 personnel.

RAF Regiment

The RAF Regiment was raised on 1 February 1942 by a Royal Warrant of King George VI as a result of the requirement to protect air installations which were vulnerable to enemy air and ground attack. As of 2006, the strength of the RAF Regiment is around 3,000, including some 300 officers and 500 part-time reservists. The Regiment is generally formed into Squadrons of 100 to 150 personnel. Currently the RAF Regiment exists to provide defence for RAF installations, and to train all the RAF's combatant personnel to enable them to contribute to the defence of their units.

As of 1 April 2007, RAF Regiment units were as follows:

Field Squadrons

No 1 Squadron	Honington	Field Squadron
No 2 Squadron (II)	Honington	Field /Parachute Squadron
No 3 Squadron	Aldergrove	Field Squadron
No 27 Squadron	Honington	CBRN Defence (RAF element of Joint CBRN Regiment)
No 34 Squadron	Leeming	Field Squadron
No 51 Squadron	Lossiemouth	Field Squadron
No 63 (QCS)	Uxbridge	Ceremonial /Field Squadron

RAF Regiment Depot	Honington
No 1 RAF STO HQ	Wittering
No 2 RAF STO HQ	Leeming
No 3 RAF STO HQ	Marham
No 4 RAF STO HQ	Honington (Survive to Operate Centre)

STO – Survive to Operate

Note: Joint CBRN Regiment: No 27 Squadron RAF Regiment provides some of the 244 personnel of the Joint CBRN Regiment alongside two squadrons of the Royal Tank Regiment all of whom are stationed at Honington.

Royal Auxiliary Air Force Regiment (RAuxAF Regt)

Airfield defence is further enhanced by squadrons of the RAuxAF Regt who are recruited locally and whose role is the ground defence of the airfield and its associated outlying installations. An RAuxAF Regiment Squadron has an all-up strength of about 120 personnel and costs approximately £500,000 a year to keep in service. As a general rule, a squadron has a headquarters flight, two mobile flights mounted in Land Rovers and two flights for static guard duties. RAuxAF Regt squadrons are as follows:

2503 Sqn RAuxAF Regt	RAF Waddington	Ground Defence
2620 Sqn RAuxAF Regt	RAF Marham	Ground Defence
2622 Sqn RAuxAF Regt	RAF Lossiemouth	Ground Defence
2623 Sqn RauxAF Regt	RAF Honington	Force Protection
2624 Sqn RauxAF Regt	RAF Brize Norton	Ground Defence

Royal Auxiliary Air Force Regiment squadrons are generally based alongside regular units in order to maximise training opportunities and give the auxiliary personnel access to equipment held by the regular unit.

Specialist RAF Regiment training for gunners is given at the RAF Regiment Depot at Honington. On completion of training at the RAF College Cranwell officers also undergo further specialist training at RAF Honington and, in some cases, the Combined Arms Training Centre at Warminster in Wiltshire or the Royal School of Artillery at Larkhill.

The RAF Regiment also mans the Queen's Colour Squadron which undertakes all major ceremonial duties for the Royal Air Force. These duties involve mounting the Guard at Buckingham Palace on an occasional basis, and providing Guards of Honour for visiting Heads of State. The Queen's Colour Squadron also has a war role as a field squadron.

Codewords and Nicknames

A Codeword is a single word used to provide security cover for reference to a particular classified matter, eg 'Corporate' was the Codeword for the recovery of the Falklands in 1982. In 1990 'Granby' was used to refer to operations in the Gulf and Op Agricola; is used for current operations in support of NATO forces in Kosovo. Op Fingle; is the Codeword for land operations in Afghanistan in support of the International Security Assistance Force. A Nickname consists of two words and may be used for reference to an unclassified matter, eg 'Lean Look' referred to an investigation into various military organisations in order to identify savings in manpower.

Dates and Timings

When referring to timings the British Army uses the 24 hour clock. This means that 2015 hours, pronounced twenty fifteen hours, is in fact 8.15pm. Soldiers usually avoid midnight and refer to 2359 or 0001 hours. Time zones present plenty of scope for confusion! Exercise and Operational times are expressed in Greenwich Mean Time (GMT) which may differ from the local time. The suffix Z (Zulu) denotes GMT and A (Alpha) GMT + 1 hour. B (Bravo) means GMT + 2 hours and so on.

The Date Time Group or DTG can be seen on military documents and is a point of further confusion for many. Using the military DTG 1030 GMT on 20 April 2007 is written as 201030Z APR 07. When the Army relates days and hours to operations a simple system is used:

a. D Day is the day an operation begins.

b. H Hour is the hour a specific operation begins.

c. Days and hours can be represented by numbers plus or minus of D Day for planning purposes. Therefore if D Day is 20 April 2007, D-2 is 18 April and D + 2 is 22 April. If H Hour is 0600 hours then H+2 is 0800 hours.

Phonetic Alphabet

To ensure minimum confusion during radio or telephone conversations difficult words or names are spelt out letter by letter using the following NATO standard phonetic alphabet.

ALPHA – BRAVO – CHARLIE – DELTA – ECHO – FOXTROT – GOLF – HOTEL-INDIA – JULIET – KILO – LIMA – MIKE – NOVEMBER – OSCAR – PAPA-QUEBEC – ROMEO – SIERRA – TANGO – UNIFORM – VICTOR – WHISKEY – X RAY – YANKEE – ZULU.

Military Quotations

Young officers and NCOs may find some of these quotations useful on briefings etc: There are two groups – Military and General.

Military

"Having lost sight of our objectives we need to redouble our efforts". *Anon*

During the Second World War Air Marshal Sir Arthur (Bomber) Harris was well known for his glorious capacity for rudeness, particularly to bureaucrats. "What are you doing to retard the war effort today" was his standard greeting to senior civil servants.

"The military value of a partisan's work is not measured by the amount of property destroyed, or the number of men killed or captured, but the number he keeps watching."
John Singleton Mosby 1833-1916 – Confederate Cavalry Leader

Tacitus (56-117AD) wrote of the conquest and occupation of Britain by his father-in-law Agricola. as follows: "He declared an Empire where there was none, and created a desert, and called it peace."

"Keep shouting Sir, we'll find you. Keep going down hill – Don't cross the river!"
LCpl Thomas Atkins

"It is foolish to hunt the tiger when there are plenty of sheep around."
Al Qaeda Training Manual 2002

"Information is something that you do something with. Data is something that just makes officers feel good! I keep telling them but nobody listens to me."
US Army Intelligence specialist – CENTCOM Qatar 2003

"If you torture data sufficiently it will confess to almost anything".
Fred Menger – Chemistry Professor (1937-)

"If you tell someone what needs doing, as opposed to how to do it, they will surprise you with their ingenuity"
General Patton

"An appeaser is one who feeds a crocodile in the hope it will eat him last"   *Winston Churchill*

"Amateurs talk tactics, professionals talk logistics." *Anon*

"More delusion as a solution" *US State Department Official – Baghdad March 2005*

"If you claim to understand what is happening in Iraq you haven't been properly briefed".
British Staff Officer at Coalition HQ 2004

"If you can keep your head when all about you are losing theirs and blaming it on you – you'll be a man my son".
Rudyard Kipling

"If you can keep your head when all about you are losing theirs – you may have missed something very important".
Royal Marine – Bagram Airfield 2002

Admiral King commanded the US Navy during the Second World War. His daughter wrote –
"He was the most even tempered man I ever met – he was always in a rage. In addition, he

believed that civilians should be told nothing about a war until it was over and then only who won. Nothing more!"

Mrs Saatchi explained her 12 month silence after her husband started living with Nigela Lawson by quoting Napoleon's dictum "Never disturb your enemy while he is making a mistake"

"We trained very hard, but it seemed that every time we were beginning to form up in teams, we would be reorganised. I was to learn in later life that we tend to meet any new situation by reorganising, and a wonderful method it can be for creating an illusion of progress, while producing confusion, inefficiency and demoralisation". *Caius Petronius 66 AD*

"A few honest men are better than numbers." *Oliver Cromwell*

"The beatings will continue until morale improves."
Attributed to the Commander of the Japanese Submarine Force.

"When other Generals make mistakes their armies are beaten; when I get into a hole, my men pull me out of it". *The Duke of Wellington -after Waterloo*

"Take short views, hope for the best and trust in God." *Sir Sydney Smith*

"There is no beating these troops in spite of their generals. I always thought them bad soldiers, now I am sure of it. I turned their right, pierced their centre, broke them everywhere; the day was mine, and yet they did not know it and would not run".
Marshal Soult (French Army) – Commenting on the British Infantry at Albuhera in 1811

"Confusion in battle is what pain is in childbirth – the natural order of things".
General Maurice Tugwell

"This is the right way to waste money"
PJ O'Rourke – Rolling Stone Magazine (Watching missiles firing during an exercise)

" This is just something to be got round – like a bit of flak on the way to the target".   *Group Captain Leonard Cheshire VC – Speaking of his incurable illness in the week before he died.*

"Pale Ebenezer thought it wrong to fight, But roaring Bill, who killed him, thought it right".
Hillare Belloc

"Everyone wants peace – and they will fight the most terrible war to get it".
Miles Kington – BBC Radio 4th February 1995

"The purpose of war is not to die for your country. The purpose of war is to ensure that the other guy dies for his country". *General Patton.*

"War is a competition of incompetence – the least incompetent usually win".
General Tiger (Pakistan) – after losing Bangladesh.

"In war the outcome corresponds to expectations less than in any other activity".
Titus Livy 59 BC – 17AD

"Nothing is so good for the morale of the troops as occasionally to see a dead general".
Field Marshal Slim 1891-1970

"It makes no difference which side the general is on". *Unknown British Soldier*

At the end of the day it is the individual fighting soldier who carries the battle to the enemy; Sir Andrew Agnew commanding Campbell's Regiment (Royal Scots Fusiliers), giving orders to his infantrymen before the Battle of Dettingen in 1743 shouted; "Do you see yon loons on yon grey hill? Well, if ye dinna kill them, they'll kill you! "

"The only time in his life that he ever put up a fight was when we asked for his resignation."
    A comment from one of his staff officers following French General Joffre's resignation in 1916.

"How can the enemy anticipate us when we haven't got a clue what we are doing?"
    Pte Thomas Atkins (Basrah 2006)

General Quotes
"All rumours are true, especially when your boss denies them"
    Dogbert – Build a better life by stealing office supplies

"If a miracle occurs and your boss finally completes your performance appraisal, it will be hastily prepared, annoyingly vague and an insult to whatever dignity you still possess."
    Dogbert – Clues for the clueless

"Don't worry about people stealing an idea. If it's original you will have to ram it down their throats."
    Howard Aiken 1900-1973 (Howard Aiken completed the Harvard Mark II, a completely electronic computer, in 1947).

Homer Simpson's advice to his son Bart:
Homer to Bart: "These three little sentences will get you through life":
Number 1: "Oh, good idea boss".
Number 2: (whispers) "Cover for me".
Number 3: "It was like that when I got here".

"Clear language, reflects clear thought." *George Orwell (1903-1950)*

"It's like the old hooker said. It's not the work – it's the stairs that are getting me down"
    Elaine Stritch – Actress 2003

"The primary function of management is to create the chaos that only management can sort out. A secondary function is the expensive redecoration and refurnishing of offices, especially in times of the utmost financial stringency".
    Theodore Dalrymple 'The Spectator' 6 November 1993.

"Success is generally 90% persistence". *Anon*

"It is only worthless men who seek to excuse the deterioration of their character by pleading neglect in their early years". *Plutarch – Life of Coriolanus – Approx AD 80*

"They say hard work never hurt anybody, but I figured why take the chance". *Ronald Regan*

"To applaud as loudly as that for so stupid a proposal means that you are just trying to fill that gap between your ears". *David Starkey – BBC (4 Feb 95)*

"Ah, these diplomats! What chatterboxes! There's only one way to shut them up – cut them down with machine guns. Bulganin, go and get me one!"
Joseph Stalin – As reported by De Gaulle during a long meeting.

"Whenever I hear about a wave of public indignation I am filled with a massive calm".
Matthew Parris – The Times 24th October 1994

"It is a general popular error to imagine that the loudest complainers for the public to be the most anxious for its welfare." *Edmund Burke*

"The men who really believe in themselves are all in lunatic asylums." *GK Chesterton*

"What all the wise men promised has not happened and what all the dammed fools said would happen has come to pass". *Lord Melbourne*

"Awards are like haemorrhoids: in the end every asshole gets one".
Frederick Raphae (author born 1931)

"When we have finally stirred ourselves to hang them all, I hope that our next step will be to outlaw political parties outside Parliament on the grounds that, like amusement arcades, they attract the least desirable members of our society." *Auberon Waugh(in The Spectator 1984)*

Extracts from Officer's Annual Confidential Reports

"Works well when under constant supervision and cornered like a rat in a trap."

"He has the wisdom of youth, and the energy of old age."

"This Officer should go far – and the sooner he starts, the better."

"This officer is depriving a village somewhere of its idiot."

"Only occasionally wets himself under pressure."

"When she opens her mouth, it seems that this is only to change whichever foot was previously in there."

"He has carried out each and every one of his duties to his entire satisfaction."

"He would be out of his depth in a car park puddle."

"This young man has delusions of adequacy."

"When he joined my ship, this Officer was something of a granny; since then he has aged considerably."

"This Medical Officer has used my ship to carry his genitals from port to port, and my officers to carry him from bar to bar."

"Since my last report he has reached rock bottom, and has started to dig."

"She sets low personal standards and then consistently fails to achieve them."

"His men would follow him anywhere, but only out of curiosity."

"This officer has the astonishing ability to provoke something close to a mutiny every time he opens his mouth".

"His mother should have thrown him away and kept the stork".

"I cannot believe that out of 10,000 sperm his was the fastest".

"The most complementary thing that I can say about this officer is that he is unbearable".

Finally

Drill instructor to an embarrassed officer cadet who appears to be completely incapable of identifying left from right – "Tell me Sir, as an outsider, what is your opinion of the human race? *Overheard at the RMA Sandhurst*

EXTRACTS FROM THE DEVILS DICTIONARY 1911

Accuracy: A certain uninteresting quality generally excluded from human statements.

Armour: The kind of clothing worn by a man whose tailor is a blacksmith.

Colonel: The most gorgeously apparelled man in a regiment.

Enemy: A designing scoundrel who has done you some service which it is inconvenient to repay.

Foe: A person instigated by his wicked nature to deny one's merits or exhibit superior merits of his own.

Foreigner: A villain regarded with various degrees of toleration, according to his conformity to the eternal standard of our conceit and the shifting ones of our interest.

Freedom: A political condition that every nation supposes itself to enjoy in virtual monopoly.

Friendless: Having no favour to bestow. Destitute of fortune. Addicted to utterance of truth and common sense.

Man: An animal so lost in rapturous contemplation of what he thinks he is as to overlook what he ought to be. His chief occupation is the extermination of other animals and his own species,

Overwork: A dangerous disorder affecting high public functionaries who want to go fishing.

Peace: In international affairs a period of cheating between two periods of fighting.

Plunder: To wrest the wealth of A from B and leave C lamenting a vanished opportunity.

Republic: A form of government in which equal justice is available to all who can afford to pay for it.

Resign: A good thing to do when you are going to be kicked out.

Revelation: Discovering late in life that you are a fool.

Robber: Vulgar name for one who is successful in obtaining the property of others.

Zeal: A certain nervous disorder affecting the young and inexperienced.

Abbreviations
The following is a selection from the list of standard military abbreviations and should assist users of this handbook.

AWOL	Absent without leave
accn	Accommodation
ACE	Allied Command Europe
Adjt	Adjutant
admin	Administration
admin O	Administrative Order
ac	Aircraft
AD	Air Defence/Air Dispatch/Army Department
ADA	Air Defended Area
ADP	Automatic Data Processing
AFCENT	Allied Forces Central European Theatre
AIFV	Armoured Infantry Fighting Vehicle
Airmob	Airmobile
ATAF	Allied Tactical Air Force
armr	Armour
armd	Armoured
ACV	Armoured Command Vehicle
AFV	Armoured Fighting Vehicle
AMF(L)	Allied Mobile Force (Land Element)
APC	Armoured Personnel Carrier
APDS	Armour Piercing Discarding Sabot
ARV	Armoured Recovery Vehicle
AVLB	Armoured Vehicle Launched Bridge
AP	Armour Piercing/Ammunition Point/Air Publication
APO	Army Post Office
ARRC	Allied Rapid Reaction Corps
ATGW	Anti Tank Guided Weapon
ATWM	Army Transition to War Measure
arty	Artillery
att	Attached
BE	Belgium (Belgian)
BEF	British Expeditionary Force (France – 1914)
BGHQ	Battlegroup Headquarters
BiH	Bosnia and Herzogovina
bn	Battalion
bty	Battery
BK	Battery Captain

BC	Battery Commander
BG	Battle Group
bde	Brigade
BAOR	British Army of the Rhine
BFG	British Forces Germany
BFPO	British Forces Post Office
BMH	British Military Hospital
BRSC	British Rear Support Command
C3I	Command, Control, Communications & Intelligence.
cam	Camouflaged
cas	Casualty
CCP	Casualty Collecting Post
CCS	Casualty Clearing Station
CASEVAC	Casualty Evacuation
cat	Catering
CAD	Central Ammunition Depot
CEP	Circular Error Probable/Central Engineer Park
CEPS	Central European Pipeline System
CET	Combat Engineer Tractor
CGS	Chief of the General Staff
CinC	Commander in Chief
CIMIC	Civil Military Co-operation
COMMS Z	Communications Zone
CVD	Central Vehicle Depot
CW	Chemical Warfare
COS	Chief of Staff
civ	Civilian
CP	Close Protection/Command Post
CAP	Combat Air Patrol
c sups	Combat Supplies
CV	Combat Vehicles
CVR(T) or (W)	Combat Vehicle Reconnaissance Tracked or Wheeled
comd	Command/Commander
CinC	Commander in Chief
CPO	Command Pay Office/Chief Petty Officer
CO	Commanding Officer
coy	Company
CQMS	Company Quartermaster Sergeant
comp rat	Composite Ration (Compo)
COMSEN	Communications Centre
coord	Co-ordinate
CCM	Counter Counter Measure
DAA	Divisional Administrative Area
DTG	Date Time Group
def	Defence

DF	Defensive Fire
DK	Denmark
dml	Demolition
det	Detached
DISTAFF	Directing Staff (DS)
div	Division
DAA	Divisional Administrative Area
DMA	Divisional Maintenance Area
DS	Direct Support/Dressing Station
ech	Echelon
EME	Electrical and Mechanical Engineers
ECCM	Electronic Counter Measure
emb	Embarkation
EDP	Emergency Defence Plan
EMP	Electro Magnetic Pulse
en	Enemy
engr	Engineer
EOD	Explosive Ordnance Disposal
eqpt	Equipment
ETA	Estimated Time of Arrival
EW	Early Warning/Electronic Warfare
ex	Exercise
FRG	Federal Republic of Germany
FGA	Fighter Ground Attack
fol	Follow
fmm	Formation
FUP	Forming Up Point
FAC	Forward Air Controller
FEBA	Forward Edge of the Battle Area
FLET	Forward Location Enemy Troops
FLOT	Forward Location Own Troops
FOO	Forward Observation Officer
FR	France (French)
FRT	Forward Repair Team
FUP	Forming Up Place
GDP	General Defence Plan
GE	German (Germany)
GR	Greece (Greek)
GOC	General Officer Commanding
GPMG	General Purpose Machine Gun
HAC	Honourable Artillery Company
hel	Helicopter
HE	High Explosive
HEAT	High Explosive Anti Tank
HESH	High Explosive Squash Head

HVM	Hyper Velocity Missile
Hy	Heavy
IFF	Identification Friend or Foe
II	Image Intensifier
IGB	Inner German Border
illum	illuminating
IO	Intelligence Officer
INTSUM	Intelligence Summary
IRG	Immediate Replenishment Group
IR	Individual Reservist
IS	Internal Security
ISAF	International Security Assistance Force (Kabul)
ISD	In Service Date
IT	Italy (Italian)
IW	Individual Weapon
JFHQ	Joint Force Headquarters
JHQ	Joint Headquarters
JSSU	Joint Services Signals Unit
KFOR	Kosovo Force (NATO in Kosovo)
LAD	Light Aid Detachment (REME)
L of C	Lines of Communication
LLAD	Low Level Air Defence
LO	Liaison Officer
Loc	Locating
log	Logistic
LRATGW	Long Range Anti Tank Guided Weapon
LSW	Light Support Weapon
MAOT	Mobile Air Operations Team
MBT	Main Battle Tank
maint	Maintain
mat	Material
med	Medical
mech	Mechanised
MFC	Mortar Fire Controller
MNAD	Multi National Airmobile Division
NE	Netherlands
MO	Medical Officer
MP	Military Police
MOD	Ministry of Defence
mob	Mobilisation
MovO	Movement Order
msl	missile
MV	Military Vigilance
NAAFI	Navy, Army and Air Force Institutes
NADGE	NATO Air Defence Ground Environment

NATO	North Atlantic Treaty Organisation
NCO	Non Commissioned Officer
nec	Necessary
NL	Netherlands
NO	Norway (Norwegian)
NOK	Next of Kin
ni	Night
NORTHAG	Northern Army Group
NTR	Nothing to Report
NBC	Nuclear and Chemical Warfare
NYK	Not Yet Known
OP	Observation Post
OC	Officer Commanding
OCU	Operational Conversion Unit (RAF)
OIC	Officer in Charge
OOTW	Operations Other Than War
opO	Operation Order
ORBAT	Order of Battle
pax	Passengers
POL	Petrol, Oil and Lubricants
P info	Public Information
PJHQ	Permanent Joint Head Quarters
Pl	Platoon
PO	Portugal (Portuguese)
PUS	Permanent Under Secretary
QGE	Queens Gurkha Engineers
QM	Quartermaster
RAP	Rocket Assisted Projectile/Regimental Aid Post
RJDF	Rapid Joint Deployment Force
RTM	Ready to Move
RCZ	Rear Combat Zone
rec	Recovery
R & D	Research and Development
rebro	Rebroadcast
recce	Reconnaissance
Regt	Regiment
RHQ	Regimental Headquarters
RMA	Rear Maintenance Area/Royal Military Academy
rft	Reinforcement
RSA	Royal School of Artillery
RSME	Royal School of Mechanical Engineering
RTU	Return to Unit
SACUER	Supreme Allied Commander Europe
SATCOM	Satellite Communications
SDR	Strategic Defence Review

SFOR	Stabilisation Force (NATO in Bosnia)
2IC	Second in Command
SH	Support Helicopters
SHAPE	Supreme Headquarters Allied Powers Europe
sit	Situation
SITREP	Situation Report
SIB	Special Investigation Branch
SMG	Sub Machine Gun
SLR	Self Loading Rifle
SMG	Sub Machine Gun
smk	Smoke
SNCO	Senior Non Commissioned Officer
SP	Spain (Spanish)
Sqn	Squadron
SP	Self Propelled/Start Point
SSM	Surface to Surface Missile
SSVC	Services Sound and Vision Corporation
STA	Surveillance and Target Acquisition
STOL	Short Take Off and Landing
tac	Tactical
tk	Tank
tgt	Target
TOT	Time on Target
TCP	Traffic Control Post
tpt	Transport
tp	Troop
TCV	Troop Carrying Vehicle
TLB	Top Level Budget
TU	Turkish (Turkey)
TUL	Truck Utility Light
TUM	Truck Utility Medium
UK	United Kingdom
UKMF	United Kingdom Mobile Force
UNCLASS	Unclassified
UNPROFOR	United Nations Protection Force
UXB	Unexploded Bomb
US	United States
U/S	Unserviceable
VCDS	Vice Chief of the Defence Staff
veh	Vehicle
VOR	Vehicle off the Road
WE	War Establishment
wh	Wheeled
WIMP	Whinging Incompetent Malingering Person
WMR	War Maintenance Reserve

WO	Warrant Officer
wksp	Workshop
X	Crossing (as in roads or rivers)

This publication was produced by R&F (Defence) Publications
Editorial Office Tel 07889 886170 Fax 01743-241962

E Mail:Editorial@armedforces.co.uk
Website: www.armedforces.co.uk

Editor: Charles Heyman;

Other publications in this series are:
The Royal Air Force Pocket Guide 1994-95
The Armed Forces of the United Kingdom 2007-2008
The Territorial Army – Volume 1 1999

Further copies can be obtained from:
Pen & Sword Books Ltd
47 Church Street
Barnsley S70 2AS

11th Edition October 2007

The front cover image was taken by Fovea, a photographic agency that specialises in military photography. Founded by an ex-soldier, the agency takes a pragmatic and practical approach to projects. Visit the webside at www.fovea.tv

HMSO Core Licence Number CO2W0004896
PSI Licence C2006009533
Parliamentary License Number P2006000197